Rogue Institution

Vigilante Injustice, Lawlessness, and Disorder at the Air Force Academy

David W. Graney

Rogue Institution: Vigilante Injustice, Lawlessness, and Disorder at the Air Force Academy

Published by Wheatmark®
610 East Delano Street, Suite 104
Tucson, Arizona 85705 U.S.A.
www.wheatmark.com

International Standard Book Number: 978-1-60494-395-5
Library of Congress Control Number: 2010925537

Contents

Introduction

"A system of morality which is based on relative emotional values is a mere illusion, a thoroughly vulgar conception which has nothing sound in it and nothing true."

—Socrates

The headline of one Colorado newspaper late November 2003[1] read: "Some Air Force Cadets Using More than Gliders to Get High." For residents of Colorado Springs, looking up and seeing United States Air Force Academy (USAFA) cadets flying high in their gliders was normal; looking on the front page of the local newspaper and reading about cadets getting high was not.

Toward the middle of the 2000–2001 school year, the first high-profile reports surfaced about possible illegal drug activity among USAFA cadets. A long list of allegations emerged: dealing drugs, using drugs, condoning the use or sale of drugs. By January 7, 2001, thirty-four cadets were either implicated or being questioned. Ecstasy was the drug of choice.

Just two years later, another round of charges involving drugs would surface. These two drug scandals spurred a media frenzy surpassed only by the simultaneous sexual-assault scandal at the Academy. The negative attention the Academy received during this time functioned as an ag-

1 John Diedrich, "Some Air Force Cadets Using More than Gliders to Get High," *The Gazette* (Colorado Springs, CO), November 19, 2003. Find Articles.com. 08 April 2009. http://findarticles.com/p/articles/mi_qn4191/is_20031119/ai_n10027593/

gravating burr under the saddle of the cadets attending the institution and their parents. Equally disturbed were the alumni and leadership of the USAFA.

Why so much dismay on the part of Academy personnel and associates? The answer varies with the group to which the question is presented, but one factor would likely be missing in most of the answers: a genuine concern over the cadets' moral and ethical deficiencies. On the other hand, the element those same answers would likely have in common is an overriding preoccupation with reputation and image. This has been just one aspect contributing to the sorry state of affairs at the USAFA for many years. An extraordinary effort to protect the Academy's image by those attending the school, family members, school officials, and alumni has fashioned an environment that values appearance over reality, opinion before fact, and career advancement over integrity.

The philosophy of minimalism and containment over confrontation and correction has always been and will always be profoundly detrimental to any institution that endorses it directly or indirectly. Although many of the cadets involved in illegal drug activity are held accountable for their actions, numerous others guilty of equal or greater crimes, such as assault, frequently get by unscathed. Not punishing those who deserve punishment breeds animosity and discontent among those making an honest effort to follow the rules, whether those rules are dictated by a school superintendent or by the law of the United States. Unfortunately, some Academy officials not only fail to prosecute the guilty but actually punish the victim. The unofficial policy concerning misbehavior at the USAFA has not been to confront and correct problems. It has been to minimize the importance of inherently important issues and contain the undesirable negative publicity that naturally follows poor performance or illegal action by any means necessary. This approach, widely utilized by USAFA leadership, has been a formula for disaster at the Academy and a glaring reminder of the dangers of dishonesty and blind acquiescence. The Air Force Academy is a rogue institution executing a failed officer-training program.

1

Clear Purpose

"I'm not concerned with your liking or disliking me . . . All I ask is that you respect me as a human being."

—Jackie Robinson

My name is David W. Graney. I am not defined by what profession I have chosen to pursue or the accomplishments I am able to list on a resume. I am defined instead by what I think, what I say, and the actions I take as a result. Situations vary, character should not. Our own character and the thoughts, words, and deeds that define it are the only entity over which we have complete control in our lives. That is why I say that neither my profession nor my accomplishments define me. They inherently cannot due to their circumstantial nature.

I was involuntarily dismissed from the United States Air Force Academy on 15 November 2002. Some might think that I am somehow less capable or honorable than an individual who was *not* involuntarily dismissed from the USAFA. This would be a legitimate partiality if the USAFA were an organization that valued strength of character and morality, and something I did was at odds with USAFA standards that attempted to enforce those ideals, but that was not the case. My experience has led me to believe that the USAFA was not an institution that valued strength of character, nor did I ever carry out any action or incarnate behavior worthy of expulsion. The motto at the Academy is "Integrity first, service before self, and excellence in all we do." It could just as easily be "Integrity when convenient, self-service, and excellence in carefully selected and/or high profile arenas." Obviously the previous statement screams for an explanation, and that is one of the functions of this piece, to explain how such a paradox can occur.

I've been asked many times to explain what happened to me at the Academy. The explanation isn't simple; there were a number of contributing factors. Graham Allison says it best in his work *Essence of Decision*: "In attempting to explain a particular event, the analyst cannot simply describe the full state of the world leading up to the event. The logic of explanation requires singling out the relevant, critical determinants of the occurrence, the junctures at which particular factors produced one state of the world rather than another."[2] Therefore, the "logic of explanation," as Graham describes it, requires that I do much more than just explain the full state of affairs at the Academy during my tenure if I am to provide a comprehensive analysis of my experience.

But there's more to it. Throughout my tenure at the USAFA, I had numerous experiences that greatly enhanced my understanding of human nature, specifically the tendency we have to subordinate ourselves to weakness in the face of adversity. I also witnessed the demoralizing effects of poor leadership, injustice, and group mentality. Accordingly, the foremost rationale for writing about my particular experience at the USAFA is to illuminate the dangers and inevitable consequences of allowing such intolerant, manipulative, and abusive environments to persist, not just at the USAFA but anywhere in our society.

In preparation for this work I read and annotated the June 2003 congressionally appointed Working Group Report, various Inspector General reports, numerous Government Accountability Office (GAO) reports, dozens of books having to do with the issues I address herein, and records from congressional hearings on the subject of Academy corruption. I even personally attended one of these congressional hearings as well as a USAFA Board of Visitors meeting in Washington, DC. I have also read or familiarized myself with the vast majority of articles on the subject from both local Colorado Springs newspapers and national news organizations. However, the crux of my preparation came through sometimes excruciating hours, days, months, and years of experience as a USAFA cadet in which I lived and breathed the Academy culture.

Many of the thoughts and experiences I will share are deeply per-

2 Graham Allison, *Essence of Decision* (Upper Saddle River, NJ: Addison-Wesley Educational Publishers Inc., 1999), 4.

sonal, and some will use that to their advantage, I'm sure. Fortunately, that is not a concern of mine, in that I hold my decision-making process to a higher standard than simply concerning myself over how others might react. I view myself as a transparent individual with little to hide, and I make every effort to say and do what needs to be said and done. "Do what is right and let the consequences follow," says one adage; I believe I've made a life of doing just that.

I should say that even though there are many cadets and school officials who lack even the most basic moral necessities, I want to make it abundantly clear that on the other hand there are also cadets and USAFA personnel who do make an honest effort to uphold standards of decency, and some of them were and still are my closest friends. On the same note, nothing that you will read here was motivated by anger, resentment, or a spirit of revenge. I have stated the purpose of this work, and I leave it at that.

The Air Force Academy was a failing institution throughout my tenure. The Academy, since its inception, has had one job: to develop and commission military officers. Every year the president of the United States commissions hundreds of new second lieutenants from the Academy who will be the first to tell you how truly special they are. The USAFA loves to self-aggrandize, its main swagger being the caliber of Air Force officers the Academy produces year in and year out. Although GAO report data show Reserve Officer Training Corps (ROTC) and Officer Training School (OTS) graduates performing at the same level in the operational Air Force as Academy grads, wherever an ear will listen there is talk of how the Academy is the premier officer development program in the country and that to wear that Academy ring is just short of a successful Air Force career in and of itself.

In actual fact, the USAFA has produced a good number of highly qualified Air Force officers *despite* its wayward training environment and military culture. Since 1955 until arguably the 2004–2005 school year, "training" at the Academy hasn't been much more than a bunch of American taxpayer (by way of the Dept. of Defense [DOD]) sponsored frat boys and sorority girls running around playing military while hazing one another out of their respective minds. Even on paper (ref. USAFA Training Manuals/codified Academy training philosophies) the military indoctrination system at the Academy has never and, to a large degree *still doesn't*, align with acceptable, proven training strategies and procedures found anywhere else in the Air Force, including other officer accession programs.

Over the years, USAFA leadership (by virtue of sheer negligence on its part) has fashioned an incredibly hostile Academy training environment responsible for a great deal of both personal injury and institutional malfunction. The irony of this moral debacle is that the Academy training module (i.e., Fourth Class System—considered by many to be "One of the greatest institutions that was ever invented" [3]) has been inarguably the *root cause* of the very misbehavior and illegal action the training is theoretically designed to prevent. Regardless of USAFA propaganda to the contrary, the Fourth Class System has historically focused on training cadets on how to be cadets, not Air Force officers. Much of the behavior deemed acceptable at the Academy would never fly (excuse the pun) in the operational Air Force. What cadets learned from the late Fourth Class System (now called the Four Class System) was how to survive in a wildly egocentric environment. They learned that it was customary to abuse fellow cadets both physically and verbally when the victimized cadets deserved it in the eyes of the collective body politic, or if the collective could get away with it. How could someone ever *deserve* to be so severely mistreated? At the Academy, consideration for such maltreatment came rather easily. Any thought or deed on the part of any given cadet that didn't sit well with that cadet's superiors effectively warranted inappropriate "training" by his or her student leadership.

The system produced an environment that bred ill feeling and discouragement among the entire Cadet Wing (student body). Cadets across the Academy suffered from extreme cases of cynicism, depression, and passive-aggression, all masked with a wide array of psychological defense mechanisms such as displacement, denial, rationalization, and repression. The psychological transformation many cadets underwent in order to survive left them broken and fragmented, mere casualties of the systemic

---

3 *Working Group Report,* "Report of the Working Group Concerning the Deterrence of and Response to Incidents of Sexual Assault at the U.S. Air Force Academy" (Washington, DC: Headquarters, Department of the Air Force, 2003), 92.

Author's Note: The *Working Group Report* integrated, by reference, privileged materials, including the statement of then-Major General Steven R. Lorenz, Exhibit 52, at 47–48.

See Also: Defense Technical Information Center, Fort Belvoir, VA. http://oai.dtic.mil/oai?very+getRecord&metadataPrefix+html&identifier+ADA488305

manipulation, downright derangement, or both that was the Academy's Fourth Class System.

Sanctioned punishment at the Academy was disorganized and ineffective. For a single offense, cadets could be punished under three different penal codes. The Uniform Code of Military Justice (UCMJ), the honor code, and conduct adjudicatory system all regulated cadet behavior. Worse yet, apart from this chaos of command, two of these three punitive schemes operated like a prejudicial Sicilian crime syndicate. and the other (the UCMJ) was completely misunderstood and underused. Mario Puzo's novel *The Godfather* would have been a better resource for honor-code policies and procedures than the Academy-issued honor manual. Lack of professionalism and an abundance of indiscretion and immaturity were the mark of most Academy disciplinary procedures, which naturally fostered an environment of distrust between cadets and Academy leadership. S. L. A. Marshall, former Army chief of staff and secretary of defense, references this type of disorder and distrust in his book *The Armed Forces Officer*:

> Lacking common purpose, and the common standard of justice, which is at the same time its derivative and chief agent, men become more and more separate entities, each fighting for his own right, each prey to his own fears, each increasingly doubting all others.[4]

It was this administrative disorder in conjunction with an antiquated and barbaric Fourth Class System that ultimately led to the Academy's provisional demise in the spring of 2003. On January 2, 2003, an e-mail went out, under the pseudonym of Renee Trindle, alleging that the Academy had a serious sexual assault problem. The writer went even further, charging that Academy leadership had grossly mishandled a number of assault cases to such an extent that various sexual assault victims had been dealt harsher punishments for minor infractions surrounding the assault than their respective assailants did for the assault itself. The e-mail went to a wide audience, including numerous high-ranking public officials, various United States senators, and the secretary of the Air Force. Shortly thereafter, a number of current and former female cadets came

---

4 S. L. A. Marshall, *The Armed Forces Officer* (Washington, DC: U.S. Government Printing Office, 1975), 68.

forward with stories of maltreatment, mismanagement, and indifference at the hands of Academy administrators. Many of these individuals were subsequently interviewed by notable media sources such as Cable News Network (CNN), *20/20*, and even Oprah Winfrey. The media frenzy was momentous and harsh toward the Academy and its handling of sexual assault. The Air Force had no choice but to respond, and not in the way they had responded to years of GAO reports pointing towards the same sexual-assault problems at the USAFA, but by *actually doing something*. What followed next was a series of investigations, administrative overhauls, and personnel adjustments, actions that would be under the collective microscope of the American people for years to come.

Unfortunately for me, I entered the Academy during the dark ages of its now fifty-five-year history. I toiled through years of high-school academics and athletics in order to have the chance to serve as a USAFA cadet, only to be thrown into this draconian environment that would constructively twist reality, alter normal perception, and uproot traditional values to replace them with its own.

I, along with my brother Chaz, arrived at the Academy on June 27, 2001, the day before Basic Cadet Training (BCT) was set to begin. We were beaming with enthusiasm for what lay ahead. For years we had studied and prepared ourselves for this day and couldn't wait to test our mettle. We stayed the night before in-processing day at the home of an Academy grad from the mid-1970s whose hollow stare could have said it all, if we hadn't been so overwhelmed with the *esprit de corps*, as they say. It was this keen patriotism and a dash of ignorance that led us to show up half an hour early for BCT and become the first and third persons to enter the graduating Class of 2005. The generous family with whom we stayed the night previous also provided us an early morning ride up to the Academy compound; it was the morning of 28 June 2001, in-processing day. On arriving at the drop-off location outside Doolittle Hall, we extended our appreciation for the family's hospitality and went our separate ways.

We encountered a very friendly environment, full of laudatory statements, as we finalized our paperwork in Doolittle Hall; that would be short-lived. My brother Chaz and I made short time weaving through the maze heading towards the bus that would take us up to the cadet area where BCT would officially start. We spent half the bus ride engulfed in the pleasantries associated with awkward and impromptu introductions.

That was the last time any of us would be allowed to communicate with each other freely in public areas apart from classrooms, church services, and athletic facilities for the next nine months. Most of us didn't even notice the cadet sitting toward the front of the bus when we boarded, although when he stood up, turned around, and began his passionate rebuttal of our worth as human beings we sure noticed him. Never had anyone so eloquently insulted my right to exist as this cadet. Clearly he had been selected to introduce us to the USAFA, not only for his well-developed capacity for insulting, but also for his love of doing so.

We sat paralyzed in the positions the cadet had commanded us to retain until the bus slowly arrived at the bottom of what was then called the "Bring Me Men" ramp. There, approximately fifty first- and second-class cadets (seniors and juniors) stood waiting patiently. As the bus came to a stop, these cadets surrounded the bus and began to beat on the windows, point at individual appointees, and mouth out all the things they were going to do to us once we exited the bus. It was a rather nerve-wracking experience as we alighted into the unknown surrounded by these new and angry faces. There were freshly painted footsteps on the pavement to guide us where to stand, and as each of us adopted a pair of footprints we became a flawlessly positioned squadron. We were introduced to the seven basic responses that would govern the way we were to address upperclassmen. The learning curve was extremely short. Exact, immediate memorization and recitation of every tidbit of information thrown in our direction was expected. Imperfect recitation of our instructions caused yelling at piercing decibel levels that shot straight through the ear-canals of ears which, as yet, were largely sensitive to unbridled yelling and screaming, a condition that would soon change almost entirely to the contrary. Thus began the initial phase of Basic Cadet Training.

2

"Cadre, Fall Out and Make Corrections"

"Living in a continual state of battle alert or hypervigilance erodes emotional stability."

MARLENE STEINBERG, M.D.[5]

Most cadets who entered the Academy prior to the year 2003 would agree that in-processing day was the longest day of their lives: head shaving, numerous air-gun vaccinations, lengthy issue of uniforms and gear, examinations, inspections, bewildering dining-facility etiquette lessons, marching, drilling, briefings, unpacking, and of course endless on-the-spot and sanctioned training sessions that carried on late into that first night at the Academy. The longest day of *my* life would come later, on one of the thirty-six-hour shifts I worked in a thirty-degrees-below-zero freezer for a seafood company in Dutch Harbor, Alaska—but in 2001, in-processing day was without question the longest day to date.

During basic training we were first introduced to the beat-down. The beat-down was a time when cadre (amateur drill instructors made up of USAFA upperclassmen) subjected basic cadets to strenuous physical activity while imparting mostly inconsequential Air Force knowledge in a largely unrestrained manner. The shenanigans always began with the words, "Cadre, fall out and make corrections." After hours of blood, sweat, and tears, someone would stop the insanity when enough cadre lost interest. Beat-downs became just as much a part of life for freshman cadets as

---

5 Marlene Steinberg, M.D., *The Stranger in the Mirror: Dissociation—The Hidden Epidemic* (New York: HarperCollins Publishers, Inc., 2000), 15.

eating, sleeping, and breathing. The first of these beat-downs came on our first night at the Academy and consisted of thousands of pushups in the dormitory hallways outside our newly assigned rooms, with swarms of cadre running around like screaming banshees. So consistent were these beat-downs that I feel quite justified in saying that Basic Cadet Training was, in effect, one large beat-down punctuated by a few administrative distractions.

The first phase of BCT was in garrison, as they say in the military; the Academy dormitories serving as the stronghold. Every morning we woke to doors rattling, whistles shrilling, and projected voices. We would pile out of bed straight into the front-leaning rest (push-up position) to await further instruction. After what always seemed like an unduly extended period of time, we would be ushered out into the darkness for the commencement of morning physical training (PT). PT consisted of running, push-ups, sit-ups, up-downs, flutter kicks, and pull-ups—the whole works. It was during morning PT that we memorized the whole repertoire of Air Force jodies (military cadences originating from the U.S. Army). We sang all about wanting to be Army Airborne Rangers, signing up for Vietnam at the Army recruiting office downtown, and of course all kinds of would-be carnal knowledge about each other's moms, girlfriends, or both.

PT led straight into breakfast in Mitchell Hall, the cadet dining facility, where the ostensibly well-mannered cadets put on a daily exhibition of some of the most uncanny behavior; chewing only seven times, resting silverware only at forty-five-degree angles, bland recitation of unfamiliar information, creepy directionless staring, aimless spot corrections, ordering basic cadets to stand on tables and sing and dance to nursery rhymes, passionately reciting squadron-specific traditionalistic chants and mantras. These things and a good many more left unmentioned combined to stir within a many cadet a spirit of disillusionment and, to the casual observer, a great deal of nervous energy. BCT mealtimes, simply put, were just weird.

Outside the psychotic atmosphere of Mitchell Hall, things were not much better. We spent most of our BCT I days hacking our way through the Academy's disjointed and largely unsupervised training environment, which had been off the deep end for years. Though BCT I was monotonous, at times excruciating, and always laborious, most of us stayed on long enough to see the coming of BCT II, the field-exercise phase of basic training.

On the last night of BCT I, we were told by the cadet commander that although we might have survived BCT I, there was no way in Hell's Half Acre (the location of the BCT II obstacle course) we were going to make it through BCT II. He told us that we weren't cut out for hard work and that we ought to not even try, that we should save ourselves the trouble and quit right there and then. So of course the entire room rang out with "ZERO FIVE [our class year] FULL OF PRIDE"—our unelected class slogan around which we were to rally in times of hardship. The cadet commander looked at us for a moment, then told us, "Zero five, you ain't got no pride," followed by, "Cadre, fall out and make corrections."

Early the next morning we loaded our gear in the back of a two-ton truck, then formed up for the march to Jack's Valley, the wooded area where BCT II was set to take place. When the gang was all there, Academy administrators and all, we marched in unison from the cadet area to Jack's Valley amid fanfare generated by civilian bystanders who had come out to both watch the spectacle and provide encouragement. Those were the last friendly faces we saw for quite a while.

Upon reaching main camp, we gathered around the flagpoles for a brief and fiery commencement speech concerning the experiences that lay ahead. Most of us listened intently as these flag-rank generals meticulously detailed what would be expected of us and what stood to be gained (or lost) out there. After an impassioned foray of American patriotism, cadre fell out and made corrections, thus consummating the inception of BCT II in the most appropriate way possible. This was a beat-down within a beat-down. By the end of it, we had assembled a bogus military campsite complete with canvas tents, boardwalks, lounging chairs, and sunscreens for lazy upperclassmen.

The next two or three weeks were spent either running up and down Colorado Rockies foothills or participating in some sort of training course. Events that transpired at BCT II courses would become class-renowned. Events that were definitely not very amusing when they occurred would serve as comic relief for months and years to come. We were introduced to widely celebrated characters, such as Assault Course Meathead, who instructed us in the correct form for certain exercises. Some from among our ranks would rise to stardom as a result of the Big Bad Basic competition. Big Bad Basic was a class-wide, single-elimination pugil-stick competition in which all basic cadets participated. Pugil sticks are rubber sticks with hard foam on each end, used to learn and practice close combat techniques with a rifle. The first rounds of the competition occurred without most people even realizing it, mainly because they took place directly after or during the assault course. Thus, most people thought it was just part of the course or were simply too tired to care.

The assault course was our least favorite of all the BCT II courses. Upon arrival at the course there would be a mass training session with three or four hundred other basic cadets. That was when Assault Course Meathead (a member of the Academy football team with a large physique and small shirt) took us through various PT-style exercises. We were all given fake M-16s, also known as rubber duckies (because they were solid plastic), and a helmet that rarely fit. Once it was our squadron's turn to go through the obstacles, we would all run over there, mouthguards in place, and begin the madness.

Personally I never completed a single obstacle of the course. The first time we went through as a squadron, I was made to do up-downs at the entrance to each obstacle but never actually allowed to enter. For five to ten minutes I simply jumped up and down until ordered to move on to the next obstacle. Up-downs with a rubber duckie in hand and wearing a mouthguard, loose helmet, and a long-sleeve battle dress uniform (BDU) in approximately 100-degree heat constituted a substantially aggravating experience. In essence, apart from accidentally low-crawling into the same pit where cadre were throwing powerful firecrackers and colored smoke bombs, my initial experience with the assault course added up to a significant number of up-downs.

On each subsequent visit to the assault course, I was singled out with the other future intercollegiate athletes in the squadron and taken to a separate location in the Hell's Half Acre woods to have our own private training sessions with upperclass athletes who would eventually become our teammates during the year. They wanted to give us their own special welcome to the Academy.

The second least-favorite course among basic cadets was the obstacle course. The obstacle course, similar to the assault course, consisted of climbing ropes, scaling walls, digging through tunnels, swinging across water traps, multiple balancing acts, and numerous other agility- and stamina-building activities. Water traps were another cadre favorite, for obvious reasons. I remember a portion of the course where, in order to cross the water trap, a participant would have to catch the rope thrown by cadre and swing across. At one point as I was approaching this obstacle fairly quickly, the cadre decided to have some fun and threw the rope too far in front of me, causing me to run full-speed into the water and face-plant in the mud on the adjacent bank. After orienting myself and crawling out on the other side, I felt a little angry; then realized the dip had actually felt good—the realization effectively squelching my frustration.

Apart from taking a boot in the face from an upperclassman attempting to kick dirt into my face and having to push a fellow cadet who was suffering from a claustrophobic panic attack through a tunnel while being hit in the head by shovels full of dirt from upperclassmen trying to bury us, the obstacle course really wasn't that awful.

The other courses we participated in when not at the assault or obstacle courses (we spent a good amount of time at those two) were distinctive in that they actually challenged the mind. We learned how to shoot M-16s at one course, carried out small-unit maneuvers and hostage-rescue techniques at another. In another course we were taught such first-aid procedures as CPR, splinting, bandaging, how to lift and carry a patient, etc. One fairly popular course required us to use critical thinking in order to carry out specific tasks, for example transporting a group from one platform to another only using a ten-foot rope. If basic cadets couldn't figure out how to successfully carry out the tasks, cadre would demonstrate. The course essentially served as a team-building exercise. It taught us to use all of our material and personnel assets.

Some of the more legendary events of BCT II, at least for our squadron, occurred during unscheduled time periods. We spent the majority of this time doing some sort of PT. In one instance, we were out in a field performing sit-ups, push-ups, pull-ups, and standing long jumps when, out of nowhere, an Apache helicopter came screaming over the treetops and straight toward us about fifteen feet off the ground. When the pilot arrived within about twenty yards of us, he pulled back on the controls and flew straight up until the machine fell to the side. He came back at us flying underneath the power lines and then began to circle around us. He came so close that the wind from his rotors actually blew some of our hats off. We later heard rumors that the pilot was reprimanded for the aerobatics, but we sure enjoyed them.

Toward the beginning of BCT II, I was asked by cadre to accompany them to the top of a nearby hill. Once we arrived at the top of the hill I was handed a shovel and instructed to dig. When I asked what they wanted me to dig they responded, "A race track." I was bewildered by the request, until they explained that I was to make a low-crawl course. According to the name they had given the project, we were going to be racing around the track at the low-crawl. I made a figure-eight that included all the necessities of a decent low-crawl course, including a tunnel and water-trap. After completing the track I was told to try it out. They timed me while I completed five laps around the track. After completing the laps, I was told that if I ever had a slower lap than had just been recorded, I would be required to do five more laps which, unfortunately, happened many times. When we came back to the tents, cadre made an announcement to the basic cadets in our squadron: "Anytime anyone screws up, Graney goes to the race track." My classmates didn't know at the time what the race track was, nor would they until cadre became bored with watching me day after day and decided to have a squadron race.

Until that time, at the sound of cadre yelling, "Graney! RACE TRACK!" I would disappear and come back a half-hour to an hour later covered in dirt from head to toe, including teeth and eyelids. I became exceptionally good at low-crawling, becoming something of a trophy low-crawler for the squadron. More than once our cadre challenged cadre from other squadrons to a basic-cadet on basic-cadet low-crawl showdown, their best low-crawler vs. ours. I'd always win, no matter how strong, fast, or athletic the other basic cadet was, simply because I was so well practiced. At my victory every time, our squadron cadre would slip into an awkward state of euphoria while I was in the background coughing up dirt. After close to three weeks of floundering around in the forest, the military monkey business came to an end, and so ended Basic Cadet Training.

BCT Debrief

I learned many things from my BCT experience. That series of events changed the way I viewed the Academy but did not entirely depreciate my positive outlook regarding it. These experiences served merely as precursors to judgments I would make in future months as a results of the compilation of issues and their intensifying and farther-reaching effects.

One such lesson I learned during this time was the extent of our vulnerability as basic cadets. From day one there was a complete lack of understanding on our parts with respect to acceptable and unacceptable behavior on the part of upperclass cadets, especially regarding the manner in which we were trained. In moments when unacceptable behavior occurred, most basic cadets not only failed to recognize it as unacceptable but were equally unaware of what to do about it. Such a situation is a recipe for disaster. No two conditions can make a person more vulnerable to abuse than, one, a basic misunderstanding concerning what qualifies as abuse, and two, a general lack of knowledge as to what entity or person to go to if there is a problem—supposing such entity or person even exists. Lack of understanding or knowledge is weakness, and as former secretary of state Donald Rumsfeld so eloquently stated during a Pentagon briefing on March 26, 2006, "Weakness is provocative."[6] Although BCT squadrons had cadre assigned to look after the physiological and psychological needs of basic cadets (squadron medical officer/first sergeant), these upperclassmen participated in the Academy's version of military training to the same extent as all other BCT cadre, so they weren't seen by basic cadets as any sort of conduit to protection. Sometimes perception is reality, which was certainly true in this case.

Another condition that made basic cadets as vulnerable as we were was the form of control cadre maintained over us. Cadre had absolute power over us during basic training. The principal source of this power was the almost absolute lack of leadership from commissioned officers at the Academy. One element of responsible leadership is oversight. As a leader, it is important to not only give commands but to know whether your orders are being carried out appropriately. During Basic I can remember only a few times when commissioned officers were actually present during training, let alone conducting oversight in any fashion. The explanation for this lack of oversight was a simple lack of concern. Leadership deficiencies would continue to be a problem throughout my stay at the USAFA. Poor leadership would allow those with malleable values to take advantage of underclassmen whenever they felt so inclined. In es-

6 Donald Rumsfeld, Pentagon Briefing, March 23, 2006, Author's notes.
See also: Ruttenberg, Jim, "In Farewell, Rumsfeld Warns Weakness Is 'Provocative'," nytimes.com, December 15, 2006. http://www.nytimes.com/2006/12/16/washington/16prexy.html.

sence, lack of leadership within a command structure also means lack of justice for those subordinate to that command.

Many cadets, because of the lawless atmosphere of both BCT and the freshman year as a whole (encouraged by the nonexistent or ineffective leadership of the institution), changed from performers to survivors. The differences between performers and survivors are often well disguised, though profound. Performers operate on the basis of a personal code of conduct well founded on ideals, principles, morals, and ethics. The actions of a survivor are rather chaotic, disorganized at best. Survivors do not focus on the legitimacy of what they are doing nor how they are doing it, only on the way it is perceived by those with whom they're trying to establish rapport. Often survivors resort to excessive flattery and indulgence (disgusting in my opinion) or attempt to make themselves look better by slandering or discrediting another.

In this sense, survivors are pathetic. We all know them, the type who will sacrifice anything to get that promotion at work: familial relationships, their integrity, morality—*anything* to get ahead or get by. Furthermore, when they do get that promotion, for example, and the money rolls in, those who lack judgment and subscribe to that definition of accomplishment (e.g., other suck-ups, brown-nosers, bootlicking apple-polishing yes-men, hopeless sycophants, or those who simply don't know better) reinforce the behavior by calling them successful, forgetting that there is no success at the expense of one's personal integrity. BCT motivated a large number of good people, scared for their own careers, reputations, and, in certain instances, safety, to subscribe to the Academy's definition of success and, even more regrettably, the Academy's terms of attainment.

This intellectual transformation only compounded existing problems, in that instead of sustained opposition to the guilty party's antics—inappropriate training carried out by upperclassmen—the perpetrators now had a theoretical support group. When a person observes a problem and chooses to be complacent in word or deed, he or she has inadvertently become an accomplice and has allowed the problem to proliferate.

A classic example involved a good friend of mine who spent a semester as my roommate freshman year. He is one of the more intelligent people I have ever known, but during BCT I he could not correctly make a facing movement. Cadre would give commands such as "About face," which meant turn around, and we would comply. Many times, when given the command to turn left my friend would turn right instead, and vice versa. He received more attention than any other cadet in our squadron during BCT I because of his inconsistent facing movements. It had nothing to do with his intelligence; it was the result of some coordination problems and persistent yelling. When we all heard left or right, he perceived himself being yelled at.

Many of my fellow basic cadets subordinated their own good judgment to the opinions of cadre and began to insult my friend privately. Then I heard a classmate publicly criticize him. I distinctly remember the upperclassman's reaction in that moment. It was not a look of, "How can you denigrate your classmate right in front of me?" It was a look of entertainment. The upperclassman smiled and changed the subject. The fallout from this course of action was that sanctions (yelling and harassment) were eased between the classmate who had publicly slandered my friend and the upperclassman who thought it was amusing. An alliance had been born between those two individuals. People are always drawn to like-minded individuals, and people at the Academy were no different. That particular cadre obviously thought very little of my friend, and our classmate took advantage of that well-known fact. He used it as a way of forming an alliance with the cadre, subsequently making his life easier. It's a classic textbook survival tactic. The list of examples for how and when classmates sold out and turned into survivors is lengthy and would be interesting to entertain, but I digress.

Recently there has been a great deal of talk concerning religious proselytizing at the Academy. I'll just say it—even if religious zealotry does show its ugly face at the Academy, it's the least of that institute's problems. However, I definitely had my fair share of run-ins with the similar issue of religious intolerance. I have never in all my life been subjected to more criticism for believing in the Almighty than at the Air Force Academy, including the time I spent as a missionary in South America. Early on in BCT I had my scriptures thrown to the floor in disgust by an upperclassman room inspector. Later, I was temporarily (it would have been permanently if not for spirited objection on my part) denied my right to attend the Christian church services of my choice. Furthermore, I was constantly harassed for my beliefs, even as I supplicated the God to whom I chose to pray.

Room inspections during BCT I were essentially a form of harassment. As basic cadets, we spent very little time in our rooms and had few possessions. Our rooms were kept in immaculate condition. Very few, if any, basic cadets actually slept under their sheets, and some even slept on the floor in order to avoid mussing their perfectly made beds. The purpose for carrying out room inspections during BCT was not to ensure basic cadet cleanliness. The objective was simply to harass basic cadets. Cadre would come into our rooms, which had been cleaned everywhere from the tops of the ceiling fans to the light-switch frames, and pick everything apart. Even though a person could prepare meals on any surface (vertical or horizontal) of our rooms and feel safe doing so, the average comment from cadre upon entering the room would be something along the lines of, "This room is disgusting." Cadre would pull all the sheets off the beds, throw the mattresses on the floor, and go through desk drawers and closets and cabinets, yelling and screaming all the while.

> *Side note*: I honestly didn't mind the commotion all that much for the reason that it was simply part of the BCT program. Cadre went to great lengths to subject us to stressful situations for good reason. It's important for military personnel to be able to handle stress. If a person has an emotional breakdown simply because of a stressful room inspection, that person is certainly unprepared for the pressure associated with any wartime scenario. I've never been shot at myself, but I can imagine having an enemy try to end your life is much more traumatic than any room inspection could ever be. Therefore, in my view, any attempt by cadre to train basic cadets to be able to conduct themselves appropriately in strenuous environments was a well-grounded endeavor. However, there are official USAFA-generated guidelines for the manner in which cadre inflict stress on basic cadets, and believe it or not, throwing basic cadets' personal effects around (such as religious items) was and still is totally out of bounds.

During this specific room inspection, one of the cadre found my Christian scripture in a drawer in my desk. Asked what the book was, I responded that it was scripture. The cadre glanced at the book then back at me, and with a straight face told me that it was indeed *not* scripture and energetically threw the Word on the ground, leaving it sprawled out on the floor, pages torn.

I was obviously disturbed by this cadet's actions. Some people don't mind when things religious are made a mockery. However, many people *are* religious, spiritual, or both, try to act according to the moral precepts to which they subscribe, and hold some things to be not just very important, but sacred. Any word or deed intended to take away from those things a person holds sacred will always be insulting. The manner in which this cadre spoke about and handled what I considered sacred scripture was extremely offensive. It was incredibly rude, ignorant, and undeniably contrary to the USAFA's own stated training guidelines.

I wondered at the time what I could possibly do about what had happened. I asked myself if there was a person to whom I was supposed to talk about it, or if I did, if it would even make a difference. The squadron first sergeant who was charged with ensuring our psychological wellbeing happened to be very good friends with the cadre who had treated me so disrespectfully, so that was obviously a no-go and, like the majority of basic cadets, I was very unfamiliar with the greater power structure outside the cadet cadre we dealt with on a daily basis. Ultimately, I did not express concern to any superior other than briefly mentioning the incident at a church service in the cadet chapel.

Knowing the atmosphere at the Academy at that time, I feel very strongly that if I had expressed my concern, chances are it would have been written off as wholly insignificant. Not only would there have been a complete disregard for the serious nature of the incident, but the fact that I had voiced a formal concern would have spread quickly between cadre, and I would have paid for it later by way of extra harassment. I make this rather speculative statement based on similar experiences that friends and associates and I had throughout our respective stays at the Academy. I chalked the incident up as a bad experience and moved on, but it wouldn't be the last time I encountered issues of religious intolerance at the Academy.

Not long after the start of the school year, I learned of a ban that had been imposed on a popular denominational Christian group until the year prior to my arrival at the institution. The church of which I speak is a highly respected, worldwide Christian denomination that for years had been banned from congregating to the extent these churchgoers would have liked, twice a week instead of one, on Academy grounds because of a cult label branded upon them. Academy officials had allegedly placed this worldwide Christian church in the same category as groups known to worship the devil. Upon learning from one of the leaders of the faith itself that the rumor of this ban was indeed based in fact, I was outraged.

I have deliberately left unmentioned this religion's formal appellation in order to avoid superfluous theological discussion, save to say that a ban on this particular religious institution was equivalent to having banned Lutherans, Baptists, or even arguably Roman Catholics. Anyone who is mildly familiar with the church of which I speak knows that there is no effort whatsoever on the part of its members to worship the devil in any manner. I couldn't imagine at the time, nor can I now, any other reason for the Academy to have specifically banned said denomination from holding meetings at the Academy other than flat-out, unadulterated, religious intolerance.

During BCT I met with spiritually like-minded individuals for services in the Academy chapel, as we weren't allowed to leave the grounds. When the school year started, the church I elected to attend was in Colorado Springs, off the Academy premises. In order to attend, I needed permission from my squadron air officer commanding (AOC), Major H, to travel off base, as freshmen were not at liberty to come and go as they pleased. When I approached Major H with the leave-of-absence form, I encountered the unexpected.

The first thing Major H did was ask me why it was necessary for me to leave the Academy to attend church. I informed him that the church I wished to attend held its services in town, and in order to attend those meetings I would have to physically leave the Academy grounds. He then asked why I couldn't just go to a service at the cadet Chapel. When I said that the services held in the cadet Chapel were for Catholics, Protestants, and Jews, he asked why I couldn't just attend one of those services. I actually had to tell him that it was because I was not Catholic, Protestant, or Jewish, and that I would prefer to attend services conducted by and for members of my faith.

He then told me he would "be gracious" and allow me to leave the Academy for one hour in order to attend my church service. One hour was hardly enough time to get to and from the south gate of the Academy compound, let alone attend a church service in town. I told Major H that I would need more time, at least a few hours, because it took some time not only to attend the service itself but to drive to and from the church building (yes, I actually had to explain that to him). He was outraged. He informed me that he was not going to sign the form and abruptly ordered me out of his office.

I left bewildered. I kept asking myself, Did that just happen? Major

H was fundamentally inhibiting my freedom of religion, and it was outrageous. I missed church the first two Sundays, then decided something had to be done. I wasn't going to miss church my entire freshman year because of my AOC's delinquency. The most absurd part was that all the other freshman cadets I knew who had expressed a desire to attend church at the same location had been granted permission with relative ease. I wondered how there could be such inconsistency in something so fundamental. Why had the AOC from my brother's squadron granted him permission under the same exact circumstances?

I had my brother speak with his AOC, who subsequently requested that I come and speak with him in his office, after which he reluctantly called my AOC and urged him to sign the form and allow me to go to church. Major H was initially surprised that my brother's AOC had signed the form. Then, out of apparent embarrassment, he began to argue his reasoning for not signing the form. My brother's AOC appeased him to a certain degree but then insisted again that he let me go to church. Major H grudgingly agreed. When I returned to Major H's office I was met with sophomoric hostility, as though I had betrayed him somehow by contacting the other AOC. He signed the form, then belittled my efforts with a tinge of malice.

I went back to my room baffled by the experience. I knew the Academy had its peculiar aspects, but it was unimaginable for me *at the time* that I would have go to such great lengths to be allowed to go to church on Sunday, and that I would ultimately be found objectionable by my AOC for doing so. It was bizarre. Lying, stealing, and cheating are the activities that should be abhorred, not trying to go to church.

Another example of religious bigotry occurred with regularity while in noon-meal formation. For noon-meal formation we assembled as squadrons out on the terrazzo, the large interconnecting courtyard of the cadet area, for attendance, announcements from the squadron cadet first sergeant, and a whole lot of nothing but standing there waiting to march to Mitchell Hall for lunch. Many times, in order to make this time pass more quickly, the first sergeant would read some jokes or tell stories submitted by cadets in the squadron. Many of these jokes were outstanding, but many other times they were completely out of line, either exceptionally crass or sacrilegious. It's one thing to tell an inappropriate joke in private with other crass and sacrilegious friends who will appreciate that sort of topic. It's another to tell jokes of that nature to a general and captive audience. I never observed much objection to these jokes, mainly because of the overwhelming culture of professional delinquency among cadets at that time. Many cadets were masters at acting mature and respectable while under the microscope, but it was just that—an act. Many of the problems at the Academy could have been largely avoided if cadets could have shown just a bit more sociopolitical initiative.

I remember on numerous occasions being slandered while saying a personal prayer before a meal. The audacity required to insult someone for praying while that person is in the act is mind-boggling, a distasteful but telling behavior. A person who insults another while he or she prays most likely has little to no respect for anything or anyone. People who do not respect the more sacrosanct aspects of life will undoubtedly disregard the less momentous rules governing social interaction. The boundless potential for malevolent behavior in these individuals is dangerous. Unfortunately, many of those cadets are now serving in the United States Air Force in various leadership capacities.

I have heard many argue the point, "You have to expect all that to a certain degree—it's the military." This is a hazardous line of thinking. Making an effort to marginalize a legitimate concern by pointing to the fact that the suspect activity happens with regularity in certain situations does not in any way change the reality that it is wrong and should not be tolerated. A person can expect to be insulted many times in life; that doesn't mean it's acceptable to go around insulting people. A person can expect that walking down a dark alley can be treacherous, yet that doesn't mean that the sorts of criminal activities that occur in dark alleys are acceptable. Yes, of course I expected to hear inappropriate commentary or be hassled for reverencing a higher power. Nonetheless, the frequency of insults and intolerance towards mine and others' faith did not legitimize that behavior. S.L.A. Marshall would agree. He states:

> War looses violence and disorder; it inflames passions and makes it relatively easy for the individual to get away with unlawful actions. But it does not lessen the gravity of his offense or make it less necessary that constituted authority put him down. ... The main safeguard against lawlessness and hooliganism in any armed body is the integrity of its officers. When men know that their commander is absolutely opposed to such excesses and will take forceful action to repress any breach of

> discipline, they will conform. But when an officer winks at any depredation by his men, it is no different than if he had committed the act.[7]

Although cadets at the Academy were not battling the enemy quite yet, passions were definitely inflamed, and the principle applies.

The final example of religious intolerance (disregard, really) stemmed from an Academy tradition. Every week during fall semester, the USAFA football team had a game; fourth-class cadets from around the Cadet Wing would create encouraging banners and post them on the wall of the staff tower in Mitchell Hall. Most often they said things like, "GO AIR FORCE, BEAT NAVY" or whatever team we were playing that week. Many times freshmen would show a little creativity and come up with something good-naturedly humorous to say about the opposing squad. But when we played universities with religious affiliations, such as Notre Dame or BYU, these banners invariably made a mockery of these schools' respective religions. Banners often disrespectfully underscored, for instance, the sexual-abuse problem within the Catholic Church or the history of polygamy associated with the Mormons. For a so-called spirit banner, these two topics should have been entirely off-limits—one would think. More disturbing was that each and every one of these banners seen hanging from the staff tower had been approved by Academy leadership.

Ultimately it took an act of vigilantism on my brother's part to quell the practice. Our first year at the Academy, we simply grinned and bore these banners, but it was a different story the next year. One day while walking out of Mitchell Hall headed back to the squadron (walking together was a deterrence measure at the Academy, like something you'd see in gangland), Chaz had had just about enough of the ignorant messages denoted on these banners and ripped one down on our way out. It didn't take long for a number of corrupt cadets from Chaz's freshman squadron to arrive on the scene.

Their hostility over my brother's actions was counteracted rather quickly by his fury. The cadets informed Chaz that the freshmen had worked very hard to make the banners. My brother informed the cadets that the freshmen's expense of great amounts of time and energy creating the banners did not legitimize their messages, and thus he wasn't going

---

7 Marshall, *The Armed Forces Officer*, 192.

to go back and rehang a banner that should never have been hung in the first place. Chaz turned around and ordered me to follow, and we left the building with the cadets still standing there. Anybody who knows my brother knows that such a situation is rarely instigated by him. It takes a fairly extreme insult or extenuating circumstance to bring out that side of my brother. The banners apparently met those criteria.

The next day, during noon-meal announcements, there was an official statement made that spirit banners should contain appropriate messages and that suspect banners would be taken down. Chaz and I just looked at each other and quietly chalked one up for the home team.

It was also during BCT that I learned of a sexual-assault response issue at the Academy. During BCT II, one of the female basic cadets in my squadron came to me and described her experience the night before. She told me she had been sleeping when someone climbed on top of her, held her down for a brief, frightening moment of forced frottage, then ran away. She said she didn't know what to do. I didn't know what she should do either. I ignorantly instructed her to inform the squadron first sergeant. She seemed very hesitant to report the incident, I believe out of fear that the person she reported it to could just as easily been the person who assaulted her.

I was left feeling miserable, realizing I could not be of any real assistance to her. I was in a completely powerless position, not just because I was a basic cadet but because I lacked sufficient knowledge of the protocol for reporting assaults, not only because we had never been trained on the subject, but also because a comprehensive assault-reporting process didn't even exist. After 2003, when sexual assault at the Academy became a matter of public concern, multiple investigations were conducted in order to ascertain from where the problem stemmed and what had been done, if anything, to correct it. The *Report of the Working Group Concerning the Deterrence of and Response to Incidents of Sexual Assault at the U.S. Air Force Academy,* hereafter called the *Working Group Report,* commented on the prevention and awareness training we received upon entering the Academy. This report stated that the sexual-assault prevention and awareness training was ineffective for the following reasons:

(1) The definition of sexual assault used in Academy Instruction 51-201 was confusing, *not in compliance with the law associated with sexual assaults* and inconsistent with the definition used throughout the Air Force;

(2) The fourth-class cadets who received the training during BCT were too tired to process the information;

(3) The self-defense training given to fourth-class women often occurred too late in the semester to be effective; and

(4) The training had little focus on the moral, leadership, or character component of deterrence.[8]

So even if my female classmate had told the squadron first sergeant about the assault, he would not have known what to do other than turn it over to his superiors, which most likely would not have led to any real results. Sexual assault at the Academy had been an accepted reality since 1993, when the first cases started to appear in significant numbers. Until recently, female cadets were told in their females-only briefings during basic training to *expect* to be sexually harassed or assaulted while at the Air Force Academy. Year after year, climate surveys administered to cadets pointing toward substantial sexual-assault problems were ignored by AFA administrators. USAFA administrators knew how ineffective the Academy's sexual-assault reporting process was but did nothing to correct its deficiencies. It was a broken system, unique from all other branches of the military, other academies, and even the operational Air Force, that jeopardized the safety of female cadets for over a decade. [Author's note: the AFA's history of sexual assault is discussed in much greater detail in a later chapter.]

Basic training is a necessary part of military indoctrination. The experience is meant to develop civilian men and women into soldiers, airmen, marines, or sailors. There is a difference between working on an aircraft carrier in the Persian Gulf and working at a real-estate company in Suburbia, America. Accordingly, those who fight our very determined enemies must be of a mental stature strong enough to withstand the emotional strain associated with that line of work. Basic training is the method used by the military to ensure its members can do just that.

It was my passion for hard work and intensity that attracted me to the military. It was this understanding that serious physical training was of the utmost importance that accounted for my superior perfor-

---

8 *Working Group Report*, "Report of the Working Group Concerning the Deterrence of and Response to Incidents of Sexual Assault at the U.S. Air Force Academy" (Washington, DC: Headquarters, Department of the Air Force, 2003), 26–30.

mance evaluations throughout BCT. Because of years of contact sports and myriad physically demanding work experiences, I valued challenging physical activity and expected as much from my BCT experience. A little rough training here and there caused me no consternation. What I did not expect or appreciate was the complete lack of respect, the nauseatingly unprofessional environment, the rampant religious discrimination, and of course the failure of the AFA bureaucracy to deal appropriately with such issues.

BCT was a stressful time during which our individual strengths and weaknesses became abundantly clear. As basic cadets we came together in order to survive a common experience and in so doing revealed who among us were the unconquerable spirits and who were not. One can create an illusion of mental toughness fairly easily when under normal circumstances, but when "s*** hits the fan," as they say, a person's true character always shines through. Basic training provided numerous opportunities for the weak to demonstrate their weakness and the strong to show their strength. The displays ranged from a classmate's pretending to pass out and intentionally rolling into a drainage ditch to avoid an afternoon run, to a cadet's unconditionally swapping his dry sleeping bag for his classmate's rain-soaked one in order to allow his classmate a decent night's sleep.

However long and taxing it seemed, after approximately six weeks BCT came to an end. Little did we know at the time, though, that what would come next would be more maddening than anything most of us had ever previously experienced—the Fourth Class System.

3

Fourth Class System

"When an idea is idiotic to begin with, its applications never make any sense."

—The Nazi Officer's Wife

The Fourth Class System was the most poorly conceived and executed idea I have ever witnessed. As Edith Hahn would say, the AFA's reproduced conception for a Fourth Class System was idiotic to begin with, and accordingly its applications never made any sense. The institution was not just entirely useless but truly counterproductive. Shortly after the conclusion of BCT we were familiarized with the Fourth Class System, an oppressive arrangement that would control (with an iron fist) our every move for the next eight months of our lives.

Upon completion of BCT II, we marched back to the Academy cadet area to start the academic year. We were officially accepted as cadets at the Air Force Academy and marched in the Acceptance Day parade. Then we had a pinning-on ceremony during which we received shoulder boards signifying our new rank as fourth-class cadets, and we underwent a name change from "basic" to "four degree." There was only one thing left to do: the beat-down.

Shortly thereafter we were introduced to our primary trainers. They were the third-class cadets, or sophomores, in our new academic-year squadrons. Our introduction to the third-class cadets in Cadet Squadron 17 (CS-17) was rather inhospitable. My classmates and I were ordered to assemble in the squadron assembly room (SAR) dressed in BDUs and wielding web-belts, canteens, and mouthguards. The introduction was an intense two- to three-hour-long physical training session, during which we learned the names of all thirty new faces and drenched our uniforms with sweat. These third-class cadets or three degrees were responsible for our indoctrination into the Academy via the Fourth Class System. They took great pleasure in detailing to us everything that was required of us as fourth-classmen.

In order to more fully appreciate the complexity of the Fourth Class System, a detailed description of a typical week in the life of a four degree during the 2001–2002 school year is necessary.

Every morning at about 05:30, four degrees would start to wake up, not because Reveille had sounded, but because we needed about half an hour to memorize all the information that we would be required to know throughout the day. We also had a set of assigned chores to complete before breakfast, such as taking out the squadron garbage or cleaning the bathroom. These things were already done by the janitorial service, but that wasn't the point. The point was to make four degrees' existence as unpleasant as possible. If a four degree wanted to take a shower before going to breakfast and class that day, he or she would have to wake up even earlier, which meant that most of the time freshmen cadets did not take showers at the start of the day. Showering at night instead of morning was a habit that carried over to cadets' succeeding years at the Academy. Since the vast majority of the school didn't shower in the morning, there was an unpleasant stench in the classrooms. They smelled because of the skipped showers and because of sweat buildup during the multiple physical training sessions throughout the day. The average fourth-class cadet's appearance consisted of an immaculately pressed and shined uniform, greasy face, and matted hair. I was one of two or three people that I knew of in my entire squadron who actually took a shower in the morning, because I was simply unwilling to subject others to my body odor.

Shortly after 06:00, freshmen would line up in the hallways at attention with their *Contrails* handbooks directly in front of their faces so they could learn Air Force knowledge while maintaining the Academy version of the position of attention. The Academy's version of the position of attention was to have one's shoulders raised and pulled back and for the chin to be firmly pressed against the chest. The position was anything but natural, purposefully degrading, and at odds with the position of attention utilized in the operational Air Force and every other branch of the military. *Contrails* was a handbook given to all incoming freshmen that contained information on the history of the Air Force, biographies on influential Air Force personnel, and significant Air Force–related historical events. It also contained information regarding the current-day operational Air Force and information the Administration wanted cadets to know about the Academy itself.

Four degrees would "call minutes" for the twenty to thirty minutes they were in the hallway until it was time to go to breakfast. To call minutes was to inform upperclassmen in one loud, unified voice exactly what was on the menu for breakfast and how many minutes were left until the start of the morning meal. The upperclassmen who enjoyed training used this time to make four degrees do calisthenics and recite Air Force knowledge until breakfast. Once the last call was made, freshmen would run back to their rooms, grab all their school supplies, and head for breakfast. Moving about the cadet area as a four degree was aggravating. Once a four degree left the dormitory, he or she was no longer allowed to talk unless specifically addressed by an upperclassman. Four degrees were required to carry schoolbags in their left hand at all times, never in their right hand or across the shoulder. Four degrees needed to be ready to salute officers passing by at a moment's notice. Allegedly, because of the speed at which four degrees traveled about the cadet area, there was not enough time for us to switch carrying hands and throw up a salute once we noticed an officer walking past, so it was absolutely necessary for us to always carry schoolbags in the left hand, even if that meant carrying a schoolbag and a laptop computer in one hand and jeopardizing an investment in the thousands of dollars.

Once a freshman cadet was actually in the hallway, apart from not being able to speak, that cadet had to walk at attention or braced up, never deviating more than one and a half floor tiles away from the wall, and always on the right side of the hallway. If it was necessary to turn around for any reason, ninety-degree facing movements were required. Four degrees were only allowed to use one stairwell leaving and entering the squadron, even though multiple stairwells existed. The stairwell designated for freshmen was the farthest stairwell from most of the places cadets needed to go on a daily basis. Even in Fairchild Hall, the academic building where cadets met for class, we were allowed to use only back stairwells, ostensibly to prevent overcrowding in the stairwells. But later in the year when four degrees were recognized as part of the Cadet Wing, these overcrowding issues apparently vanished. After Recognition (the three-day training session after which the Fourth Class System effectively comes to an end), four degrees could use any stairwell they liked and, miraculously, overcrowding was never an issue.

Whenever a four degree passed an upperclassman assigned to the same squadron, either while in the squadron area or on the terrazzo, he or she was required to sound off by giving a spirited verbal greeting incorporating the upperclassman's name and rank followed by an energetic shout-out to the squadron, for instance, "Good morning, Cadet (insert name here)! Mean Seventeen!" Any other upperclassman received a Sir or Ma'am instead of the name. If a four degree got the name or time of day wrong, hesitated to the slightest degree, or didn't sound enthusiastic enough according to the upperclassman, an on-the-spot training session would ensue. Once we made it out of the squadron, all four degrees were required to run to their destinations. Not only did four degrees have to run to their destination, but they had to run the strips. The Academy terrazzo was a large square. Inlaid in the terrazzo were smaller squares outlined by marble tiles. Fourth-class cadets could only run on these marble tiles and the marble strips that would take the four degree on the longest route possible to reach the destination. While running on these strips with schoolbag in left hand, four degrees were required to come to a walk while greeting every upperclassman they passed and then return to double time (military terminology for running). As every cadet at the school went to meals and class at the same time, a four degree would pass large numbers of upperclassmen on the terrazzo, thus having to start and stop repeatedly and yell the entire way to the destination.

Few times in my life have I felt genuinely humiliated, but because the Academy was a hotbed for negative sentiment, it probably doesn't come as a surprise that the majority of these humiliating experiences took place at the USAFA. Once, while attempting to run the strips, I crossed paths with a little girl and her mother who were visiting the Academy. I didn't even notice them until I was on my way back to the squadron area. The little girl, feeling intimidated by all the men and women in uniform walking around, was trying to stay out of the way, so she had pressed herself up against the granite wall bordering the terrazzo where, in a normal world, she would have been out of the natural flow of traffic. As I began running, I heard the mom call out to her daughter to come away from the wall so I could pass. As many children would do, the girl protested and stubbornly maintained her position. Following a stern gesture from the mother, the girl grudgingly moved but wanted to know why it was necessary. Her mother hesitantly informed her that four degrees were only allowed to run on those marble strips she had been standing on, and that if she hadn't moved I couldn't have gotten where I needed to be. That statement and the absolute bewilderment on the girl's face caused me to feel truly humiliated. I felt so ridiculous! Here I was, a nineteen-year-old man performing an activity of absolutely no value whatsoever, and consequently being called out for it by a little girl no more than six or seven years old.

I imagine moments like the above and the attendant pressures of the Academy are what caused a cadet in the earlier years of the Academy's existence to kill himself. On the interior wall of the southwestern wing of Fairchild Hall is a mural for a previous graduating class. The mural is a remembrance of significant events during that specific class's tenure at the Academy. Apparently, they found it necessary to commemorate the fact that one of their classmates had loaded his M-14 rifle with a No. 2 lead pencil and shot himself with it. His portion of the mural shows him sprawled on the floor with blood pouring from his nose, the rifle next to him. The fact that the mural contains a graphic depiction of the suicide of an Air Force Academy cadet is sick and wrong. That whoever painted or created it thought it appropriate to incorporate that event into the mural in such a barbaric way is cause to wonder. The fact that Academy leadership allowed it to stay—and in such a highly visible location—is even more thought provoking. But again I digress.

Once we four degrees arrived at Mitchell Hall, we would pick up breakfast and sit down at randomly assigned tables (mandatory breakfast- and squadron-assigned seating came later). Four degrees would eat in the same manner as we had in BCT, sitting on the first one-third of the seat, back straight as a board, hands positioned on thighs, eyes staring at the eagle picture on the plate in front of us. Just as in BCT, four degrees were allowed seven chews for each bite. After asking permission to be excused from the table, four degrees would stand up and leave Mitchell Hall still squaring corners and walking at attention in the direction of their first-period classes.

After four hours of academic instruction, all four classes would return to their respective squadrons to prepare for the noon-meal formation. For many upperclassmen, the thirty minutes prior to formation out on the terrazzo was their favorite part of the day. It was a time to take the stress they accumulated from the rigorous Academy curriculum and let it out on four degrees. We always had intense beat-downs and then headed out to form up. As we stood in formation, cadet leadership would take accountability (report how many cadets were physically present and how many were absent but accounted for). We marched to lunch in order of how well each respective squadron was performing militarily. If your squadron was performing poorly, you would end up being in the last group of people to enter Mitchell Hall for lunch. My freshman squadron marched last for many months in a row for a number of reasons. The main reason was that the vast majority of three degrees in our squadron, college sophomores, were on alcoholic probation for underage drinking. The cadet squadron commander was on alcoholic probation as well, after just about killing himself with alcohol poisoning, along with his cadet squadron leadership friends after each of them took 22 shots of whiskey and blacked out during his twenty-first birthday party downtown. They survived the incident because someone was conscious enough to call 911.

I remember seeing the people assembled each day to watch noon-meal formation while visiting the Academy and wondering how anyone could enjoy it. Maybe I should have been content that at least *someone* was enjoying it, but it's hard to do that when the other person's enjoyment is contingent upon your displeasure. After marching to Mitchell Hall to the sound of the Cadet Drum and Bugle Corps' rendition of the Air Force anthem and other famous marching songs, we would enter what could reasonably be labeled a madhouse. The decibel level upon entering a room with 4,400 cadets yelling and being yelled at would be startling for many, unsettling for some, but for the cadets who ate lunch that way each day it was standard. After reaching the table at which a four degree was assigned to eat, he or she would immediately begin pouring upperclassmen's drinks according to their previously stated preferences. While pouring drinks at attention, the four degree would have to recite inconsequential information called four degree knowledge. This information included sports trivia, current events, the exact number of days until graduation for all four classes, the date of the next Air Force Day, and what significant event had transpired on that day that put it into the history books. The preparation that occurred in the early morning hours was often for this specific noontime meal occasion. If a four degree arrived at the table and did not impress the upperclassmen with his or her recital of all the information the group had been ordered to memorize, then the upperclassmen would make the four degree pay for it by essentially not allowing that cadet to eat lunch, all the while further damaging that cadet's increasingly insensitive hearing.

Although Academy regulations stated that the table commandant was responsible for doolies (freshmen) getting enough to eat, usually it was quite the opposite. The table commandant was usually the person most inclined to train freshmen and, as a result, was also the most culpable party with respect to freshmen not being allowed to eat. Table etiquette and decorum dictated that if a four degree was being addressed by an upperclassman, that person must stop eating and attentively listen to what was being said to him or her. Accordingly, in order to not allow the freshman cadet to eat lunch, upperclassmen would just take turns yelling at the four degree and he or she would spend the entire meal listening to upperclassmen yell and scream or make derogatory comments, all the while not eating lunch. This happened so regularly that some four degrees (including my brother and me) would go weeks and sometimes months without eating a decent lunch.

Once the noon meal concluded, four degrees would attend a short period of military training before afternoon classes began. By and large, this time was reserved for either the proctoring of four-degree knowledge tests or practicing for or participating in a strange activity referred to as a knowledge bowl. Upperclassmen took knowledge tests very seriously, and consequently so did most four degrees. Each week for approximately eight months in a row, we were instructed to study and internalize certain information for the knowledge test that week. The information was sporadic but almost always had something to do with the Air Force Academy or the Air Force at large. All thirty or so of us four degrees would assemble in this tiny room with paper and pencil in hand in order to take the knowledge test. One upperclass cadet, usually a three degree, would come in, tell us all to shut our mouths, and then ask the first question with an air of distaste. After asking the first question, the next thing out of the three degree's mouth was always something to do with how bad we smelled. It was true; four degrees, having not taken a shower in the morning and sweating through their uniforms from running to class and intense calisthenics during regularly scheduled and on-the-spot beat-down sessions, did smell rather unpleasant.

It was always mildly amusing to see the faces of fellow classmates, who loved all the tenets of the Fourth Class System, beam brighter than the noonday sun after each question because they knew the answer before the proctor even finished asking the question. The only questions to which I had an answer before they were asked were questions referring to when fourth-classmen could participate in certain activities. They would always ask such questions as "When can a fourth-class cadet talk in public areas?" The correct answer was always "Never," mainly because four degrees were restricted from just about everything other than using the restroom, studying, being trained, eating, and breathing. Therefore, answering "Never" to those types of questions was always a safe bet.

If a normal U.S. citizen walked into the SAR where knowledge bowls took place and witnessed the mannerisms and verbalizations transpiring within the room, that person would most likely stare blankly, utterly captivated by the scene. The civilian would be amazed that people defending our country were acting in such a ridiculous manner. Knowledge bowls were competitions in which four degrees would compete against four degrees from other squadrons to see who knew more about the Fourth Class System, the history of the Air Force, and the primary functions of Air Force aircraft and their respective crew members. There were home and away competitions, either in our SAR or the opposing squadron's SAR. It was always the same thing; we would line up at attention outside the SAR, steadfastly reading our *Contrails*, while the three degrees and other training staff would walk up and down yelling at us that this was our time—much as a West Texas high-school football coach would do in the locker room before game time. The nature of the training staff's comments depended on the previous knowledge bowl performance. If we had performed well the week before, the comments would range from, "You got lucky last week," to "Get up for this, you are the better squadron, prove it today." If we had lost the week before or performed poorly, comments would range from, "You were horrible last week, and we all know what happens when four degrees don't perform," to "You had better do better this week or there will be serious repercussions. Trust me, you do not want to repeat last week's mistake."

When both squadrons arrived, we would enter the SAR screaming our squadron's purposefully antagonistic motto, newly contrived on a weekly basis depending on which squadron we were up against that week. Once we had all filed into the room, our squadron would stand next to the opposing squadron and continue yelling our motto as loudly as possible, trying to outmatch the other squadron. Minute after minute would pass with us just yelling at attention, waiting for the knowledge bowl to start, while training staff walked around with very serious expressions on their faces.

After deciding that they could wait no longer, someone would take control and silence the four degrees. Two rows of chairs were positioned in the center of the room facing each other. When the competition began, the first line in formation would file into our row of chairs, the opposing squadron into theirs. One upperclassman would sit in the middle and ask the questions. While the upperclassman was asking the question, four degrees would assume a position that would enable them to throw their fist out in front of them as quickly as possible, indicating they knew the answer. Once the first cadet to respond was acknowledged, all the four degrees in that row would immediately shoot back into the seated position of attention while that particular cadet attempted to answer the question. If that cadet answered correctly, his or her squadron would be awarded a certain number of points. Thus went the competition.

I always felt incredibly out of place at knowledge bowls. I hadn't joined the Air Force to act in such a bizarre manner. The decorum associated with knowledge bowls was absurd, and I couldn't help feeling ridiculous throughout the entire experience. Accordingly, I never answered questions and tried to fly under the radar as much as possible. Although I rather despised knowledge bowls, one in particular actually managed to bring a smile to my face; it was the knowledge-bowl competition with my brother's squadron. Neither my brother nor I ever fully participated, and, to the best of my knowledge, neither of us had ever actually answered a question, so when our two squadrons met, training staff thought it would be entertaining to have a Graney vs. Graney showdown. Ordinarily the chair closest to the knowledge-bowl proctor was reserved for the four degree in each squadron who knew the answer to every question. Therefore, training staff figured it would be amusing to place two cadets, twin brothers at that, who were notorious for their limited participation in knowledge bowls, in the hotseats for an epic consolation round. My brother's eyes met mine from across the aisle, each of us with a look of mutual understanding. We sat down, and on the last question of the round, which happened to be a "When may four degrees—" question, I triumphantly answered, "Sir the answer is never!" and the whole room went crazy.

Training staff from my squadron were out of control, hugging each other in sheer bliss. The scene on the other side of the aisle was quite the contrary: melancholy faces, subdued, disgusted with my brother's performance. Chaz and I knew that I would go back to my squadron temporarily favored by my upperclassmen, while he would go back as a perceived loser. The situation took on a strangely humorous undertone for us, as the upperclassmen were making a huge deal out of the event, while we were both too bitter about the absurdity of the event in general to care one way or the other.

After the afternoon military training time we would all go back to class for the last two or three academic periods of the day. Once classes finished up, intercollegiate athletes would go down to the Cadet Field House for practice. If a four degree was not an intercollegiate athlete, his or her afternoon consisted of one of three activities: military training sessions, intramurals, or studying—for the lucky ones.

Three degrees in our squadron tried to conduct training sessions every day after school, just as when they were four degrees, but new school policy had created what was known as excellence time, and that seemed to impede them. In order to turn every afternoon into a training session, upperclassmen now had to submit paperwork to the AOC detailing what they were planning on doing for training and its relative purpose. Consequently, the Class of 2005 was not trained after school with the same frequency as the year before, because across the Cadet Wing people simply did not enjoy paperwork. At around 17:30 hours, intercollegiate practices would have wrapped up, and dinner would be served. Dinner was on a first-come, first-served basis similar to breakfast. After dinner on Tuesdays and Wednesdays, squadrons would assemble for another military training session, normally conducted in the SAR. This training would span the seven o'clock hour as planned, but four degrees did not usually arrive back to their rooms until around 20:30 hours, as on-the-spot training took place en route.

Most cadets at the Academy take more than eighteen credit hours each semester. Twenty to twenty-two credit hours a semester is more normal than it is abnormal. Difficult curriculum and little time to study accounted for our Cadet Wing's 2.3 average GPA. When arriving back at our rooms after all other training was supposed to have concluded, we had an incredible amount of studying to accomplish in very little time. Most colleges recommend that students study two hours for each hour of class time. If four degree cadets had tried to follow that advice, they would have had to study continuously until well past noon-meal formation the next day. Instead, four degrees had to go into crisis management mode. The most important or critical studying came first, then on down the priority list. These late-night study sessions never ended as a result of actually finishing all the required homework. Study sessions ended when the cadet reached the point of exhaustion, the point at which all attempts to continue studying became futile. This would usually occur around 01:30 in the morning. It was always mildly depressing to hear Taps sound at 22:30 hours, when you knew you were just getting started. Many times cadets really would be just getting started then, because in addition to studying for class the next day, four degrees had to shine their shoes, iron a new uniform, create a handmade grade card for the weekly room inspection carried out by their personal trainer, clean the room if necessary, take a shower if he or she hadn't done so that morning, check squadron e-mail, visit with the personal trainer if requested to do so, and plan for the next day. That's a typical weekday in the life of a four degree. Weekends were spent similarly, either being trained or attempting to catch up with schoolwork.

Apart from all the inconsequential activities and trivial rules and regulations governing our every move, the most aggravating aspect of the Fourth Class System by far was the way we were treated. There was a complete and utter lack of respect for us from upperclassmen, who did and said just about anything they desired. Frequently those desires were misguided, against school regulations, and even contrary to the laws of the United States. The Fourth Class System is a two-part process involving not only the activities and decorum required of four degrees, but also the way upperclassmen interact with freshmen. The problem with the late Fourth Class System at the Academy was not simply the mistaken adherence to inconsequential training practices—it was the way those practices were carried out on four degrees. I remember reading this passage out of the *Academy Training Philosophy (ATP) Handbook*:

> Before they (upperclassmen) arrived at USAFA, they never treated anyone with as much disrespect as they treat fourth-class cadets, and upon graduation, they will never treat anyone as they did at USAFA.

Such a bold statement tells us that even though the writer didn't necessarily know the past experiences of specific cadets at the Academy and most certainly could not have known how these cadets would behave in the future, he felt confident making this statement in light of the severity and longevity of abuses delivered by upperclass AFA cadets. Furthermore, more than one person at the Academy must have agreed to the validity of that estimation, since it was included and highlighted in the official ATP handbook! I could not agree more, based on my own experience at the Academy. I find it disturbing that even though Academy administrators agreed with the contention enough to include it in the ATP, nothing was ever done about it; that level of inaction is slightly creepy. S.L.A. Marshall, once again, had this to say:

> ... It might be well to speak of the importance of enthusiasm, cheerfulness, kindness, courtesy, and justice, which are the safeguards of honor and the tokens of mutual respect between one person and another. This last there must be if people are to go forward to together, prosper in one another's company, find strength in the bonds of mutual service, and experience a common felicity in the relationship between the leader and the led.[9]

What Marshall describes above is so antithetical to common practice at the USAFA that for a moment the quote itself seems naïve and idealistic. But Marshall was not a romantic, nor did he speak in rhymes and riddles. He spoke in plain English and to the point. The drastic contrast between Marshall's model of decent human interaction and the way AFA cadets treat each other speaks to how pervasive and elaborate the abuse has become at the Academy; the root cause, of course, being the Fourth Class System.

---

9 Marshall, *The Armed Forces Officer,* 41.

4

Vicious and Illegal Indulgence

"Hell is the impossibility of Reason."

—Platoon

Nothing sums up the essence of the late Fourth Class System more perfectly than the above movie quote. Most of the more stressful situations in our lives are caused by the inability or unwillingness of some entity to be reasonable. One cannot dispute irrationality with rationale, illogic with logic, or the unreasonable with reason. There will always be friction between the sensible and the senseless. Only when the absurd become aware of their absurdity can those who endorse purposeful thought and action have any influence over them.

A shrewd deliberator knows the best way to dismantle the opposing argument is to expose its falsely-reasoned basis. The principal tools of debate are facts, comparisons, and cause and effect. When attempting to bring an entity to agreement, there is nothing more aggravating than that entity's inability or unwillingness to accept the facts of the matter or a refusal to acknowledge well-founded conjectures regarding cause and effect. When this is the case, exasperation and hopelessness are often the result. Hopelessness leads to depression. In summation, many of the hopeless situations people end up in and the debilitating effects of depression consequently suffered are caused simply by the absence of reason. The number of examples is overwhelming, because humans have a boundless capacity for unreasonable behavior. We have the unique ability to bring about incredible good in the world. We can also cause more calculated pain and suffering than any other species on earth. The Fourth

Class System had fashioned a morally depraved, senseless climate, one that caused exceptional psychological and sometimes physical damage to many cadets. The system and all its intricacies produced entire generations of graduates unwilling to acknowledge the facts concerning their alma mater or compare theirs to other officer training programs, graduates who disregard the true causes and effects of Fourth Class training methods as practiced on them and eventually by them. Many of these officers served as one of the main factions opposing change at the Academy, even when it was obviously necessary. By the time they came together to oppose needed changes, these former four degree cadets were serving in capacities such as AFA superintendent, commandant, and air officers commanding; as members of the Association of Graduates, and at Air Force Headquarters. The degenerate culture at the Air Force Academy continued largely because of the adherence by these men to the unwritten but officially sanctioned implementation of the Fourth Class System.

In order to appreciate the pointlessness of the Fourth Class System, it's important to know its history and to compare it to the practices of other service academies, in this case the United States Naval Academy (USNA a.k.a. Annapolis) and the United States Military Academy (USMA a.k.a. West Point). The USMA was founded in West Point, NY, in 1802.[10] From the time of its inception until the time of the Civil War, there was no systematic or sanctioned Fourth Class indoctrination program at the institution—only what was called "deviling,",which occurred during basic training and consisted of minor pranks played out on new cadets by upperclassmen. Deviling included activities like cutting tent strings, stealing freshmen's clothes, pulling cadets out of their tents, and other inconsequential activities, and would end at the start of the academic year. Toward the Civil War these pranks became more widespread

---

10 Government Accountability Office Report, "DoD Service Academies: More Changes Needed to Eliminate Hazing," GAO/NSIAD-93-36 (Washington, DC: U. S. Government Accountability Office, November 1992), 11.

See also, referenced in GAO Report:

S.E. Ambrose, *Duty, Honor, Country: A History of West Point* (Baltimore, MD: The Johns Hopkins Press, 1966).

P. Benjamin, *The United States Naval Academy* (New York: G.P. Putnam, 1900).

Captain W.D. Puleston, *Annapolis:Gangway to the Quarterdeck* (New York: D.Appleton–Century Co., 1942).

among the corps of cadets and slightly more dangerous. Over time, an entire set of unwritten laws developed that regulated the way upper and underclassmen were allowed to interact. Military Academy leadership viewed the evolving condition as the emergence of hazing and made efforts to contain it. USMA and USNA superintendents in the early 1870s both spoke out against the practice, calling it "essentially criminal," a "vicious and illegal indulgence," and a "cruel and senseless practice." The proliferation of hazing at the academies and their respective superintendents' opposition to the practice caused the U.S. Congress to pass legislation that both defined and criminalized hazing. Even though it had been outlawed, hazing continued and even worsened around the turn of the century. Steps were taken by Congress in the early 1900s to put an end to hazing at the academies, but its efforts were largely unsuccessful due to noncompliance by graduates, faculty, and even cadets during congressional hearings and investigations. The uncooperative spirit demonstrated by these groups was motivated by their fervent commitment to protect hazing at the academies, as well as those responsible for it. When congressional efforts to stop the practice proved ineffective, hazing at our nation's service academies became an accepted reality. The practice and all its particulars would evolve into the Fourth Class System, incorporating many of the same traditions, protocols, and codes of behavior as the previous modus operandi. The Fourth Class System and the reasoning given for its alleged necessity have changed and evolved over the years, but since its inception hazing-type behavior has always been at its heart.

Up until the conclusion of World War II, the Air Force as we know it today was the Army Air Corps, a strategic component of the Army. In 1947, at the request of many distinguished Army Air Corps leaders, the Army Air Corps became the United States Air Force, an entirely separate branch of the military. Shortly thereafter, the newly commissioned Air Force began preparations for its own Academy. On 11 July 1955, after significant deliberation about the appearance, location, and construction of the institution, the first class of 305 male cadets was sworn in. Because of the father-son-like relationship with the Army, much of the decorum, etiquette, and training practices found in the Air Force originates from the Army (hence Air Force cadets singing Army jodies). Just as these aspects of the operational military were passed on to the Air Force, so the Fourth Class System from the USMA was transferred over to the Air Force Academy.

When I was a cadet at the Air Force Academy, this was the stated purpose of the Fourth Class System:

> To lay the foundation early in the cadet's career for the development of those qualities of character and discipline which will be expected of an officer. These qualities must be so deeply instilled in the individual's personality that no stress or strain will erase them.[11]

There is no doubt that certain traits were deeply instilled in us, but character and discipline were not among them. Character is not something you learn upon entering the adult world. One does not graduate from high school, move on to college or the career field, then subsequently become a person of character. Character is something that is firmly established years before entering adulthood. Important, life-altering decisions are made as an adolescent as well. In fact, some of the most life-altering decisions occur in adolescence. Decisions such as where to go to college, what career to choose, and what kind of lifestyle to lead are often made in the later adolescent years and dramatically affect the rest of a person's life. In order to make the appropriate decision when these choices present themselves, character and discipline are a necessity and ideally have already been developed by parental involvement, instruction, and constructive criticism.

When people enter the adult world and find themselves in difficult situations where they must make moral judgments, their preexistent character shines through, and they make the choice accordingly. The character strengths and flaws an individual has upon entering the Academy are the same qualities he or she leaves with, unless during the cadet years, that person made a personal decision to change them. Four-degree training at the Academy allows a cadet's true character to surface. The real purpose of the Fourth Class System had nothing to do with the information found in the standard issue *Contrails* handbook and cannot be condensed into one paragraph.

The Air Force Academy's ultimate mission is to train cadets to be effective officers in the United States Air Force. The Air Force Academy's mission is theoretically no different from that of reserve officer

---

11 United States Air Force Academy Cadet Handbook, *Contrails* (USAFA, CO: United States Air Force Academy, 2001–2002), 16.

training corps (ROTC) units found at colleges throughout the nation or in officer training school (OTS), called officer candidate school (OCS) for the Navy, Marine Corps, and Army. Each and every one of these programs is designed to produce officers to serve in leadership capacities in the United States Armed Forces. Accordingly, the training administered by these programs should have everything to do with the stated objective. Any training conducted that does not facilitate officer development is both unnecessary and inappropriate. Lack of sufficient officer-development training at any one of these institutions creates a precarious situation for our country wherein we would have men and women insufficiently trained to fulfill their enormously important roles as leaders of the most powerful air, sea, and land force representing the most powerful nation in the world.

When we combine insufficiently trained leaders, immense military power, and profound responsibility, we set ourselves up for wrongdoing and injustice not only to our countrymen but to those countries with which we interact. This undesirable scenario should be avoided at all costs. The burden rests on both the Department of Defense (DOD) and the American people to carefully monitor the situation at our service academies and ensure that our future leaders are being properly trained. If it becomes known that there is some sort of problem with the way our military personnel are being trained, for the security of this nation and others it should be corrected.

The Fourth Class System insufficiently trained future officers, thus producing thousands of officers who entered the operational Air Force without a real concept of leadership or strength of character; the only exceptions, of course, being those individuals who had developed leadership skills and strength of character prior to attending the academy—and those who wisely learned what *not* to do from deficient upperclassmen and officers at the Academy.

A system that is built around illegitimate activities or ideologies will never be reasonable or justifiable. The very fact that the Fourth Class System originated from a practice created by a group of misguided and foolish young cadets and was banned when first discovered by the leadership of each service academy and later outlawed by United States legislators is the *largest testament to its illegitimacy*. Nowhere along the line did any individual with the appropriate power to do so, within the leadership structure of either the military or United States government, decide that there needed to be a Fourth Class System at service academies *where there once was not.* Imprudent cadets around the time of the Civil War decided there would be Fourth Class Systems at the academies. It was these cadets and their successors who defined what fourth-classmen could and couldn't do, how they would interact with upperclassmen, and how they would be punished for noncompliance. Academy leaders were left out of the process entirely. By the time these leaders attempted to stop the practice it was too late. It had already become a firmly established way of life among cadets. Instead of enforcing their authority and eliminating the practice, next-generation leaders at the academies must have just accepted it as a categorical imperative and issued official doctrine as to its relevance to training future military officers. It is important to understand that it *is for this reason*, more than any other, that the Fourth Class System can be regarded as illegitimate.

On the surface, tradition is the culprit behind the Fourth Class System's preservation. Academy personnel take great pride in the traditions of their institution and expend large amounts of time and energy ensuring that these traditions are maintained. In 1992, when the GAO recommended that the Air Force Academy make changes to its Fourth Class System similar to those the naval and military academies had already made, the Air Force Academy refused. One USAFA cadet's reaction to the GAO recommendation is the perfect embodiment of the Academy administrators' mindset:

> "Don't mess with it [the Fourth Class System]. There are plenty of schools around where people can go and be treated like you would like this place to treat them. We are the last of a dying breed. Please, leave us alone, look away, and let the tradition continue.[12]

The Fourth Class System was the most championed tradition at the Air Force Academy. All sorts of officers and upperclass cadets were willing to emphatically swear by and testify to the great value of the enterprise. I say upperclass cadets and not cadets in general, because the vast majority of four degrees at the school not only lack an appreciation for the Fourth Class System but openly despise it.

---

12 GAO Report, "DoD Service Academies: More Changes Needed to Eliminate Hazing," 76.

Cadets across the board understood that the Fourth Class System turned what was supposed to be an officer-training school into a fraternal proving ground. The system made the institution into a government-sponsored fraternity. Upperclassmen used four- degree training as a means to haze incoming freshmen. The purpose of four-degree training was never to enhance a four degree's ability to perform effectively as an Air Force officer, but to prove to upperclassmen that he or she belonged at "their" school. Accordingly, those four degrees who were determined unsuitable (by upperclass cadets) for attendance at the AFA were constructively removed, either by making that fourth-classman's life so miserable that he or she left voluntarily, or by employing a practice known as pencil whipping that would ultimately lead to the cadet's involuntary removal from the institution. Pencil whipping is making someone look bad on paper. This can be done on performance evaluations, or by documenting when a person makes some sort of mistake (no matter how insignificant), and then ensuring that documentation makes its way into the person's personnel file. Sooner or later, all the negative documentation adds up, and administrative action has to take place to address the person's allegedly poor performance. These are the two methods employed by upperclass cadets when attempting to get rid of a disliked four degree: creating an unbearable environment by constant and severe hazing or pencil whipping them to the point of no return. The real purpose of the Fourth Class System was to empower upperclass cadets to harass freshmen cadets whenever and in whatever manner they desired.

Although both factions (upperclassmen and the Academy administration) share the blame, I believe that cadets are the principal force behind the continuation of the Fourth Class System. I have said on numerous occasions that the Academy was an elaborate behavioral-science laboratory; the Cadet Wing as a whole, and each and every cadet serving as one intriguing case study after another. Even as a professionally uneducated, casual observer, I was enthralled by the insights I gained into human behavior. I can only imagine how interesting the behavioral standard at the Academy would have been to someone like Sigmund or Anna Freud, who spent much of their lives analyzing and theorizing about human behavior. If the two were alive today, they would have a psychoanalytical field day upon discovering how apposite their theories on defense mechanisms are among cadets at the Academy.

Given the very low probability that any large group of people capable of original thought will claim to agree unanimously on anything in the absence of coercion, the almost universal willingness of the upperclassmen of the AFA Cadet Wing to testify to the utility of such a harsh system indicates, to me at least, that there is something more than steadfast loyalty to tradition at play. How these cadets go from near-abhorrence for the Fourth Class System as freshmen to absolute reverence for the system as upperclassmen is, of course, worth considering.

I would argue that the catalyst behind the upperclassmen's approval of the Fourth Class System was in large part their defense mechanisms. The survivors of whom I spoke earlier are these upperclassmen. In order to deal with the anxiety created by the disagreement between their innermost thoughts and feelings, which questioned the legitimacy of the Fourth Class System, and Academy propaganda that conversely championed the value of same, these individuals allowed various defense mechanisms to become deeply imbedded in the fabric of their beings. It is my opinion that the Freudian defense mechanisms at work here are displacement, denial, rationalization, and repression. I also believe two other defense mechanisms, cognitive dissonance and dissociation, first envisaged by Leon Festinger and Pierre Janet respectively, are equally applicable. Displacement is defined as follows:

> A defense mechanism whereby a motive that may not be directly expressed appears in a more acceptable form.[13]

One prominent example of this is a man who kicks his dog because of his dislike for a boss at work. Another example of this could be the grade-school student who verbally or physically harasses a younger and weaker child in response to his own victimization at the hands of the playground bully.

To contextualize this modus operandi with respect to the Air Force Academy takes very little ingenuity. Generally speaking, although no longer subject to the harassment associated with the freshman experience, upperclass cadets are disgruntled, so they harass the new freshman cadets. It doesn't take superior intellect or much empirical observation

---

13 Edward Smith, Susan Nolen-Hoeksma, and Barbara Fredrickson, *Atkinson & Hilgard's Introduction to Psychology,* 14th ed. (Florence, KY: Thomson Learning, Inc., 2003), 461–463.

to realize that the more disenchanted the upperclassmen were about their own plight at the Academy, the more severe was the training. Just like the man and his dog, upperclassmen channel their frustration onto fourth-class cadets. In this respect, the Fourth Class System serves as an indisputably inappropriate stress reliever for upperclass cadets. As stress is an ever-present aspect of Academy life, and harassing freshmen is so effective in the assuagement of this stress, upperclassmen embrace the system at least partially for its therapeutic effects on their psychological wellbeing. Say the upperclassman is having a bad day. While hazing some four degree, he or she can say, "At least my life doesn't suck that bad," to use the exact words I heard on multiple occasions from the mouths of various upperclass cadets.

Along with shifting aggressive impulses to the less threatening target (freshman cadets), upperclassmen also suffered from a harmful case of denial. Denial has been defined as follows:

> A defense mechanism by which unacceptable impulses or ideas are not perceived or allowed into full awareness.[14]

Because voicing any opposition to the Fourth Class System as a freshman was equivalent to career suicide, many cadets ultimately began to refuse to accept the reality that indeed there were significant problems at the institution. They would first deny it to upperclassmen (the target audience) by their two-faced display of unyielding support and appreciation for the system, then, later, on a more personal level to family and friends.

After fervently denying the existence of real problems at the Academy for some time, their arguments would ultimately become so sincere and convincing that even *they* believed them. These cadets' decision to turn their backs on reality has allowed two ill-fated situations to persist: the unwarranted continuance of the Fourth Class System, and a sharp decrease in cadets' *willingness* and, more significantly, their increasing *inability* to accurately perceive reality.

Part of the denial attributed to these upperclass survivors was the repression of the guilt naturally associated with immoral or illegal behavior, such as conducting illicit four- degree training. Hazing was and

---

14 Ibid., 461, 462–463.

still is both immoral and illegal, yet it has been universally endorsed by Academy administrators, mainly by inaction when decisiveness and legal or administrative action were absolutely necessary.

Upperclassmen not only repressed guilt about their mistreatment of fourth-class cadets but also rationalized their behavior in an effort to legitimize their actions. This process of rationalization and repression fostered the delusional mentality so prevalent throughout the upperclass ranks at the Academy.[15]

Upperclassmen who were the worst abusers of four degrees were often those who had taken the most abuse as freshmen. These individuals were fanatical about the way they conducted training and how often it took place. They would sacrifice their own grade point averages (GPA), military performance averages (MPA), and/or physical education averages (PEA) in order to haze fourth-class cadets as often and as severely as possible. Their passion was pain—you could see it in their eyes. They were psychologically disturbed, in large part due to the inappropriate training they had received as freshmen at the hands of upperclassmen who received similarly inappropriate treatment when they themselves were four degrees. When they talk about the "long grey line" at the Military Academy and the tradition of excellence that it engenders, the "long blue line" at the Air Force Academy could be this never-ending cycle of abuse passed down from class to class by those who were the greatest recipients of abuse. It's nauseating that it has gone on for so long relatively unmolested by any entity strong enough to stop it.

When I first voiced opposition to the Fourth Class System, I was bombarded with what upperclassmen believed to be legitimate purposes of the Fourth Class System. Not one of these explanations for the necessity of the Fourth Class System ever held up with me because of the erroneous framework upon which the assertions were based. These upperclassmen's explanations attempted to justify the system at large and individual aspects of the system as well. For example, I was told that chewing only seven times at meals ensured that I wouldn't take too large a bite and jeopardize good table manners, which would be catastrophic in the presence of a high-ranking officer. It would only make sense then, if that were indeed the case, that *all* cadets should be required to chew

15 Ibid., 461–462, 627.

only seven times, because it would be important for upperclassmen also to have good table manners.

I was told it was important to press my chin against my chest when standing at attention because that's the position I would need to assume when ejecting from an aircraft, but upperclassmen never held that position of attention, and they were much closer to flying airplanes than were freshmen. The same goes for memorizing random four-degree knowledge. We were told that the reason we memorized days until graduation, sports trivia, and other inconsequential information was because when at pilot training we would be required to memorize what is called BOLD FACE. BOLD FACE is a list of operational procedures for every situation that could arise while flying, most especially emergencies during which there isn't much time to think. Flight instructors require pilot trainees to memorize BOLD FACE word for word. Memorizing four-degree knowledge was allegedly preparing us for that endeavor, but once again, members of all three upper classes were closer to pilot training than we were, yet it was not necessary for them to practice this type of memorization.

I was told on numerous occasions that going through the Fourth Class System was excellent preparation for being a prisoner of war, and that Academy graduates who had spent time as prisoners of war had even mentioned that they were grateful for their Fourth Class experience, because it helped them cope with a similar environment at the POW camp. If that doesn't tell you all you need to know about how disenchanting the four-degree year is, I don't know what will. POW camps are essentially hell on earth, on average, far worse than any civilian prison experience. That being said, the way POWs were verbally degraded, demoralized, demeaned, and dehumanized (during the time period in review) was in actuality similar to the way we were treated as freshmen, eerily enough. Consequently, I agree wholeheartedly with the assertion that the four-degree experience was first-rate POW preparation.

Nonetheless, the purpose of an officer-training program is not to train people to be able to deal with the pressures of a POW camp, nor is it to experience all the pain and suffering a future service member could face in battle in order to be able to handle that sort of pain while in combat. For example, childbirth is a painful experience, but a woman does not need to have her lower lip pulled up over her nose (an experience one woman likened to childbirth) in order to prepare for the pain associated with childbirth. Moreover, many service members who did not go through a Fourth Class System also survived POW camps, and most importantly, both DOD and Academy officials have *actually stated* that preparing four degrees for POW camps is not an appropriate training objective of the Fourth Class System.

I was told that it was necessary for four degrees to carry their bags in their left hand in order to be able to salute officers walking past, but upperclassmen who were also obligated to salute officers were able to do so quite easily while wearing their bag on their shoulder. We were told that we were restricted from using most of the more convenient stairwells at the Academy because of crowd-control purposes, but once we were recognized as members of the Cadet Wing, we were allowed to use those stairwells even though the volume of personnel moving about the Academy was essentially the same.

We were told that we needed to wear four shirt garters (elastic straps that connected a person's shirt to his socks) at all times in order to present a satisfactory military uniform, but upperclassmen as well as officers and enlisted personnel throughout the operational military easily maintain proper military appearance standards without them (my father, a career Army officer, had never even heard of shirt garters until I mentioned them to him while at the Academy). I was told that it was important to be yelled at and hazed on a continual basis in order to be capable of functioning within a stressful environment, yet it was my feeling that incessant yelling did more to damage my hearing, career motivation, and academic performance than it did to increase my capacity to handle stress.

The United States General Accounting Office did its own review of the training situation at the academies in November of 1992—long before I showed up. Most of the conclusions drawn from that report acutely coincide with the opinions I formed while at the Academy. Regarding the issue of incessant yelling, the GAO report said,

> Our point is that hazing-type treatment is an inappropriate and unrealistic form of stress. The kind of stress imposed on Fourth Class Academy students bears little relationship to the kind of stress encountered by active duty officers....[16]

16 GAO Report, "DoD Service Academies: More Changes Needed to Eliminate Hazing," 66.

> Our review indicates that hazing can have detrimental effects on cadets and midshipmen. A strong correlation exists between self-reported frequency of exposure to hazing-type treatment and measures of a number of negative outcomes; such as higher levels of physical and psychological stress, lower academic performance, attrition from the academies, and lower career motivation.[17]

The list of four-degree training activities goes on as do the clearly reasoned and evidentiary rebuttals to their legitimacy. Overall, *no aspect of the late Fourth Class System and not much of the current Four Class system (as it is called now) at the Air Force Academy served or serves any legitimate future officer-training purpose whatsoever.* Even though there was no real officer-development aspect to the four-degree training, there were real consequences. Just as the GAO report states, there is a definite correlation between how much hazing a person is subjected to and the person's academic performance, stress level, attrition from the academies, and motivation.

I believe that there are several other consequences inherent in the Fourth Class System that are not as apparent, yet are as detrimental, if not worse. These stem from the allowance and endorsement of verbal abuse by school administrators. School administrators would argue emphatically that they would never endorse verbal abuse and that *this person* is throwing out misguided allegations, but when you allow fourth-class cadets to be screamed and yelled at by upperclassmen who may, while yelling and screaming, say anything they want, whenever they want, for as long as they want, you are endorsing verbal abuse.

For years and years Academy officials have tried to make parents and any other interested parties think that they are serious about enforcing their strict no-hazing policies; very few times have cadets at any of the service academies actually been dismissed for hazing. When fourth-classmen are hazed, no one cares. Upperclassmen obviously don't care, or they wouldn't be doing the hazing. The squadron AOCs don't care, because they view cadets who complain as weak, contemptible, and probably deserving of the extra attention. Parents don't hear about it very often because of the restricted communications four degrees have with the outside, and when they do hear about it, the Association of Graduates

17 Ibid., 55.

steps in and tells the parents that it's all part of the system, that it's just a game, that they'll get through it, and that they'll understand and appreciate the whole experience once the training has concluded.

Therefore, the four-degree system is perceived by many as a rock that you can either break yourself against or leave be—an invading force you either die fighting or submit to and survive. If they do not want to be singled out or go insane, many freshmen just accept the Fourth Class System as necessary in a way that they are then too inexperienced to understand but will come to understand later. These cadets still don't welcome the abuse, but they subordinate what their own conscience tells them about the validity of the training to the ideology espoused by their trainers. In this manner they blindly follow and allow themselves to be controlled physically and psychologically. This survival tactic has a profoundly detrimental impact on that person's future leadership potential. That people would subordinate themselves in such a manner might seem strange to an outsider looking in, but if you look at the helpless situation four degrees find themselves in and consider the alternative, it makes sense. The alternative course of action, which is to never fully accept the way you're being treated, is full of heartache, much more so than if you had chosen survival. The *Contrails* handbook says it is the fourth-classman's responsibility to be an assertive follower. *Contrails* defines an assertive follower's obligation this way:

> Follow the legal orders of those senior in position and rank. Demonstrate assertive followership skills in support of unit mission objectives.[18]

In order to make it through the Fourth Class year without being singled out regularly, a person could not be an assertive follower. The training that occurred during the four-degree year was generally against the Air Force Academy's stated regulations. The ATP was seldom adhered to, and its influence on training was largely unrecognized by most cadets and Academy officials. In fact, not only did cadets and administrators at the Academy not adhere to their own training philosophy, but most of these individuals did not even know that the ATP handbook existed.

The ATP handbook stated very clearly that upperclass cadets were

18 United States Air Force Academy Cadet Handbook, *Contrails*, 17.

not to insult, demean, or demoralize four degrees either by word or deed, that upperclassmen were not to use physical training as a punishment, and that training was supposed to be conducted in a positive manner. There could not have been a larger disparity between the manner in which we were *actually* trained and the manner in which we were *supposed* to be trained according to ATP. In fact, the ATP handbook went into great detail concerning the widespread and flagrant abuses of the Fourth Class System attributed to upperclassmen. That being said, technically an assertive follower would not allow himself or herself to be trained in an inappropriate manner; but of course, there was no doubt in any person's mind that it was impossible to not be trained in such a manner, because any attempt to step out or refuse to participate in four-degree training would have quickly ended an Academy career.

Accordingly, cadets had to choose how much they were willing to tolerate. Some very high-profile four-degree cadets had very little tolerance for the four-degree training and subsequently received hundreds of demerits—enough demerits to constitute expulsion—except that some of the cadets of whom I speak were protected because of their standing on the AFA football team. The level of protection one had as an intercollegiate athlete depended on how highly regarded your sport was in the minds of Academy officials, as well as your respective importance to that team. The cadets who were the most openly defiant of the four-degree system were generally those athletes with the highest level of protection. The most defiant of these cadets during my tenure at the Academy is now playing in the National Football League.

If you were a person with no protection of the kind I just described, rebellion was not tolerated, and you would be promptly removed from the Academy for such. Each cadet knew how much protection he had and most times acted accordingly. Not too surprisingly, the individuals who resorted to survival tactics were, more often than not, those individuals who did not participate in intercollegiate athletics. These individuals had to find their own way of surviving. Not only did these cadets have no protection from intercollegiate athletic status, but on average they were subjected to more abuse because when the athletes were at their respective afternoon practices, these cadets were having some sort of beat-down in the squadron area. Accordingly, four-degree athletes thought that they were better than the other four-degree cadets in the squadron because they could get away with not participating in Fourth Class System training to the same degree as required by nonathletes. Conversely, nonathletes came to despise athletes because of their privileged status and then would rationalize the injustice by telling themselves that they were better cadets (militarily) and were going to make better officers. This long-standing, festering sentiment at the Academy was the reason for the rift between athletes and nonathletes, a situation that was widely acknowledged by both cadets and school officials, yet as one would expect, nothing was ever done to correct the problem. Academy leadership was much more concerned with doing well in sports than solving inequalities (reference the astronomically high government salary enjoyed by the head coach of the AFA football team). Even if there had been an effort to correct the problem, it couldn't have been done without eradicating the Fourth Class System from which the problem arose.

With an entire Cadet Wing just trying to survive the cadet experience, there is very little opportunity to learn real followership or leadership. Cadets learn to be great survivors above all else. After employing all kinds of survival tactics as freshmen, they go on to their upperclass years with the same mentality. Then, instead of surviving the four-degree experience, they begin the effort to avoid being dismissed for honor violations, academic/military/physical performance, etc. Phrases, for example, "Collaborate to graduate," arise that perfectly embody the mission of cadets at the Academy, which is to do only that which is necessary to survive the next three years and graduate. This is obviously a pathetic situation for an officer-training program to find itself in—everyone at the institution merely trying to survive, a whole group of highly skilled social survivalists going on to lead military forces in situations where mere survival is seldom the only priority.

The priority while serving in a leadership capacity is to effectively carry out mission-essential activities in a morally justifiable, ethically sound, reasonable manner. In order for cadets to be ready for that kind of responsibility, it is necessary to create an environment that encourages the development of leadership qualities that will enable future officers to accomplish mission objectives when placed in a leadership capacity and not simply survive the next haze. The Fourth Class training system at the Air Force Academy encouraged an environment that produced survivors, not leaders, and the consequences of such a training failure should be obvious.

The Fourth Class System was supposedly a leadership laboratory.

School administrators believed that the system gave freshmen the opportunity to learn how to be assertive followers, while upperclassmen learned valuable leadership skills. The problem with the whole scenario was that there was never any opportunity for real leadership or followership. What the Academy would label leadership opportunities, I would label inappropriate training. The way in which we were "led" as freshmen would not be tolerated under any circumstance in the operational Air Force. Officers in the operational Air Force cannot yell and scream at their subordinates, make threatening gestures, nor make them do hours of push-ups or up-downs. It's simply not the operational Air Force officer's job to verbally and physically abuse subordinates at his or her discretion, nor is it his or her prerogative to constructively fashion an unbearable environment for subordinates whom the officer regards as poor performers in order to encourage these individuals to leave the Air Force. Officers are not to order subordinates to jump up on lunch tables and sing and dance to "I'm a Little Teapot." Officers are reprimanded if it becomes clear that they are attempting to pencil whip a subordinate. Officers are not allowed to insidiously defame subordinates to other officers or incite these fellow officers to abuse a subordinate whom they happen to dislike. Simply put, if USAFA graduates led airmen in the operational Air Force in a way even remotely similarly to the manner in which they "led" fourth-class cadets at the Academy, they would either be harshly reprimanded, demoted, asked to resign, sent to a court-martial, or even incarcerated.

The result of the so-called leadership laboratory the AFA talked about was anything but proper leadership or followership training. Real leadership does not entail *giving* inappropriate orders, and likewise true followership does not entail *following* inappropriate orders. To reiterate—what was learned at the Academy as a result of the Fourth Class System was an acute ability to survive inhospitable environments and a well-developed capacity for abusing others. Neither of these is a stated objective of the Air Force Academy, nor should they be. The cultural delinquency here is obvious; we have a program that functions counterproductively. It not only fails to meet its stated objectives, it actually fosters undesirable qualities in our future leaders. Nonetheless, the broken system has been allowed to persist relatively unabated for generations and will most likely continue for years to come.

When sexual assault became a nationally recognized problem at the Academy in 2003, many people began trying to figure out why such a high percentage of female cadets fell victim to sexual harassment, assault, or both. I don't see it as being that complicated. Unruly environments are perfect breeding grounds for illegal action. A few years back I spent more than a year in Buenos Aires, Argentina. I lived in various neighborhoods (*barrios*) with varying levels of security. One of the *barrios* was extremely dangerous, and I tried to avoid it as much as possible. The *barrio* was abnormally dangerous because the Buenos Aires police department had essentially given up on enforcing the law there. I was actually friends with a police officer who was in part responsible for controlling the crime that went on there. He told me that neither he nor any of his fellow officers responsible for the *barrio* were willing to even enter that part of town while in uniform. His reasoning was that every time a police officer had gone into that *barrio* in the past months and years, they had been shot at or killed. He told me that he didn't get paid enough to risk his life going into that *barrio.*

The obvious result of the police department's unwillingness to secure that *barrio* was that every mischievous sprite in west Buenos Aires with criminal intentions gravitated in that direction in order to conduct "business." This migration created an incredibly dangerous environment for both the people who, unfortunately, lived there and those who had to either pass by or through for any reason. I was one of those individuals who had to pass through that *barrio* on a constant basis, and I'm sure my life was in jeopardy on multiple occasions, even when I didn't realize it. If I had been robbed walking through that *barrio* I would not have been surprised and would probably have been happy to be alive were I to survive.

The point is that it should not surprise anyone when crimes take place in unruly environments. A training violation here and there is not something to be concerned over. However, a systematic refusal to abide by stated regulations *is* something to worry about, and when it's allowed to continue no one should be surprised if the situation worsens and the consequences of its not being remedied become more severe.

I had a very low tolerance for the way I was treated as a four degree. I despised the way upperclassmen interacted with me and my classmates. I hated the four-degree activities I was subjected to. Ironically, though, a quote by Major General John M. Schofield that we were required to memorize, which came right out of our *Contrails*, wholly vindicated my discontent. Schofield stated,

> ...He who feels the respect which is due to others, cannot fail to inspire in them respect for himself, while he who feels, and hence manifests disrespect towards others, especially his subordinates, cannot fail to inspire hatred against himself.[19]

I was one of those mistreated subordinates Schofield refers to in this quote. According to Schofield, who was a highly respected (and still a widely quoted) military officer, it would be very unusual for a service member in my position to *not* despise superiors guilty of such mistreatment. Nevertheless, I was in just as helpless a position as any other four degree at the Academy and accordingly submitted to the training, although theoretically dragging my feet the whole way. My Basic Cadet Training strategy had been to fly under the radar, bide my time, and come out on the other end. I attempted to employ the same strategy during the academic year, which ended up working just about as well as it had during basic training. It didn't.

---

19 Ibid., 63. (Quote taken from his graduation address to the West Point Class of 1879)

5

Becoming a Target

"To break a man's spirit is the devil's work."
—George Bernard Shaw

Becoming a target at the Academy could be a self-inflicted wound in certain cases, but generally speaking, the events surrounding a cadet's target development were largely out of his or her control. Some four degrees became targets because they looked funny. Some because they had funny names. Some female cadets became targets because they were attractive, like the female cadet who had to obtain two restraining orders against the captain quarterback of the football team and ultimately move to a new squadron. According to Academy climate surveys conducted when I was a cadet, about 25 percent of male cadets didn't think that females belonged at the Academy; hence female cadets were targets for certain upperclass cadets before they even showed up at the Academy.

The list of potential target development conditions was endless and mostly circumstantial, though one thing was sure: there was always a target. Every squadron had "that guy" who always drew more attention during training sessions. Harsher words were always spoken when addressing that guy, training violations were abundant when that guy was present, and that guy also made the lives of other four degrees in his or her squadron easier. By being subjected to training that would normally have been distributed amongst multiple cadets, that guy drew negative attention away from his or her classmates. For that reason, it was always good to have such a person around, just not *too* close. If that guy got too close, you risked being swept up in the insanity of that guy's world, which was not a good thing if you were trying to avoid greater hardship. Accordingly, freshmen cadets didn't mind having a target amongst them as long as it wasn't they and he or she was far enough removed. I became that guy about a month into the academic year. Not only did I become that guy within my squadron, but I became the forerunner amongst those guys throughout the entire Cadet Wing, rivaled only by my twin brother. Apart from the fact that my last name rolls off the tongue rather melodically even when yelled at the highest decibel possible, there were other reasons for my target development.

Many of my classmates, in an effort to appease upperclassmen, would take the Fourth Class System far into the realm of absurdity. These freshmen would overemphasize their enthusiasm for the Fourth Class System by exaggerating the basic four-degree requirements. For instance, some four degrees would yell louder when greeting upperclassmen, run faster on their way to class, and volunteer for extra physical training. On the surface it would appear that these individuals were making their lives more difficult, but these classmates understood that even though they were making their day-to-day life more strenuous, they were actually creating a more painless and secure existence in the long run. Many upperclassmen would see cadets like those I just described and think, "Now, there are some four degrees who understand what this place is all about," and accordingly treat those cadets in a more hospitable manner. Ultimately, these cadets would be grouped with freshmen whom upperclassmen perceived as performing well at the Academy, thus elminating any possibility of them becoming targets.

I developed an intense distaste for the Fourth Class System only days after it began, so I could never bring myself to do more than the bare minimum. In the normal world, doing the bare minimum has a negative connotation. Many times the person who does the bare minimum can have a detrimental effect on both the organization of which he or she is a part and on his or her own personal development as well. However, the Academy wasn't the normal world. When an activity is inherently worthless, whether a person participates with gusto or with apathy doesn't matter, because either way, the activity is still worthless. Therefore my lack of enthusiasm and bare-minimum effort was wholly justified by virtue of the fact that the system itself was worthless. Nevertheless, there was an unintentional, albeit fairly obvious, disparity between my level of enthusiasm for the Fourth Class System and that of many of my classmates.

Upperclassmen who felt that taking part in the four-degree system was a valuable enterprise concentrated their efforts on four degrees who, in their minds, demonstrated a lack of motivation. According to these upperclassmen, for a freshman to not exaggerate the basic four-degree requirements meant there was a lack of motivation. Lack of motivation was considered to be the result of ideological noncompliance. Ideological noncompliance was regarded as fundamentally blasphemous and thought to be a threat to the integrity of the institution. Not only did these upperclassmen consider differing opinions concerning the value of the four-degree system blasphemous, they considered them flagrantly insulting and offensive *on a personal level* because of their own admiration and appreciation for the Academy's version of military indoctrination.

The philosophical inflexibility of these upperclassmen was the result of the natural human tendency to legitimize time spent, invested efforts, and sacrifices made. No one likes to feel that he has wasted his time, made a meaningless effort, or sacrificed for naught. The more time, effort, and sacrifice an individual invests in a worthless endeavor, the more it hurts when he or she realizes it. Because it hurts to invest oneself in a meaningless cause, many people attempt to legitimize the *cause itself* instead of confronting reality, and in so doing defy reason.

For example, say a person is tasked to chop down a tree using the back side of an axe. That person can bang away at the tree indefinitely but will never chop down the tree. It matters not whether the person goes about the task lethargically, striking the tree only a couple of times, or vigorously, striking it 50,000 times—either way the tree will be left standing at the end of the day. The person who exerted more effort trying to down the tree will be more prone to legitimize the task than the person who put forth minimal effort. The former of these two individuals might rationalize that because of the effort to down the tree, he is now physically stronger from swinging the axe, strength that would not have been gained if the task had not been presented and the effort had not been made, but the fact that this person gained strength through his efforts to down the tree in such a manner does not in any way make attempting to chop down a tree with the back side of an axe a worthy endeavor. The obvious reason for the activity's glaring illegitimacy, bearing in mind the objective (to down the tree), is that after all that effort and perceived physical reward, the tree remains relatively undisturbed.

The upperclassmen who, as freshmen, put forth the *greatest effort*, invested the largest amount of time, and sacrificed the most for the Fourth Class System were also the upperclassmen who had the *greatest appreciation* and admiration for the system. After making it through their freshman year, these upperclassmen, instead of accepting the reality that their efforts toward officer training were largely in vain, legitimized their training by attributing most of their good qualities as future leaders to four-degree training. Hence, fundamentally, they aligned their *own self-worth* with that of the Fourth Class System. Consequently, they interpreted any affront to the merit of that system unconditionally as an affront to their *individual worth*.

I carried out the duties required of fourth-classmen but did not do so with the same level of enthusiasm as many of my classmates, which led many upperclassmen to view me as ideologically noncompliant. This philosophical divergence on my part regarding the value of the Fourth Class System was considered offensive by many upperclassmen in my squadron for the reasons stated. My dissimilarity played a significant role in my becoming a target.

Not far into the academic year, my discussions about the four-degree system in the Academy library became dangerously well known. Four degrees in my squadron and others would talk amongst themselves about specific statements made, arguments put forth, and the ideological enlightenment taking place during our impromptu conversations. When upperclassmen heard about these conversations, my name was thrown around because I casually led these discussions by expressing my abnormally intense abhorrence for the Fourth Class System. Upperclassmen would not have heard of our discussions, had it not been for some four degree either not fully understanding how quickly rumors and gossip moved through the Cadet Wing or who was trying to, as we used to say, pimp their classmate. Pimping your classmate was a phrase coined by cadets at the Academy that played into my performer vs. survivor theory. Pimping your classmate entailed doing or saying something to gain favorability in the minds of the upperclassmen at the expense of your classmate. Pimping your classmate was a classic survivor tactic.

Informants are generally regarded as distasteful, yet no one can argue that their informant status gains them many temporal advantages, thus making their existence temporarily more comfortable. In any case, regardless of the motives of the informant, my opinions regarding the Fourth Class System became a subject of inquiry, and I became a person of interest. Even so, until approximately a month into the school year, what upperclassmen "knew" of my opinions was still based entirely on four-degree hearsay; a condition that soon changed due to the conniving and manipulative actions of a particular upperclassman.

About a month into the school year I was summoned into the room of said upperclassman. I reported in with a "C4C Graney reporting as ordered" and was met with an abnormally casual adherence to Academy military decorum. He waved me off with a gesture, insinuating the frivolity of reporting in and inferring that this was going to be an informal engagement. He instructed me to sit down and relax, which was unusual instruction from this cadet in particular, but having been ordered to do so, I sat down and relaxed. He told me there were rumors regarding my attitude toward the Fourth Class System that had caught his attention. He explained that he, being the one ultimately responsible for my military development at the element level, felt it imperative to discuss any concerns regarding four-degree training. He started out by asking me directly what I thought about the Fourth Class System. At this point in the year I clearly understood the passion many upperclassmen felt for the four-degree system, and by every account this cadet was no less zealous than his fanatical friends. I took a moment to formulate a response, then told him that I didn't think it was a particularly good idea to discuss such things and that it didn't really matter what I thought anyway, in that my job was to follow and not campaign for or against four-degree training. It was the most diplomatic, nonconfrontational answer I could think of without lying straight up about the way I truly felt. This upperclassman was not satisfied with that response and again asked me what I thought, this time assuring me that everything I said would be off the record, just between us. He said he wanted to know because he cared and wanted to make sure that I was realizing the full benefit of four-degree training. At that point I still didn't feel entirely comfortable sharing my feelings, but I did.

I was eighteen years old at the time, and at that age I believed people until they gave me a reason not to. At that age I maintained an unpolished understanding of the more finite aspects of social interaction. I have always made a concerted effort to act with prudence and speak after appropriate forethought, but at that time I was inexperienced, as are most young adults with respect to the adult world and how it operates. This inexperience led me to do and say things at that age that accrued wisdom and understanding would not presently allow. So I laid out a comprehensive rebuttal to the legitimacy and value of the Fourth Class System. It was intriguing to see his face transform from, "I just want to know so I can help you," to "Wow, I really wish I could end your pathetic existence." Once I had concluded one of the most well-spoken narrations of my life, he responded with a few hollow, mostly inaudible responses. He was attempting to maintain his sympathetic demeanor, but he couldn't hide his newly acquired disdain. I could read the resentment and hysteria on his face as clearly as words on a page.

I left the room halfway invigorated, because for the first time I had spoken my mind to one of the people responsible for the system's enactment. The other half of me was disenchanted, aware I had just made an enemy. Not only had I made a new enemy, but the new enemy was my element leader, the first-class cadet in charge of my whole existence at the Academy, and he was vindictive. The next day during morning minutes I had a whole swarm of upperclassmen around me asking what my problem was, asking why I didn't like the four-degree system, then answering for me before I had a chance to respond, using my own words verbatim that I had said to my element leader the night before. I came to find out that immediately following our "confidential" meeting, my element leader had e-mailed all the seniors, juniors, and sophomores in our squadron informing them in great detail about what I had said to him under the auspices of confidentiality.

At first I was a little perplexed that he could be so malicious. The same cadet who, according to the Academy Training Philosophy handbook, was largely responsible for helping me develop those qualities of character necessary for an effective Air Force officer, had deceived me, undermining any trust that ever existed or could ever exist between us, and actually instigated the situation that was ultimately responsible for ending my first attempt at a military career. I became the target of unrestrained hazing from that day forward. Every day from then on, I was that guy who was subjected to rampant and concentrated training violations; that guy who made everyone else's life easier by being subjected to training that would normally have been disseminated across dozens of four-degree cadets, the guy who couldn't eat lunch because he was being yelled at for the space of the meal, the guy who received Forms 10 full of demerits for every minor infraction an upperclassman could think of or find in the long list of 34th Training Wing regulations, that guy on whom upperclassmen could take out their aggressions, the cadet they could hate and treat as if he were the root of all evil, that cadet to whom you say or do just about anything you want to and face only negligible opposition from anyone, because the people responsible for stopping unbridled abuse of fourth-class cadets harbor equally hateful feelings toward that particular cadet.

Needless to say, it was an extremely unfortunate situation to find myself in. And the situation only deteriorated as the year went on. There were two reasons for this. The first was the fact that upperclassmen, realizing that they were free to do essentially anything they wanted in regard to my training, became more and more rancorous with respect to the things they said to me and put me through. The other factor was a combination of significant events that both laid the foundation for additional abuse as well as incited more upperclassmen to participate. The abuse I was subjected to became more and more painful as the year progressed, until it was almost unbearable. I was criticized on numerous occasions throughout the year for allegedly having attitude problems. The irony of that accusation was that it was my unassailably constructive attitude alone that enabled me to withstand and overcome months and months of the very same abuse responsible for my allegedly bad attitude.

It shouldn't be too surprising that the cadet who revealed the contents of our confidential meeting ended up being involuntarily removed from the Academy because of a separate honor-code violation. However dishonorable he may have been, he had already set in motion my target development, an uncontrollable impetus that quickly became a maddening display of human weakness and group mentality. Once upperclassmen target a four degree and determine it necessary to facilitate that cadet's removal from "their" institution, that cadet's Academy and future Air Force careers are in serious jeopardy. That cadet's main objective, from that point forward, most times is to merely survive until graduation and to overcome the incredibly malevolent efforts to the contrary on part of select upperclassmen.

One situation that exacerbated the way I was treated by upperclassmen had to do with academics. During BCT I, cadets are given a number of tests to assess their mathematical proficiency. I, never having taken calculus or precalculus, was placed in the lowest math class at the Academy called Math 130, which was essentially trigonometry/precalculus, but I was signed up for calculus as well. I went to the math department and tried to convince them to let me take one math class at a time—the lower math first, of course, so I would be prepared for the more advanced calculus class later on. I was told that my concerns were inappropriate and that with a reasonable effort I would do fine.

I had graduated from high school with a 3.91 GPA. I knew how to be a good student. I also knew that attempting to take the lower-level course and the advanced course at the same time was generally not a good idea and at most institutions wouldn't even be allowed without administrative consent. My objections were given no consideration, and I was abruptly shown to the door. I never felt comfortable with the material in either class, and when midterm grades came out I was not only failing my two math classes but chemistry as well. I had been spending so much time and energy trying to figure out what was going on in math classes that I had neglected my other courses. Consequently, my midterm GPA was not so good. I was in what salty cadets called the square-root club. I'll let you figure that one out.

The math-class debacle was not the main reason I had such a low GPA, though. Ever since my target development, I had been spending large amounts of time being hazed. Many times this training interfered with study time, which was already scarce to begin with, and when I was left alone I was so wound up and frustrated that focusing on mathematical derivatives proved rather difficult. I would compare the situation to coming out of a rugby game, sitting down on the bench, and attempting to read and understand Kant's *Grounding for the Metaphysics of Morals.* On multiple occasions during precious Academy-mandated study times I was hand-creating, with exact precision, grade cards for room inspections. Frequently I was required to not just produce one acceptable grade card like my classmates, but three at a time. Many of my classmates spent precious study time creating their grade cards as well, but as a target I was required to create and recreate these grade cards multiple times a week, even though each card was noticeably flawless. I spent many study sessions at attention while my trainer did a long, even by Academy standards, room inspection. When walking through the hallways during study time, I was stopped and trained longer than other four degrees. I was told to counsel with my trainer more often because of my "lack of motivation." All these second and third efforts by upperclassmen to haze me added up and had an extremely detrimental effect on my ability to succeed academically as a four degree.

The November 1992 GAO report has something interesting to say about this particular situation:

> In general, cadets exposed to higher amounts of hazing-type treatment were more likely to have grade point averages below 2.4, particularly at the Air Force Academy.[20]

The interpersonal stress I was feeling due to the constant abuse profoundly affected my academic performance. When midterm grades came out, the first-class cadet responsible for passing out grade reports entertained his classmates by yelling my GPA throughout the squadron. He also made personal visits to his friends' rooms so they could discuss my lack of accomplishment and reconfirm to each other that I was a poor performer and didn't belong at the Academy, thus increasing the quantity and severity of hazing I was subjected to later. The November 1992 report could not have better summed up the conditions responsible for my deteriorating environment at the Academy:

> From our examination of hazing-related disciplinary cases, we found that many recipients of more intense or frequent hazing-type treatment are individuals who were perceived by upperclassmen as poorly motivated or poor performers. The situation can, to some extent, become a self-fulfilling prophesy. When fourth-class cadets or midshipmen are "identified" as being poor performers, they attract more attention and pressure from upperclassmen, which often compounds rather than solves their performance problems. For example, at a hearing for an Air Force Academy fourth-class cadet who had exceeded the limit on demerits, it came out that he had been singled out for repeated individual attention by upperclassmen because of a reputation for being arrogant during Basic Cadet Training.
>
> Since the cadets and midshipmen who receive more intense or frequent hazing-type treatment are often those reputed to be poor or marginal performers, there may be a tendency for Academy officials to see the recipients of such treatment as those who did not belong at the

20 GAO Report, "DoD Service Academies: More Changes Needed to Eliminate Hazing," 60.

> Academy and to view the ultimate outcome as appropriate, however inappropriate the actions that led to that outcome may have been. [21]

Let me reiterate the "self-fulfilling prophecy" idea from these paragraphs. Upperclassmen chose to target me because of what they perceived as a lack of motivation and poor performance on my part. Even though there was no tangible evidence (initially) of subpar performance, the hazing campaign they carried out and the negative effect it had on my academics turned me into a documented poor performer. So just as the GAO report says, target development leading to target neutralization (destroying the target) is many times a self-fulfilling prophesy.

The one protection I had working against the hazing campaign when it first began was my intercollegiate status. I was not recruited to wrestle for the Academy, though I had every intention of trying out and making the team once I arrived. One of the daily activities during BCT I was intramurals. Every basic cadet participated in a sport of some kind. If a basic cadet was going to be playing basketball at the intercollegiate level, he or she would play intramural basketball, and the same went for other sports. For intercollegiate athletes it was a time to meet your teammates and begin to prepare for the upcoming season. It was also a chance for coaches to see some talent. I ended up defeating two or three recruited wrestlers rather handily, which encouraged the assistant wrestling coach to invite me to come out for practice when BCT was finished. I took him up on the offer and decided to make a quick pass by the head coach's office in order to ask what I would need for practice (my only possessions at the time didn't include wrestling equipment). The head coach just gave me an ugly look and snapped, "Who said you could try out?" I told him that his assistant coach had invited me, to which he said, "Just make sure you show up."

Our off-season conditioning for wrestling was considerably intense. Three times a week we would go on a run straight up Stanley Canyon, a few miles down the road from the cadet area. The run was about three and a half miles and had about a 30-degree incline almost the entire way. The end point was a reservoir at which you hoped to arrive before the coach, because if you didn't or were passed by the coach at any time along the way you would have to run it again the next day. So as you were run-

21 Ibid., 74–75.

ning up this mountain, sometimes throwing up along the way, you had to worry about this man, the Olympic and National medalist who ran 100-mile races for fun, running behind you with every intention of making you run again the next day.

The wrestling season didn't become any less intense once we actually started wrestling. The first day of live wrestling, I was placed in a group of three with two of the best wrestlers on the team. We did live take-downs for two hours straight, two minutes in and one minute out. Needless to say it was incredibly exhausting. On top of that I was being almost completely dominated by these two wrestlers, which of course just makes a person feel even more tired. I'm pretty sure the coach put the other freshmen wrestlers in similar situations to ascertain which guys really wanted to wrestle for the Air Force Academy. It was intense but invigorating; I loved the physical challenge and remained optimistic about the season.

In an effort to incite team camaraderie, the team all sat together at lunch, which meant no training while we ate; most people are aware of how important food is to a wrestler. It was a great situation that soon ended. When my grades came out, the coach told me to spend more time on academics, effectively ending my freshman wrestling season right when competition was set to begin. Not participating with the wrestling team meant that I no longer sat "at ease" at the wrestling tables, no longer missed out on afternoon training sessions in the squadron, and lost my only protection against target status. It also meant that I was spared from contracting skin herpes.

The wrestling team very rarely washed the mats, a situation that allowed skin diseases to proliferate. I remember wrestling around one day and noticing a spot of my own blood on the mat from a nosebleed of two weeks before. I was disgusted. While serving as captain of my high-school wrestling team, I never allowed practice to start until the mats were washed. Just as the football team somehow got away with restricting our access to the intercollegiate gym for a week, in order to allow them to work out undisturbed by other intercollegiates, this was just another indication that wrestling was not a priority sport at the Academy. One of the wrestlers on the team contracted herpes while at a weekend tournament and never had it properly treated. The team trainer, in an effort to allow the infected wrestler to go on competing, simply covered up the infected area with some sort of makeup. This cadet, with the assistance of the filthy mats, then spread herpes to the majority of the team. After seeing what the infection had done to my ex-teammates' faces and necks, I wasn't so upset about having had to leave the team prematurely.

When I was removed from intercollegiate status the floodgates opened. As soon as it was revealed that I was no longer an intercollegiate athlete, a weeklong beat-down was announced to welcome me back to afternoon squadron training. Upperclassmen sent an e-mail out to all the four degrees in my squadron claiming that we were going to have what they called "Power Week," because of some infraction on Graney's part. I hadn't made any infraction, and most four degrees knew it. The reason for this weeklong training session was to celebrate, in true Air Force Academy Fourth Class System style, the return of C4C Graney, whose return they had been anticipating. Power Week came and went. As I was being trained by five and sometimes ten upperclassmen at the same time, their contentment with respect to their newly acquired, unadulterated access to me was obvious. My return to squadron lunch tables was equally memorable in that I was immediately placed at the training table, the table at which all the worst upperclass trainers sat. I stayed there, despite an AFA mandate requiring freshmen to rotate lunch tables each week, until Recognition, which was several months away at the time.

Lunchtime quickly became my least favorite occasion. Lunch actually took on an entirely different meaning in my world. The dictionary describes lunch as "a meal eaten in the middle of the day." The definition of lunch for me at the training table could have been defined as "a time when verbal abuse is pervasive, when food is plentiful, yet unavailable to the exploited, intended for the consumption of the browbeaters, but not the browbeaten." Many times the training would become so loud that upperclassmen from other tables, not even particularly opposed to training at lunch, would come over and voice their objections. Most often these upperclassmen would simply yell in opposition from their table. These objections never even subdued the level of intensity at the table, and in most cases just aggravated the situation. One day, my brother Chaz, who had also been sitting at his squadron's training table for weeks on end, was physically assaulted by upperclassmen—something that, up to that point, hadn't happened to me yet. Chaz described the experience:

> I sat with Cadet W, Cadet A, Cadet Y, Cadet F, and others for almost a month straight, during which they put a lot of stress on me. I have no problem with that because that is the purpose; however, many of their

actions were grossly in violation of training standards. During my stay I was called many offensive and vulgar things. The AFCWI outlines training violations in great detail. "Verbal abuse is defined as any language or tone of voice that is unnecessarily out-of-control, defamatory, profane, insulting, demeans the subordinate, or minimizes a cadet as a human being. Abusive comments made in jest are also prohibited." Once Cadet W said, "We should make Graney go up to the staff tower and tell everyone how small his dick is." When I brought up the issues I had with Cadet W to the AOC and others, Cadet W called me a "pussy" because I had "told" on him. Later on in the year he said to me, "Graney, you are such a worthless piece of crap." Those are some of the verbal comments that were made to me among others. The more serious issues I have concerning training violations happened on Wednesday Dec. 12th. That day when I got to (the) table I immediately started getting yelled at by Cadet W, Cadet F, and Cadet A. At that point it wasn't much different than any other day, except this day they decided it would be okay to physically push me around (and they were right because they received no punishments for their actions). Cadet W walked behind where I was standing and hit me with his shoulder so I fell forward, causing me to put my hand on the table to stop myself from falling forward. At that point I realized that this was not right; however, I continued to fill drinks and recite knowledge. No sooner had I stood back up again than Cadet A began grabbing my parka and tried to physically pull it off of me, yanking me around in the process. I shrugged his hand off and started to take my own parka off without any assistance when Cadet A again grabbed my clothing, only this time it was my scarf, and started ripping that off. I again shrugged him off and continued to do what I was supposed to be doing when Cadet W walked back to his seat and in the process again put his shoulder into my back, causing me to fall forward. After this I was told to sit down, so I sat down, and no sooner had I sat down than I was told to "get the hell out of here" by Cadet F, so I got up and began to put my jacket on. Then Cadet F grabbed my jacket and threw it in my face, swearing while he did so. I left the table at that point. Now, this is a serious issue. I was assaulted by three different individuals, one of whom was the Group Training Officer, who should be held to a higher standard anyway. The AFCWI also details how touching a subordinate is a training violation. "Directly touching or causing a substance to touch a subordinate/trainee is inap-

> propriate and will not be tolerated." I was not only touched but pushed around and taken advantage of by three individuals who are halfway through their two-degree year. There is not a chance that they didn't know that they were in direct violation of training standards but decided to do what they did regardless. These individuals are all guilty of serious training violations; however, nothing was done to punish them for their actions other than a verbal warning not to do it again. Not even one Form 10 was issued to any of these individuals for any of the acts described above.

Just as my brother stated in this memorandum for record (MFR), not one of these cadets was dealt any judicial or nonjudicial punishment (NJP). My brother reported this situation to his AOC, who then decided to condemn my brother for not having used his chain of command in reporting the incident. Therefore, instead of effectively dealing with three cases of illegal physical contact, Chaz's AOC gave him a tongue-lashing for not using his chain of command. If there were a textbook on how to be an ineffective leader, this case would be a perfect example of failure of leadership. Not only would it be an example of how to neglect one's command responsibilities, it's also illegal. When you are in some sort of supervisory position in the military and one of your subordinates comes to you a victim of a crime and you do nothing, that is illegal; you are in essence abetting a crime and could be appropriately labeled a criminal yourself.

The fact that my brother and I were twins also added to our mutually deteriorating situations. As twins, you are recognizable to twice as many people, often people you've never seen before. Twice as many people think they know you because they know your twin. Twice as many people either hate you or love you; twice as many friends, twice as many enemies. With respect to our particular situation at the Academy, the twin factor worked against us, in that twice as many people were making it a priority to ruin our lives, individually if not collectively.

One other noteworthy issue that influenced my target status had to do with an incident involving a significant case of fraternization. After terrorists flew planes into the World Trade Center towers in New York City, a Pennsylvania field, and the Pentagon in Washington, DC, the Air Force Academy went on lockdown. The Academy and the Colorado Springs area in general, being home to the North American Aerospace

Defense Command (NORAD) and various other military installations, was considered a likely target for terrorism.

Even in the movies, rogue states had listed Colorado Springs as an important military target. I remember watching *Sum of All Fears* in a Colorado Springs movie theatre when, all of a sudden, while the Russians were talking about where they would strike first in the event of nuclear war with the U.S., Colorado Springs, CO, came up, which caused quite an uproar in the theatre. Anyway, because Colorado Springs was a prime terrorist target and we as a country had just experienced the worst terrorist attack in American history, the Academy greatly enhanced its security measures.

We were not allowed to leave the Academy grounds. There was 24-hour surveillance of who went in and out of every building on campus, including our dormitories. In every building we entered, we had to display our military identification cards. If a cadet happened to not have his card with him, he was detained by security forces and escorted to wherever he claimed to have left the card. There were even reports of suspect activities on and around the Academy grounds. Posters with the face of some man with a Middle Eastern name were put up, and we were told to stay on the alert and immediately report to security forces if we saw him or any other suspicious persons or activities.

According to the heightened security measures, someone had to monitor not just the entries to the dormitory buildings themselves but the entrances to individual squadrons within the buildings as well. Those points of ingress had to be manned by cadets from the respective squadrons near those entry points 24 hours a day. This was a strain on upper-class cadets, who were solely responsible for maintaining that level of security, many times at the expense of their academics. Most times they would attempt to study out there in the hallway in a little chair facing the stairwell, though obviously it wasn't the most conducive place to study. Fortunately, it only lasted a number of weeks, after which things seemed to settle down a bit. It was during this time of heightened security and nervous tension that the first Quote of the Day (QOD) emerged.

As I entered the squadron late one mid-September night, the cadet monitoring the entry decided to throw out the insult that I would later select as the first QOD. This cadet, who had admired and congratulated my intensity and attitude toward BCT I/II training, had (unbeknownst to me) become jaded by all the anti–C4C Graney sentiment and propaganda. The anti–C4C Graney sentiment was the result of the actions of the upperclass cadet I'd had the supposedly confidential meeting with regarding my attitude toward the Fourth Class System. That confidential meeting had only happened days prior to this time. As I passed this friend-turned-foe, he told me to hold up a second. As I stopped he exclaimed with great passion, "Cadet Graney, you are the worst cadet in the entire Cadet Wing," then went back to reading. Slightly perplexed by this cadet's subordination to group mentality, I turned away and continued on to my destination.

As my roommate and I sat there looking at each other in our respective rolling chairs thinking about what had been said to me, it dawned on me that that was the *quote of the day*. I had a whiteboard hanging outside the door to which I gave new purpose; it would become the Quote of the Day Board. From that day forward, without naming the individuals to whom the quotes belonged, we posted the most outrageous commentary of the day. Naturally, being in a place where irrationality prevailed, these quotes were consistently preposterous, to the point that casual observers would initially question their authenticity, only to be left dumbfounded to find that someone was not only capable of saying something so asinine but had actually chosen to do so.

The Quote of the Day Board continued into my sophomore year and would eventually become so famous that cadets from other squadrons would actually go out of their way en route to class to get their daily kicks and giggles. Many times while sitting in my room as a sophomore, I would hear footsteps passing my room accompanied by a burst of laughter. I guessed the laughter was caused by the QOD, in light of the comprehensive shortage of anything else reasonably amusing at the Academy.

After seeing his comment up on the QOD board, the cadet previously mentioned became irate and told every cadet he encountered in succeeding moments that he wanted to see Cadet Graney and roommate as soon as possible. It was only after our respective intercollegiate practices, dinner, and a two-hour squadron beat-down that we heard of this upperclassman's desire to see us. Upon hearing about his desire to visit with us we went straight to this cadet's room. Apparently this upperclassman had forgotten that he had wanted us to come by, because when we reported to his room he was right in the middle of fraternizing with two freshmen classmates of ours who were supposed to be on competition rest for their game the next day. Competition rest was supposed to be just that, rest. A cadet on competition rest was off-limits for any training, in order to be physically prepared for his or her competition the following day. However, our two female classmates had decided to spend their competition rest fraternizing with this upperclass cadet, while the rest of their classmates where down in the SAR going through a two-hour physical-training session.

Fraternization was an extremely effective survival technique, employed principally by female four degrees. Upperclass cadets were much more lenient on freshman cadets with whom they were fraternizing, obviously. That's why fraternization was against Academy regulations. It's hard to find a professional work environment anywhere in which fraternization is acceptable, because everyone knows that fraternization directly leads to unfair management practices. Fraternization generally involved a freshman female and an upperclass male, but I knew of a case in my sophomore year where a three-degree female cadet was having an intimate relationship with her squadron Military Training Leader (MTL), the active-duty enlisted man responsible for overseeing the squadron's military development. That specific female three degree also received unparalleled military performance evaluations, to no one's surprise.

When we knocked on this upperclassman's door, there was scurrying around in the room, a silent pause, and then the door cracked open to see who it was. Once the upperclassman saw us, he quickly shut the door, though before he could do so both my roommate and I clearly saw through the darkness two of our female classmates laid out on both his and his roommate's beds with the movie they had been watching paused. When he shut the door, my roommate and I exchanged a look of mutual distaste for what we had seen. A few moments later the upperclassman emerged from his room, shut the door behind him, and attempted to regain face as he started lecturing us about the QOD and our lack of respect for upperclassmen. Before he could finish, my roommate defiantly asked him why our two female classmates were lying on his bed watching a movie when they were supposed to be on competition rest. My roommate intentionally asked the question loud enough so that our two misguided classmates in the room could hear him. The upperclassman immediately began screaming at my roommate, telling him that the discussion was about my roommate and me—*our* deficiency, *not his*. After about a ten-minute lecture the upperclassman gave us this incredibly disdainful look, told us that he was finished, and ordered us back to our room. Once again we were back in our rolling chairs, looking at each other, utterly speechless.

The fallout from this encounter was significant. My roommate and I were now eyewitnesses to a dismissible offense. This upperclassman could have been indicted for fraternization as well as condoning an honor-code violation. It was essentially lying for those two freshman cadets to say they were on competition rest while fraternizing with an upperclassman in a separate room. The upperclassman, by allowing (if not requesting) these freshman cadets to lie, was condoning an honor-code violation. How did this incident contribute to my deteriorating situation at the Academy? I would answer that question by asking another. What does a Mafia boss do with key witnesses to crimes for which he or his operatives are responsible? He has them whacked. He neutralizes the threat by eliminating any potential witnesses. The Godfather calls up someone nicknamed "The Beast" or "Mickey I-kill-people-for-a-living" and pays him to find the witnesses, kill them, and then dispose of the bodies in the East River.

This upperclassman obviously didn't have my body dumped in the river, but that wasn't necessary. He could eliminate me as a threat to his Academy career by using the approved mechanisms of the Fourth Class System. More than that, he wouldn't even seem abnormal for doing so because of the number of upperclassmen already attempting to remove me from the Academy. Not surprisingly, I received two Forms 10 from this cadet immediately following this incident for a couple of bogus infractions. However, more detrimental even than the Forms 10 campaign he mounted against me was his private and public slander. As the squadron superintendent, this cadet was the highest-ranking second-class cadet in the squadron. Therefore he was able to influence many of his classmates, who would not otherwise have involved themselves in hazing campaigns, to become actively engaged in target-elimination activities by engendering an environment where the target cadet is ostracized from his classmates, issued numerous Forms 10 with accompanying demerits, and physically and emotionally harassed to an unmanageable level, all with the intention of realizing the cadet's voluntary or involuntary removal from the Academy. In the professional world they call it constructive termination. I ultimately received twenty-six Forms 10 for mostly insignificant infractions. The average four degree in my squadron received one or two throughout the space of the year. The greatest evidence to this paradigm shift could be what this *same* cadet said about me in a performance evaluation during BCT II:

> Outstanding performance militarily and physically. Performs well on courses and flight activities. Well motivated. Sounds off very strong. Above average basic cadet.

Above average basic cadet! Incredibly, despite no change of behavior, I allegedly went from an "above average basic cadet" to "the worst four degree in the entire Cadet Wing." Amazing how that happens.

I would describe my freshman year as pure insanity caught spiraling out of control. No matter what I did, things just grew worse as the year progressed. The longer I was subjected to mistreatment, the more embittered and indignant I became. This state of being was interpreted to be that poor attitude upperclassmen had been talking about all along, when in reality my resentful attitude was a consequence of severe mistreatment for months on end, not a result of any inherent attitude deficiency of mine. I was labeled cynical by upperclassmen, my AOC, and my MTL. Then again, as George Bernard Shaw once said,

> The power of accurate observation is often called cynicism by those who do not possess it.

My poor academic performance was interpreted as evidence of my inability or unwillingness to perform in a manner consistent with Academy standards, when in reality it was a result of constant training violations that greatly interfered with my studies. With newfound "evidence" of my alleged lack of performance and unsatisfactory motivation to be a cadet at the Air Force Academy, the hazing and pencil-whipping campaigns that had been raging for months appeared more and more legitimate as I appeared more and more illegitimate.

One could liken my situation as a freshman at the Academy to a situation I experienced while working on a horse ranch during my high-school years. My coworkers and I trained horses for the majority of the day up in the corral, where it could become fairly hot. After some rough physical labor of the kind that takes place on horse ranches, I suffered a splitting headache. The combination of hard labor and an abnormally hot day caused me to become noticeably dehydrated, yet I continued working, subsequently developing heat exhaustion. I went back to my room feeling miserable. I took a second to rest, then went to dinner, where I must have eaten the wrong thing, because I got food poisoning. I remember having an irritating tingle in my throat around dinnertime, and I went to the infirmary. They sent me away with instructions to drink water and get some rest. I drank a little water, not enough, and tried to rest, but one of my roommates stayed up until the wee hours of the morning with the light on working on some personal project. I felt terrible when I rose early the next day. I meant to go out to care for the horses, but instead I went straight to the restroom and threw up maybe fifteen times, then started dry heaving.

My head and throat were on fire, and I was having trouble breathing. I tried drinking some water, but my throat hurt so badly I couldn't swallow. I tried to go down and drop feed for the horses and clean stalls, but found myself too weak to even think about picking up a bale of hay, much less the heavier alfalfa. Once my colleagues came down, they took one look at me and told me to go back to my room and rest. Back in my room, I was delirious. I couldn't tell the difference between inside and outside, upside and down. As soon as my head hit the pillow, my world started spinning so fast I threw up again. My condition continued to worsen, as because of my throat irritation (I later found out I had strep throat) I shied away from eating or drinking, thus depriving my body of the necessary nourishment.

Realizing the fix I was in, my brother (who had been working as a lifeguard near the ranch) tried in vain to feed me Jell-O and have me drink fluids, a gesture of kindness I only vaguely remembered because of my feverish, confused state. I couldn't even sit up without someone helping me. I'm not sure why they waited three days to take me to the hospital, but when they did I was taken straight from the normal waiting area to the emergency room. They laid me out on a bed and hastily pumped vitamins and antibiotics into my bloodstream by way of two IVs, one in each arm. I spent the night at the hospital, and the nurses called my parents and told them if the people who had brought me to the hospital had waited another twenty-four hours I could have died.

Both experiences—my freshman year at the Academy and this spell of intense sickness at the horse ranch—worsened as time went on. In both cases I underwent intense hardship. But the foremost similarity between these two experiences is that once the negative force was set in motion, the individuals responsible for my welfare did next to nothing to stop the situation from deteriorating out of control. I had been labeled a target early on in my Academy career. Everything that transpired after my target identification was affected, if not defined, by the fact that dozens of upperclass cadets were masterminding the conditions that would play a major role in my involuntary removal from the institution.

6

Honor and Conduct Adjudicatory Processes

"Confidence, not fear, is the keynote of a strong, convincing doctrine."

—S. L. A. Marshall[22]

When I think of the Academy's honor and conduct adjudicatory processes, I see immaturity, lack of perspective, and flat-out incompetence. Standing before a cadet honor board was like a scene straight out of George Orwell's *Animal Farm*. In order to become a part of the Cadet Wing, all cadets must swear to live by the honor code. Every cadet must take an oath not to lie, steal, cheat, or tolerate anyone who does. The honor oath continues: "Furthermore, I resolve to do my duty and live honorably, so help me God." Oath aside, sometimes a cadet's actions, statements, or both are at odds with the honor code, and for this reason cadet honor boards exist. Just as criminal and civil courts exist to ensure that the laws of the United States are upheld and that justice is served, honor boards exist to ensure that cadets adhere to the honor code and that violators are properly dealt with.

Just like the AFA's hazing scheme, i.e., freshman indoctrination, the principle behind the honor system and the protocol for its administration at the institution were originally designed by cadets at the USMA who lacked the authority or necessity to do so. A code of honor among officers in the military was around long before the USMA came into existence. The USMA at its inception informally adopted this code of

22 Marshall, *The Armed Forces Officer*, 160.

honor, but there was no methodical honor system until the late 1800s, when some overambitious cadets began forming what were called vigilance committees. These vigilance committees, by their own prerogative, would investigate alleged honor violations and submit their findings to the cadet chain of command. If the cadet chain of command determined them guilty, these cadets would then be pressured to leave the Academy. I can only imagine the means by which these cadets were pressured to leave. Academy administrators never officially recognized these committees, but they tolerated them, which in essence sanctioned their decisions. It wasn't until Douglas MacArthur took over as superintendent of the Military Academy after World War I that a formal student honor committee was established. At the onset of its establishment, the now officially sanctioned honor committee codified the existing unwritten rules governing honorable conduct.

Before the establishment of unofficial vigilance committees and later official honor systems, when cadets had any sort of disagreement with each other over matters of integrity or points of honor, the offended party would call out the offender, and the issue was dealt with through a good old-fashioned fistfight or duel of some kind. The parties involved would have it out and then return to their business, unless someone died, which was the end result of one physical confrontation regarding an alleged infringement of the Naval Academy's honor code in 1905. Consequently, the president of the United States at the time, Teddy Roosevelt, had the honor code abolished, only to have a very different version reinstated forty-five years later by Admiral Barry W. Hill. The practiced definition of honor changed as years went by. For example, at the Naval Academy for a time, honorable conduct was actually interpreted by cadets to mean *never* turning in your classmates for *any* offense.[23] When the Air Force Academy came into existence in the mid-1950s, a panel was formed with the purpose of establishing an honor system at the Academy. They studied numerous institutions from around the country, both military and civilian, but ultimately introduced an honor system very much like the one in effect at the USMA. Despite the numerous changes in statement, interpretation, and application of the honor code, toward the end of the

23 Government Accountability Office Report, "DoD Service Academies: Comparison of Honor and Conduct Adjudicatory Processes," GAO/NSIAD-93-36 (Washington, DC: U.S. Government Accountability Office, November, 1992), 11.

20th century all three academies had firmly established, closely analogous honor systems, which are still in place today.

Cadets at the Air Force Academy participate in four years of honor-education courses. Honor education is part of the Academy's character-development program and begins as soon as newly appointed cadets enter Basic Cadet Training. During BCT, we took numerous breaks from physical training to learn about the honor system. As basic cadets, our lessons predominantly revolved around lying, stealing, cheating, and toleration of such actions. The instruction came in the form of lectures, speeches, skits, filmclips, case studies, and scenarios. as well as Cadet X letters. Cadet X letters were letters describing actual honor cases, either in the past or currently being adjudicated. I was baffled as to why it seemed necessary to teach us such things at our respective ages. To me, it seemed unwarranted, as I had been taught to be a person of character and integrity all my life. I had been trying to live honorably long before I ever knew the Academy existed, not because I faced expulsion from my home with some equivalent of a dishonorable discharge if I failed to do so, but because living honorably was the right thing to do. During these lessons we were asked such questions as, "If you look at someone else's paper while taking an exam, is that cheating?" I was immediately reminded of the lessons I had taught elementary schoolers at church. As a Sunday-school teacher, I was given a manual that contained suggestions for teaching certain concepts. When the time came to teach these kids about honesty, the manual provided numerous questions with simple answers meant to help them understand and practice honesty. I remember presenting this scenario:

> You are out playing baseball with your friends in the back yard when one of your friends hits a home run. The ball goes so far it breaks your neighbor's window. Your friend who hit the ball gets scared, yells "RUN," and all your friends take off, leaving you alone in the backyard.
>
> What do you do?

After thinking for a second or two, the seven- and eight-year-old children in my class answered in concert, "Tell the neighbor you broke his window."

If this same question had been asked during an honor lesson at the Academy, it would have generated a heated debate. There would have been arguments for and against informing the neighbor about the damage you and your friends had caused. Some would say, "I didn't break the window, and besides, I'm not going to tell on my friends. I wouldn't tell on my friends, because when you go into combat, it's not going to be any superfluous adherence to some code of personal ethics that's going to get you through the tough times, it will be your friends." Some would argue, "You have to turn in your friends, because if you don't you are guilty of toleration. You are tolerating a moral infraction, and that is an honor-code violation." Some would say, "I've been taught my whole life that it's okay to protect friends and family, so I'd never tell on my friends no matter what the situation, much less for breaking some dude's window." Some would say, "Yeah, I've been that guy who turned in friends for screwing up, and all I got for it was hatred and heartache. Let me tell you, it's just not worth it. When your friend breaks the window and tells you to run away, RUN AWAY!" The cadet honor instructor would then describe what the Academy expects of cadets enrolled in the institution and what the appropriate action in this particular situation would be, the idea being that, because of this honor education, they would be better suited to choose the correct course of action in the future if faced with a similar situation. Many of the children I used to teach at church had a greater understanding of what honorable living entails than many of the adults I knew at the Academy.

The Academy's honor system is an almost entirely cadet-run operation. Cadets from each squadron elect other cadets whom they want to be cadet honor officers. It is from these honor officers that honor-board members are chosen. When an alleged honor violation occurs, seven cadets are chosen from this group to adjudicate the honor case, along with a voting field-grade officer. The idea behind the honor system is to have cadets policing cadets. In order to maintain the high moral standard that the institution espouses, any cadet has the right to accuse any other cadet of violating the honor code. Cadets also have the option of turning themselves in, which has happened on numerous occasions. Once a cadet does accuse another cadet, an investigative team made up of two to three upperclass cadets looks into the matter and determines if there is enough of what the Academy refers to as evidence to recommend the case to an honor board, though what these investigative teams consider evidence would seldom hold up in any U.S. court of law. Because most honor violations are in essence he said/she said disputes, the evidence these investigative teams collect is almost entirely hearsay or testimonial in nature.

The accused cadet must be informed that he or she will be going before an honor board at least two days before that board convenes, to allow the cadet to prepare a defense. Once the board convenes, the lead investigator presents all the evidence and makes a statement as to why he or she recommended that the case go before the board, thus slanting the board toward a guilty verdict before the case even begins. Once the hearing does convene, in light of the extremely limited legitimate evidence usually accompanying honor cases, the board members must attempt to determine who is and isn't telling the truth.

Honor boards at the Academy use a nonadversarial model that's more administrative than judicial.[24] The individuals who ultimately make the decision in the case are also responsible for questioning the parties involved. As board members present questions and listen to arguments, they try to be attentive to the accused's and accuser's body language. They question the credibility of these cadets by looking at their past performance. Since almost all honor-code violations depend on the intent behind a cadet's actions, the board must determine if there was intent to deceive, to gain personal advantage by deception, or both. Once these boards finish the questioning, they proceed to a closed session to cast their votes.

Six of the eight honor-board members must agree for a cadet to be convicted of an honor-code violation. The board members are instructed to weigh their decision using the standard of proof beyond a reasonable doubt. They must be entirely convinced or satisfied *to a moral certainty* that the cadet violated the honor code.[25] Although reason would lead one to believe that being entirely convinced of someone's guilt based on mostly hearsay and testimony would be difficult or impossible, honor boards do it all the time.

Once the board members settle on a verdict, they send the case to the commandant with their recommendations. The commandant has the authority to overturn the board's decision, but statistics show that historically commandants have concurred with approximately 95 percent of honor-board decisions. In essence, it is the verdict the cadet honor

24 Ibid., 33.

25 Ibid., 27.

board reaches and not the commandant that determines a cadet's future. A group of college-age kids are making a decision that will affect this person for life, often based on little, if any, concrete evidence.

The cadet honor board has made some very poor decisions in the past. The worst recent decision is arguably that affecting former cadet Andrea Prasse, who was involuntarily removed from the Academy eight days before her projected graduation date.

Another cadet at the Academy had been seeking a romantic relationship with Andrea, but she was not interested, to say the least. Not only was she not interested, but in order to quell his incessant sexual advances, she attempted to report the ongoing harassment and sought a no-contact order to prevent him from communicating with her. His reaction was to accuse her of an honor-code violation. He accused her of copying the design she used for a class project from another source, even though according to the stated guidelines for the project, students were *allowed* to copy other designs. Even though the board found the charge to be unfounded, they expelled her anyway after concluding that she had originally told the cadet she had not copied the design. Andrea's teacher testified on her behalf, stating very clearly during the hearing, "I do not suspect Andrea to be guilty of lying or cheating." In addition to the statement of the teacher who assigned the project that Andrea had done nothing wrong, two of her classmates also could have vouched for her and entirely cleared her name, but Andrea was not allowed to call them as witnesses even though part of the due-process protections that the honor system supposedly upholds is the right to call witnesses and personally cross-examine them if so desired. Additionally, according to its own statutes, an honor board cannot find a cadet guilty solely based on the word of another cadet. Andrea says in her own words,

> I didn't lie or cheat. My teacher says I didn't lie or cheat. My group members say I didn't lie or cheat. And then this one cadet says that I did, and they find me guilty beyond a reasonable doubt.

Even though the case against her was obviously ridiculous, honor-board members concluded, supposedly beyond a reasonable doubt, that she was guilty of an honor-code violation and recommended her expulsion from the Academy. The commandant, who for the most part does not overturn cadet honor-board decisions no matter how flawed their conclusions, went right along with the board's decision. After carefully reviewing the recommendations from both the honor board and the commandant, the superintendent, who possesses ultimate authority and responsibility at the Academy, is required to take a look at the entire case and make his own decision. This decision is final, the nail in the coffin for most cadets who make it that far into the cadet honor or conduct adjudicatory processes.

I'm sure if one looked at the statistics on how many times the superintendent (three-star general) didn't concur with the commandant's (one-star general) recommendations regarding honor and conduct cases, the number would be infinitesimal. It was no different in Andrea's case; the superintendent concurred, and she was forced out and told that she would have to serve three years as an enlisted airman in the Air Force to pay for her Academy education. She did not receive her degree in aeronautical engineering from the Academy or her commission when the rest of her class did, including the cadet who falsely accused her. The cadet who falsely accused her also happened to be one of the seventy-two cadet honor officers responsible for enacting the honor system at the Academy. His influence was felt among his peers, who were undoubtedly friends, close associates, or acquaintances at the very least. I recognized the majority of the faces and names of the 1000-plus cadets in my class. I can only imagine how close-knit the cadet honor officers' group was, with only seventy-two members. The board had been stacked, and everyone knew it.

Andrea and her parents spent the next year and a half battling with the Air Force Academy, who refused to budge. During this time Air Force Academy officials made some comments that would make even the most optimistic proponent of the American justice system cringe. Colonel Mark Hyatt, who was the director of the Academy's character-development center at this time, stated in a CBS news interview, "I am convinced there are not any innocent cadets that are convicted." Other Academy officials in the same interview said the honor system has *never* produced a wrongful conviction.[26] The absurdity of these comments would be striking to even the most unlearned individuals regarding law and order. Not only does it defy reason to believe that any system of adju-

---

26 Jaime Holguin, "Expelled Cadet Awaits Pentagon Ruling,"*CBSNews.com*, Sept. 25, 2002. http;//www.cbsnews.com/stories/2002/09/25/eveningnews/main523248.shtml.

dication has *never* produced a wrongful verdict, but to think that a system run by people who lack experience, maturity, and competence and who determine guilt and innocence according to their *perception* of intent has never made a mistake is incredibly foolish.

After being removed, Andrea sued the AFA for wrongly suspending her. She gained the support of U. S. senators Russ Feingold and Herb Koyl as well as U. S. Representative F. James Sensenbrenner, Jr., all of whom urged the Air Force to overturn the judgment against her. She volunteered at her local fire department in Wisconsin and then eventually enrolled at the University of Wisconsin–Madison in a master's degree program in engineering physics and astronomic science. She was admitted into the program despite not having an undergraduate degree! In the winter of 2003, when sexual assault became a huge issue at the Academy, Andrea joined voices with the numerous female cadets coming out with their stories. This of course was not the first time Andrea had mentioned sexual harassment—she had been kicked out for it. The Air Force Academy offered her a compromise. They offered to grant her a degree and commission if she agreed to six months of probation, remedial training, and mentoring. Andrea rejected the offer as inappropriate. Taking the offer would imply admission of guilt, and she wasn't guilty. One hundred thousand dollars in legal fees and months of lost income later, the secretary of the Air Force exonerated her completely, gave her an undergraduate degree from the Air Force Academy, and allowed her to be commissioned an officer in the United States Air Force. Andrea was commissioned in a private ceremony in her back yard in Wisconsin.

Her case is one of two out of 1000 since 1996 to be overturned by the secretary of the Air Force. In other words, once most cadets have been stuck by the honor system, they're stuck.[27] Andrea's first lawyer, Lester Pines, said of her case, "What happened to Andrea was a complete perversion of what anyone would call justice or due process." The sad truth is that Andrea's case is not unique in its lack of these crucial elements.[28]

27 Meg Kissinger, "From Outcast to Officer, Fight with Academy Ends in Exoneration," *The Milwaukee Online Journal,* Aug 1, 2004. http://www.jsonline.com/news/wauk/aug04/247965.asp.

28 Bruce Murphy, "Air Force Overrules Cadet's Suspension," *The Milwaukee Journal Sentinel,* Dec 23, 2003.

Many cadets have been victimized by fellow cadets' misuse of the honor system, with no national recognition and much less favorable outcomes.

Take what happened to a teammate of a close friend of mine, Cadet S. As Cadet S and I were on our way to dinner one evening during our sophomore year, he told me what had happened to one of his gymnastics teammates. I knew it was going to be a dark story when S told me that the reason he wanted to tell me was because the whole scenario reminded him of my freshman year. Apparently, Cadet S's teammate was not very well liked in his squadron. An athlete, he was probably automatically hated by the upperclassmen in his squadron who were not intercollegiate athletes. He was a gymnast, which would indicate to most that he was very strong; the very fact that he was physically strong probably made some upperclassmen dislike him because they were never able to train him enough to see him quit. According to Cadet S, this freshman had been caught riding the elevator at one point, which four degrees were not allowed to do. That very well could have set off some fireworks among the many upperclassmen who were pathetic enough to actually be upset about something that insignificant. Whatever the reason, this freshman was disliked and became a target for abuse from upperclassmen. Subsequently, while participating in squadron morale activities, he was physically assaulted and battered.

Most of the typical morale activities squadrons participated in were eventually banned from the Academy: hall brawls, midget tossing, slip and slide, the gauntlet, etc. Ultimately, the only squadron morale activities allowed were activities like TOP GUN comprising beach volleyball, an unattended barbeque, aviator sunglasses, white t-shirts, and the *Top Gun* soundtrack playing on someone's radio. Hall brawls were outlawed for reasons that go without saying (they were exactly what they sound like). Midget tossing entailed from two to four cadets throwing a cadet small in stature down the hallway onto piled-up mattresses. School administrators had to ban the activity when a female cadet, involuntarily selected as the midget, had her back broken in the process. Slip and slide entailed soaping down the tile dormitory floors and then running and sliding as far as possible on your knees or belly. Suffice it to say, although very entertaining, it too was discontinued.

It was during the gauntlet that Cadet S's teammate was allegedly assaulted. The gauntlet entailed pushing a person down the hallway in a rolling chair, football or lacrosse helmet strapped on, while cadets lining both sides of the hallway pummelled the individual with pillows. It was all fun and games for this freshman until he laughingly made his way out of the gauntlet. Two cadets were awaiting his arrival at the end of the hallway. After he rolled past, these cadets shut the emergency doors behind him and attacked. It was all very well choreographed; the cadet pushing the chair ripped the kid's helmet off while dumping him on the tile floor. The impact with the floor broke open the skin on his cheek, and the two cadets began kicking him so violently they broke his collarbone. They left him lying on the floor, where somebody found him moments later. He was taken to the cadet clinic where he received multiple stitches in the cheek and a sling for the arm on the side of the broken collarbone. I know, because I saw him walking around wearing the sling and a huge bandage on his face.

It would not be hard to guess the reaction of this kid's intercollegiate gymnastics coach upon hearing what had happened. The coach, in a rage, called the victim's AOC and let him have it. The AOC eventually agreed to meet with the four degree and the upperclassmen to ascertain what had happened. The result of this meeting is not so easily explained, though. The AOC's solution was to have this fourth-class cadet apologize for the incident in front of his squadron, thus directly accepting responsibility for what happened. Now, one could say something's not right with this story, and clearly one would be correct. First of all, upon hearing what had happened, the doctor who treated the victimized four degree at the cadet clinic should have at least called the kid's AOC (if not the security forces) to inform him that he had a very serious issue on his hands. Second, the AOC should have initiated a formal investigation into the affair in order to determine if this cadet was telling the truth; if so, then criminal assault charges should have been brought against the perpetrators. If the cadet victim was found to have lied about being attacked, he should have been sent before an honor board according to Academy policy and recommended for expulsion. Third, no matter who might be at fault, in a case like this it is completely irresponsible to have either involved party make a public statement regarding the issue to people who have nothing to do with the case.

Having been the victim of a similar situation, I'd be willing to bet that there were some ulterior motives involved with the AOC's decision. The three upperclass cadets were all seniors. AOCs generally let first-class cadets attempt to run the squadron, and surely this squadron was no different. These three upperclassmen probably had some significant role in the squadron chain of command, and the AOC really didn't want to create an issue with these upperclassmen whom he trusted and respected, especially on behalf of some freshman who, according to what these three upperclassmen had told him, was a poor performer. The AOC probably viewed the freshman cadet as contemptible and unreliable. I would conjecture that this AOC was no better trained to deal with issues of this nature than all the other untrained AOCs serving at the Academy at that time. He probably wanted to see the issue disappear so he could resume his late morning to early afternoon self-appointed work schedule, like the majority of his AOC counterparts. He probably thought this was a case of cadets getting a little rowdy and that the parties involved just needed to apologize, shake hands, and move on. These rather speculative remarks do not originate from the cynical perspective of an outcast but from the real-life circumstances surrounding my own physical assault and battery while a freshman at the Academy.

This has to do with the honor code for a number of reasons. First of all, the system failed to reveal that his attackers not only lied about their intentions during the assault but also about the who, what, when, and where of it. Secondly, this cadet who made an admission of guilt under a considerable amount of duress would never have been able (even if he were to have come to his senses) to file assault charges, because as soon as he did so, he would have been brought up on honor charges—that is, if he remained at the Academy long enough to give it any thought. As soon as he told the authorities he had been brutally victimized, they would have brought up the fact that he had made a public disclosure of partial responsibility for the incident at such-and-such time on such-and-such date, and that approximately 120 cadets would be willing to testify to the fact. I would like to think that it was out of simple incompetence that this cadet's AOC instructed him to accept responsibility for his own victimization, but because of my own experience I have a hard time believing that.

If that's not a sufficiently clearcut case of misuse and complete failure of the honor system, I have a few more, in one of which I was involved. There was a case at the USMA where a fourth-classman, who had recently received cookies in the mail, was asked by an upperclassman if he had any cookies left. The four degree answered that his cookies were all gone. Later it was discovered that the cookies were in fact not gone. The cadet was convicted of an honor-code violation and removed from the Academy. Another cadet at West Point was forced to leave for quibbling over his status as a nonvirgin. In one final example; an upperclassman and freshman cadet made a bet which the freshman ultimately lost. As a condition for losing the bet, the upperclassman ordered the freshman to buy him some food from a snack bar off-limits to four degrees. While purchasing the food, a suspicious cadet in line behind him asked if he was a freshman. The four degree's options at that point were to either say yes and receive demerits for breaking an Academy regulation or attempt to play it off and say no. Either way, he was acting under orders, but in spite of that, after saying no he was charged with an honor violation and forced out of the Academy.[29] I can relate to this kind of trivialization of the honor system.

During the forty days prior to Recognition weekend, my room had become a hangout spot for upperclassmen at all times of the day; as long as I was there, of course. A room built for two or three inhabitants was host to from ten to fifteen raging upperclassmen on a fairly continual basis. After seeing what had happened to me during first semester, none of the other freshmen in the squadron wanted to room with me for the spring semester; though one of my classmates was at least *willing* to room with me—the same kid who had been extensively harassed during BCT for his facing movements. Needless to say, this cadet and I spent many hours being trained together. The target status that we had both individually acquired quickly become one giant, collective training priority and, better yet, in a centralized location—our room. Our room essentially served as the forward operating base (FOB) for four-degree training. Many squadron-wide training sessions originated in our room and then spread throughout the squadron. Other freshmen would come running, supposedly to our rescue, only to find the room so crowded with upperclassmen that they couldn't even make it through the doorway. These four degrees would then retreat to the hallway, where they ended up being trained by upperclassmen who couldn't fit into the room either.

Accordingly, I made every effort to avoid being in my room or the squadron area in general. I had to go to great lengths to make it through

29 Government Accountability Office Report, DoD Service Academies "Status Report on Reviews of Student Treatment,"T-NSIAD-92-41 (Washington, DC: U.S. Government Accountability Office, 2 June 1992), 9–10.

the squadron hallways to my room, collect my study materials, and get out; sometimes this process took as long as two or three hours because of upperclass cadets' intentionally long and agonizing training. Once I finally made it out of the squadron, I would run over to the only place where I could actually study: the Academy library. I would isolate myself in the upstairs corner by a window looking out over Colorado Springs. When I needed a study break, I would take a second to gaze out at the city lights. I remember thinking how peculiar it was that two diametrically opposed, neighboring worlds could operate so oblivious to each other. I usually studied at the library until forced to leave. I closed out the library in order to avoid, as much as possible, the inevitable harassment I would be subjected to when I returned to the squadron.

One night, after making it from the entrance of the squadron to my room (20 yards or so) in relatively good time (15–20 min.), I was visited by an upperclass cadet whose imbedded hatred for me had just recently surfaced. The visit came after Taps, when both I and this upperclassman were supposed to have retired for the evening. Instead of being dressed in an officially sanctioned AFA uniform required of four degrees 24/7, I was wearing a hospital scrub top that looked almost identical to the standard-issue USAFA pajamas, just with shorter sleeves. I only wore it when I was either moments away from or actually sleeping, and only for the purpose of being able to sleep better. Additionally, if this upperclass cadet had not been committing a violation himself by coming into my room uninvited after Taps, he would never have known I had the scrub top. He came back the next day with a Form 10 for unauthorized possession of civilian clothing and required that I hand over not only the shirt but any and all additional contraband. The only unauthorized item I had in my possession was the shirt, which I obediently handed over, but he was utterly convinced I had more contraband that I wasn't telling him about. Therefore, during academic call to quarters for the next four days, and then a couple of days on the weekend he conducted absurdly thorough room inspections in hopes of finding the additional contraband that he just *knew* I had.

On the third or fourth day of these inspections, I came back to my room to find this upperclassman waiting for me with a devilish grin on his face. As I entered my room he asked me if I still thought I had no contraband. I hadn't been lying the last dozen or so times he had asked me that question; therefore, nothing having changed, I answered mechanically, "No, sir, I do not have any contraband." His cheerful demeanor turned to sheer bliss. As he collected himself, he asked me if that was my final answer, to which I answered in the affirmative. Before I could finish answering, he went as far as to ask me if I'd be willing to put it in writing. This time I hadn't even begun answering before he interrupted me in order to say that he wouldn't need it anyway. After telling me that I was going to "regret that," he informed me that he had found a DVD underneath the table against the wall, and that not only was I going to be receiving another Form 10 for having more contraband, but I was going to an honor board for lying to him about it. As he left the room he squealed over his shoulder in a less than masculine tone of voice, "That sucks," and left the room still smiling.

I can remember times at the Academy when certain emotions largely impeded my ability to speak. Just as bewilderment had impeded my speech after the comment "Graney, you're the worst cadet in the entire Cadet Wing," unprecedented frustration struck me silent this time. My roommate and I stared at each other with a mutual lack of understanding how anyone could enjoy being so conniving and malicious. We also could not figure out where the movie had come from. After a considerable amount of thought we realized it had to have been left there by a classmate of ours the night before. It was *very uncommon* for freshmen to come by our room because of how *common* it was for upperclassmen to be there. We later deduced that this freshman who had visited us had only done so to avoid being seen with the movie while passing through the squadron. While seeking refuge in our room (it had to have been his last option), apparently he had concluded that shoving the DVD under the table in our room was better than being caught with it in the hallway. When we asked this cadet about it later, he claimed he had forgotten the movie. Either way, I still had a situation on my hands. I approached this upperclassman later and explained to him what happened. He of course would hear nothing of it. "Sorry, Graney, not my problem. You're the one who decided to lie about it, not me. The only option you've left me is to turn you in, sorry."

I wasted no time establishing contact with my first-class cadet neighbor, the same guy who'd conceptualized the BCT II race track I had constructed and upon which I low-crawled for lengthy periods of time. Ironically, this same cadet who was responsible for many truly aggravating hours of low-crawling during BCT II had actually become, throughout the course of the year, a dispassionate mentor-protector of sorts for me. This cadet also knew me to be a person of unquestionable integrity from interacting with me each Sunday at church. There was no doubt in his mind that what I told him had happened was the exact truth; I had never given this cadet or any other cadet or school administrator a reason to doubt my integrity, nor did I throughout my entire tenure at the Academy. This cadet immediately went to the accuser's room and, after a heated debate, was able to talk the three degree out of charging me. If this first-class cadet had not stood up for me, I would have been charged with an honor-code violation and told to pack my bags.

The irony is that this third-class cadet, the same cadet who went to great lengths to pencil whip and work to remove me from the Academy in due course left the Academy himself. He voluntarily out-processed approximately three months after this incident because the Academy "just wasn't for" him. I would later learn that this same cadet had been severely harassed while a freshman, which didn't exactly shock me. It's that type of background that supports my theory of displacement as the best explanation for this behavior. While at the Academy, I often used the term "third-grade mentality" to make sense of the mistreatment propagated from year to year, a condition I observed in the majority of upperclass cadets. "It happened to me, so it's going to happen to you"—that was the mindset.

This is obviously not how the honor system is meant to operate. The honor system is not to be used as a tool to either enforce Academy regulations or remove disliked cadets. It is supposed to be a moral standard; the cornerstone for honest and upright living among cadets. Questioning with the intent to ensnare a cadet in a lie or enforce a regulation is specifically outlawed at the Academy. The academies even created a label for that type of questioning: going fishing. But just as with most things that are outlawed at the Academy, cadets do it anyway. Why? Because Academy officials very rarely punish upperclassmen for abusing either the Fourth Class System or the honor code. The school administration does not care if freshmen are subjected to hazing or misuses of the honor system, so when they become upperclassmen they haze and misuse the honor system as well.

The perfect analogy would be that of the parental couple that unconditionally defends its child's bad behavior. Let's say the child acts up in school, causing the teacher to call the principal who then calls the parents. The parents, in order to protect their own illusion of respectability, disparage the teacher in front of the principal no matter what their child has done. The child could have gone up and slapped the teacher, yet, these parents say the teacher probably deserved it. No matter how absurd or inappropriate their child's behavior, they always find a way to divert responsibility onto those trying to stop it. When the child realizes that his parents will never question anything he does, the behavior worsens.

Everyone knows that such children often end up in a juvenile detention center or the state penitentiary, after doing something for which the parents couldn't find an excuse. It's no different at the Academy. The Academy propaganda department (i.e., public affairs) paints a picture of accountability among cadets and school administrators. They try to convince people that not only do cadets not haze or misuse the honor system in the first place, but if a cadet were to do so, the Academy would not tolerate it for one minute. Nothing could be further from the truth. I am aware of numerous cadets who openly admitted to having stacked a board (both honor and squadron commander review boards [SCRB]) in order to sway an opinion either in support of an accused friend of theirs or to facilitate the deserved or undeserved dismissal of a widely disliked cadet.

If one were to compare how often cadets are hazed at the Academy with how many times cadets are charged with training violations, a gross disparity would come to light. If the frequency of hazing incidents were compared to the number of cadets actually removed from the Academy for hazing, the disparity would be even greater. Just as the behavior of the child in our analogy deteriorates as that child realizes that there is no parental restraint, cadets haze and misuse the honor system to an even greater extent when they realize the absence of restraint on the part of Academy administrators.

The honor incident having to do with the contraband (movie) found in my room wasn't my first nor my most precarious run-in with the honor system. About two and a half months earlier I had gone in front of an honor board as the accuser. Every freshman at the Academy used to be assigned a three-degree personal trainer, and it had nothing to do with Winsor Pilates. This third-class cadet, to whom a four degree was assigned, was responsible for ensuring that one particular freshman cadet was performing academically, militarily, and physically. However, all these personal trainers really did was conduct room inspections and remind the four degree how much of a disgrace he or she was to the trainer. After I became a target, my personal trainer became the ringleader for all those cadets in the squadron who sought enthusiastically to effect my removal from the institution. He made every effort to be on my case for something or another at all times of the day or night.

One night on a nontraining weekend, I had to use the restroom at the end of the hallway. It was an hour or so after Taps on a Saturday night, when most upperclassmen had left the Academy grounds for the weekend, so the dormitory hallways were deserted. I made my way to the bathroom still wearing my class A uniform, used the facilities, and was buttoning the last button on my jacket on my way out the door when from all the way across the squadron my three-degree trainer came running. He had seen me leave the restroom without my uniform properly secured. Once he reached me, it was clear to me that he had been drinking heavily. He almost fell over while running down the hallway to yell at me, then had difficulty stopping. His eyes were glazed over. He was incoherent, and his breath smelled of alcohol. He was swaying back and forth, slurring his speech, repeating himself and using excessive profanity, even by Academy standards. His saliva landed on my face as he passionately disciplined me for not having my uniform secured before exiting the restroom. Realizing that he was nearly passing-out drunk, I took the initiative of steering us toward our rooms, a rather daring act that went almost entirely unnoticed. Walking away from an upperclassman while being trained would have been considered incredibly inflammatory under normal conditions, though he didn't even notice; the part of his brain actually functioning was apparently completely absorbed in the tongue-lashing he was dishing out.

He continued yelling as we walked side by side down the hallway toward our rooms. Once we reached his room, I stopped and faced him, hoping he would recognize his room and go in. After standing in front of his room for several minutes I realized he had no intention of retiring for the night. I then attempted to steer us nonchalantly toward my room, where I was planning to make my escape, but when I went to return to my room he immediately got in the way and scolded me for walking away from him. He told me that it was "things like that" that caused upperclassmen to hate me, and that he was embarrassed to be my trainer, that I was a disgrace to him. It was the fourth or fifth time he had told me that since the charade began at the bathroom door. Realizing that there really was no end in sight to this tirade, I risked upsetting my trainer even more by moving toward my room for a second time. He became even more upset and placed his body between me and my room. I physically walked right through him, igniting the real fireworks. The entire way to my room he was yelling into my ear for me to stop. I ignored his orders and proceeded. While I was walking and my trainer was yelling, a random cadet walking through the squadron decided to intervene. This random upperclassman told me to stop, then got in my face and asked me why I had not stopped when ordered to do so by an upperclassman. I was hoping that this upperclassman would usher my out-of-control trainer elsewhere once he recognized my trainer's extreme drunkenness, but instead he chose to speak some harsh words to me and take off. He scolded me for not obeying a direct order from an upperclassman, then disappeared. My trainer's screaming turned into an extremely insulting one-way conversation. I stood there in front of my room for close to forty-five minutes listening to his speech about my insignificance to the United State Air Force. A first-class cadet who, after forty-five minutes of high-powered criticism, decided she had heard enough, came out of her room and asked my trainer to go back to his room. His entire demeanor changed at this request. He turned and appeased her by informing her that he would go back to his room in just a second and that he was sorry to have disturbed her. She took him at his word and returned to her room.

As soon as she closed her door, he was back in my face telling me the same nonsense as before, just at a slightly lower decibel level. A few moments later the first-class cadet again intervened, this time only poking her head out the door to see if he had gone back to his room. She was a little frustrated to see him still standing there but did nothing but watch from her doorway. Having made eye contact with her and sensed her permission to end the engagement, I escorted my trainer back to his room. I led him back by the arm—against his will, but with very little opposition on account of the firstie's watchful eye. On reaching his room I opened his door, placed him in his room, and shut the door. As I walked back to my room I reestablished awkward eye contact with this first-class cadet, who didn't utter a sound as if out of respect for the frustration I was feeling.

On returning to my room I encountered my wide-eyed roommate, curious to know what the hell had just happened. My emotions must have been written all over my face, because he sank into a subdued posture suggesting, "I'm not here, do what you need to do." He retired for the night without saying a word, and I sat motionless in the dark, staring out the window at the deserted terrazzo. I honestly don't know how long I sat there totally absorbed in thought. The headache I had experienced while listening to my trainer's endless criticism couldn't compete with the flood of thought that completely monopolized my mental faculties.

It was during this moment of intense contemplation that I came to know beyond the shadow of a doubt the frivolity of the four-degree experience. The same guy who thought it was okay to break the law (underage drinking/public intoxication) had spent over an hour correcting me for not having a button done up on my uniform. The guy who made a complete fool of himself was simultaneously describing to me *how foolish I was* for not embracing the Fourth Class System. The guy who thought it was acceptable to break just about every training regulation at the Academy had spent a large part of the night telling me how unacceptable my behavior was in light of the same regulations. The same guy who was supposed to be responsible for ensuring that I demonstrated proper conduct was unquestionably exhibiting, according to the Uniform Code of Military Justice (UCMJ), unbecoming conduct. Worst of all, though, was that the guy who was supposed to be doing the leading had to be led by the arm to his room by the guy who was supposed to be following him.

Later on in the year, after being asked by my AOC, Major H, what kind of trainer I was going to be as a three degree, I responded that my leadership style would in no way resemble the way I was led as a freshman. Hearing this, Major H asked what was so wrong with the way I had been led. The interlude where I had been trained after Taps on a non-training weekend by a drunken cadet was only one of the many reasons I provided. It was moments like that that caused me to reject any desire to emulate the manner by which I was trained. It was such asinine questions in conjunction with repeatedly negligent behavior on the part of my AOC that made me not want to imitate *his* leadership style either.

Later on the evening of the incident, my optimism made way for cynicism. My focus had already switched from somehow benefiting from the Fourth Class System to merely living through it. After this incident, that focus changed from perseverance to crisis management. I resigned myself to minimize the personal deterioration brought on by the perverted ideology of the Fourth Class System and Academy culture at large. It took extraordinary personal resolve to resist becoming jaded, though

I could think of nothing more important at the time, nor was there any pursuit in which I would invest more energy.

The day after the incident, I was asked by my cadet squadron commander to detail in a memorandum for record (MFR) exactly what had happened the night before. Apparently the female first-class cadet who had witnessed the whole thing had notified him that an investigation might be appropriate. I wrote up the MFR and handed it to him. He had also asked for an MFR from my trainer. Evidently, my trainer must have neglected to include anything in his MFR about his drunkenness, because when I brought it up it became an honor issue. Honor-cadet investigators asked us both about the inconsistency between our stories. Neither of us budged, so the case was sent to an honor board. I was told a few days beforehand that I was going to be testifying and should prepare myself to do so. I didn't consider preparation to be necessary, as all I had done in my MFR was tell the truth, and that's all I planned to do before the honor board. I knew that any statement contradictory to what I said had happened was a lie. Besides, I would have had no idea how or what to prepare even had I wanted to.

Consequently, I just showed up in my service dress on the day and time and at the location specified. I sat down by myself in the waiting area, not really knowing what was happening. No one asked me to take a seat. No one informed me when I would be going in or where exactly the board would be. I just sat there patiently, looking around the room and waiting for something to happen. After some time I started to wonder if I had come on the wrong day or if I was in the right place, but then a door opened and the first-class cadet who had been there that night stepped out, looked at me with a blank expression on her face, then exited left. The door stayed open for a second or two, during which time I wondered if I was supposed to just walk in or wait for someone. I stayed put until a minute or two later, when a board member appeared in the doorway and told me to come in. As I walked up to the door and into the room I could feel the hostility in the air. Still, I had no cause for distress, as I had done nothing wrong. The only thing I had done was endure multiple training violations. Furthermore, I wasn't even the one who had reported the incident; the female first-class cadet had. My only involvement in the whole scenario was having been abused and then having written about that abuse the day after, at the request of my squadron commander.

I walked into an environment heaving with egotism. As I looked around the room at the board members' faces, it was hard not to notice the arrogance they radiated through their expressions and body movements. Even then, I had little reason to care, because I still felt as though this issue was about my trainer and not me. I was directed to a seat that, to my surprise, was next to the seat occupied by my trainer. I couldn't understand why they would have us both in there at the same time. Even as young and inexperienced as I was at that stage of my life, I had no trouble grasping the fact that it was probably not a good idea to have the accused sit right next to the accuser. As I approached my seat, my trainer gave me what I call the ugly look. I had to wait for my trainer to take his arm off the back of my chair before sitting down, another form of surreptitious intimidation.

I sat down, still rather calm and collected despite a growing feeling of disharmony with my surroundings. A cadet at the end of the table informed me that the meeting was being recorded and that I needed to speak "loud and clear" in order for the tape to be audible upon review. He first asked me whether I knew why I was in front of an honor board. I responded that I did not know for sure, though I had a suspicion that it had to do with the portion of the MFR I had submitted in which I wrote that my trainer had been drinking. He then informed me my suspicion was correct, that there was no mention of drinking in the MFR submitted by my trainer. His followup question was, "With Cadet Z sitting right next to you, are you still willing to say that he was drinking?"

I sat back for a second, realizing how ridiculous a situation this cadet had engendered by asking that question. It was one of the most flagrant attempts at coercion I had seen in a long time. My response was to sit up in my chair and say, "I don't really care who the hell is sitting next to me. I said he was drunk in the MFR because he was drunk, and for no other reason." My response obviously outraged the questioner, who then initiated what became a highly critical personal attack. He began asking me questions about my performance as a four degree. He asked me about the number of upperclassmen in my squadron who considered me a poor performer. During this line of questioning, I was asked, "Cadet Graney, don't you think based on your four-degree performance that you could have *deserved* a little extra training?" I listened, absolutely amazed that this meeting, like most other officially sanctioned activities at the Academy, had become just another venue to harass four degrees. We had all come to this meeting to see if someone had lied about underage drinking, but we were now entertaining the perceptions upperclassmen in my squadron had about my performance. This wildly misguided cadet must not have been familiar with the idea of relevant evidence. Section IV Rule 401 of the *Manual for Courts-Martial United States* (2005 Edition) defines relevant evidence this way:

> "Relevant evidence" means evidence having any tendency to make the existence of any fact that is of consequence to the determination of the action more probable or less probable than it would be without evidence.[30]

What this upperclassman failed to understand (or care to recognize) was that whether or not I deserved extra attention as result of allegedly poor four-degree performance neither pertained to nor negated the disputed fact that my trainer was drunk and out of control on a nontraining weekend after Taps.

To this upperclassman's question I responded, "Sir, I don't see the purpose in asking me that. How does whether or not I deserved additional training have anything to do with determining if my trainer is lying about his underage drinking?" To this the upperclassman replied furiously, "Cadet Graney, we ask the questions, you answer them!" It was at that precise moment that I realized how immature and incompetent cadet honor boards really were. They were willing to pass judgment on who was telling the truth based solely on my allegedly poor performance as a four-degree cadet and the above-average military-performance rating maintained by my trainer. The whole scene was such a joke. Very little time was spent asking why I thought he was drunk or in cross-examining my trainer on his story. I heard no questions along the lines of, "Cadet Z, what had you been doing before this incident occurred?" or "Is there anyone who can corroborate your story?" The whole line of questioning revolved around why I was a bad cadet, why I needed extra training, and then convincing me of that fact. It even got to the point where, out of frustration, the field-grade officer on the board threatened to send *me* to an honor board for lying about my trainer's sobriety! Hearing that, I expressed my disappointment with both their adjudicating abilities and standard of justice. I

30 *Manual for Courts-Martial United States* (Washington, DC: Department of Defense, 2005), Section IV Rule 401, pages 111–119.

told them no one had ever honestly questioned my integrity ever before, and that there was no more reason to do so now than there had ever been in the past. Additionally, I told them it was rather insulting for them to have done so, especially under such discreditable terms.

I was asked to leave at that point, a request with which I gladly complied. It was just as Andrea Prasse's lawyer had said: "… complete perversion of what anyone would call justice or due process." I left the room hysterical. I couldn't believe that what had just happened had really happened. It was a maddening display of irresponsibility by all parties involved; not just the 19- to 21-year-old cadets on the board, but the field-grade officer as well, who so willingly went along with the extravaganza. I went straight from the honor board to the cadet weight room, where only after four or five hours of heavy lifting did I begin to calm down. I filed the experience away as just another story to tell my equally unimpressed friends and colleagues and continued on.

Not surprisingly, my trainer was exonerated. Nonetheless, he didn't escape completely unscathed per se. He was restricted from training for a short period of time as punishment for conducting training after Taps and on a nontraining weekend. Of course, the fact that he couldn't technically train me for a short while did not in any way stop my situation from worsening as result of the incident. My trainer went around and told all his friends that I had "tried to get [him] kicked out of the Academy" by accusing him of an honor violation. So they came after me. More and more random upperclassmen whom I had never seen before started training me for no apparent reason.

The most obvious correlation between the incident with my trainer and the intensified training made itself evident at the close of the second Academy-wide four-degree training session referred to as a wing round robin. Round robins entailed en masse training of four degrees from each squadron for about an hour in each of the other squadron areas by their respective training staffs. I had been called out for additional training in the majority of the squadrons we visited that day, but none more intensely than the last. Two cadets from that squadron immediately singled me out for some focused, personalized training. The entire time, they were overly anxious and determined to make me hurt physically and emotionally. They took turns leading calisthenics until I was completely exhausted. After the bell rang to indicate the end of the round robin, they had me stand up and brace myself at attention. All three of us were struggling for air, pulses raging, and sweat streaming down our faces. After five hours of similar physical training my BDUs were just as wet from sweat as they would have been if I had been doused with a firehose. As we stood there looking at each other, one of these cadets broke the silence by coming up to me and whispering in my ear, "That's for Cadet Z."

Later in the year, strangely enough, my trainer would end up getting into trouble not just for underage drinking, like almost the entire sophomore class in my squadron, but for devising his own mind-altering concoctions with over-the-counter prescription medications. When last I heard, he had been kicked out of the Academy shortly after the beginning of his second-class year. I wonder if I was the only one unsurprised by that course of events. He had already done irreparable damage to my Academy experience and my Air Force career. What did it matter if he was ultimately removed for the same sort of drug abuse I had called him out on? Seeing the people responsible for building a case for my own removal from the Academy end up being removed themselves was something I never quite got used to, even though it happened repeatedly.

I've shown multiple examples of cadets being more than willing to use the honor system as a tool in their efforts to remove people from the Academy or to enforce certain regulations. But there are just as many, if not more, cadets unwilling to participate in the honor system. The reasons for their refusal to comply with the honor system are many, though from my experience I say that the most prevalent reason cadets are unwilling to turn in other cadets is loyalty. No one appreciates an informant. Informing on classmates is looked down on by most cadets at the Academy no matter what the issue. When cadets have issues with other cadets' behavior, they usually tell those cadets to take it elsewhere rather than inform on them.

The second most prevalent reason is fear of reprisal. I was the victim of reprisal on numerous occasions for merely *knowing about* honor-code and training violations. When I stumbled across that upperclassman fraternizing with my two female classmates, I was subjected to intense reprisal action even though I didn't even turn him in. Imagine what would have happened if I had turned him in! I don't have to imagine too much. Not only was I the victim of severe reprisal, I knew of other unfortunate cadets who had suffered similar treatment as a result of complying with the honor system.

As soon as my freshman year began, one of the three degrees in our squadron was kicked out of the Academy. We were all naturally curious to know what he was being kicked out for and, much to our chagrin, we eventually found out. We learned that he had been removed for lying and for instigating a blanket party by going into a cadet's room, throwing a blanket over him, and then punching and kicking the cadet under the blanket as hard and for as long as the assailants deemed necessary. This cadet and his friends had been turned in by an associate. Once this cadet and his friends found out who had turned them in, they threw a blanket party for the informant. The blanket party just expedited the removal of these cadets, though it's a great example of why many cadets, especially four degrees, do not turn in other cadets for honor-code violations. Another fear among cadets is that if they turn another cadet in for an honor-code violation, that same cadet might know of some honor-code violation that the accuser committed and then turn him or her in as well, thus jeopardizing both cadets' careers.

The third most prevalent reason cadets don't turn in other cadets for honor violations is conflicting priorities. The average cadet has an incredible amount of work to do on a daily basis. Accusing someone of an honor-code violation and having to deal with all the documentation and meetings associated with carrying out an honor investigation would take precious time out of a cadet's schedule, time that many are unwilling to give up. If it's a matter of enforcing the honor code or earning a decent grade, most cadets will go with earning a decent grade.

Apart from the vast majority of cadets' not fully complying with the honor system, many legal professionals have challenged the legitimacy of certain aspects of the system as well as the necessity of the honor code in its entirety. The April 1995 Government Accountability Office, National Security and International Affairs Division (GAO/NSIAD) 95-49 report [31] organized the profusion of complaints various legal counselors had at the time with the honor system into six categories, the first of these being the honor system's lack of adequate standards of evidence or formal evidentiary procedures. Rules that would apply to most courts of law regarding what is and isn't legitimate evidence are not applied in honor-system procedures. The Academy gets away with it because it

---

31 GAO Report, "DoD Service Academies: Comparison of Honor and Conduct Adjudicatory Processes," 38–42.

claims the honor system is administrative and nonjudicial, but the result is the allowance of hearsay, conjecture, and other forms of questionable evidence. There's a reason courts of law do not allow submission of hearsay and conjecture as evidence; they are inherently unsubstantial. The fact that cadet honor boards allow this sort of evidence to be presented is inherently injudicious. Experts have noted that in the preponderance of honor cases there is considerable insufficiency of hard evidence (physical or documentary), a condition that leads board members to make most of their decisions based on their own uneducated or biased or immature perceptions regarding whom they consider guilty after listening to argument for and against the accused.

The second concern is that honor boards are too dependent upon subjective inferences of intent. In almost every honor case, the key factor in determining a cadet's guilt is the intent behind the action. If a cadet's actions violated the honor code by no intentional motive to deceit on part of the cadet (i.e., his or her intentions were not to break the honor code), the action itself does not constitute an honor violation. Therefore, honor boards must spend the majority of their time attempting to determine the intentions of accused cadets. However, such an undertaking is extremely difficult, if not impossible—especially for young people. The April 1995 GAO/NSIAD-95-49 report says it like this:

> Defense attorneys question whether students in their late teens and early 20's have the maturity of judgment and perspective to make such highly subjective judgments where the consequences can taint an individual for life, noting that it seemed ironic that the honor system was virtually the only area of Academy life where Academy authorities treated students as though they were responsible adults.

There's absolutely no question in my mind that Academy cadets do not have the maturity of judgment and perspective to make highly subjective judgments. Even if they were as capable as the average adult or even someone professionally trained to detect deceit, the chances of their correctly determining whether someone is lying are about the same as the chances that they will settle upon a false determination.

Another criticism of the honor system is that students are penalized for defending themselves. The GAO/NSIAD-95-49 report gave this explanation:

> One defense attorney stated that accused students were, in effect, penalized for conducting a vigorous defense and trying to prove their innocence. This reportedly occurs because Academy officials tend to take the admission of guilt and the expression of willingness to accept the consequences as the primary evidence of remorse and commitment to live honorably. This sets up the ironic situation where, given the same circumstances, a guilty person is more likely to be retained at the Academy than an innocent person.

Before I went before the military review committee (MRC) toward the end of my Academy career, I was told by a legal professional to go in with as apologetic a demeanor as I could possibly muster. I was told to take responsibility for everything, to plead for forgiveness and ask for a second chance. The reason he gave for advising me to take that course of action was almost word for word what the GAO says. He told me that the board would view any attempt at defending oneself as a lack of remorse and a lack of willingness to take responsibility for one's actions. He told me that even though he believed I had been greatly wronged by the Academy up to that point, for the sake of my future Academy career it would be wise to do as he instructed. I was blown away that not only had I spent my entire Academy career being mistreated (abuse that brought on the MRC in the first place), I was now being advised for the sake of continuing my Academy career to go in and actually apologize for having been abused and mistreated.

Experts also argue that students have been removed from the academies for trivial offenses, and that the severity of some honor punishments exceeds the severity of the offense. The same GAO report came across this outrageous circumstance:

> One defense attorney noted that some punishments appear disproportionate to the offense, particularly when one looks at the punishments across adjudicatory systems. We were referred to the following two Naval Academy cases that were adjudicated in the same year by the same Academy officials.
>
> One case involved the honor system. A plebe (freshman) was being questioned while serving noon meal to the upperclass midshipmen at his table. An upperclassman asked him what he had done over the weekend to improve his physical fitness. Although under no obligation

> to have engaged in physical conditioning, the plebe answered that he had gone running on Sunday. In response to follow-up questions, he cited where and when he had run. He then asked to discuss it later with the questioner. When his request was denied, he stated that he had answered incorrectly and that he had not been running. He was charged with the honor offense of lying, was found guilty, and was separated from the Academy.
>
> The other case involved the conduct system. Several midshipmen went to a Navy athletic contest at another university. They had been drinking prior to the game at the home of one of their classmates. After the game, one of the midshipmen (a sophomore) physically struck a woman in a wheelchair in a university dormitory. He was picked up by campus police and later released into the custody of several classmates. He then went into the local community, where he encountered a 12-year-old girl who was babysitting for her next-door neighbor. He began to curse and verbally abuse the girl and struck the girl's mother when she told him to leave. He then attempted to follow the girl into the house where she was babysitting. He broke into the house by kicking in a plate glass exterior door. Once inside, he broke several windows and was found by the police where he had passed out on the floor and he was arrested. He was found guilty of five conduct offenses at the highest level of seriousness and the lesser offense of underage drinking. He was retained at the Academy.

I wish there were a way to have a moment of silence in a book; if there were, I would request one now with respect to the intellectual and moral negligence of the Academy officials adjudicating these two cases. How anyone could determine that the honor violation committed by the first cadet was a more severe offense than that of the cadet in the second case is truly mind-boggling. It illustrates a complete lack of judicial capability and shows the grave inconsistency within the Academy's systems of adjudication.

The last of the six major concerns experts raise has to do with whether a separate honor system, in its entirety, is necessary at all. Just as 85–90 percent of officers serving in the military did not need to go through an Academy-like Fourth Class System to be commissioned officers, neither did they need an honor system like those of the academies to ensure their honesty and integrity. Very simply, if rigid honor systems like those in place at the academies are not necessary at institutions that produce 85–90 percent of commissioned officers, why are they necessary at the academies? The operational military has no comparable honor system either; even though the consequences of dishonorable behavior and disorderly conduct have widespread implications.

How can the operational military ensure honorable behavior and orderly conduct without an honor system? The military operates under the Uniform Code of Military Justice, which deals out real punishments for real crimes and indiscretions after conducting actual investigations in accordance with legitimate adjudicatory processes. If the operational military can operate without an honor system, and so can ROTC and OCS/OTS, it would follow that the academies don't need a separate honor code. If one were to say the current honor system at the Academy is absolutely necessary, reason suggests that it would also be necessary for all ROTC detachments, at OCS/OTS, and the officer corps in the operational military. All have similar objectives and moral obligations; thus, the ethical requirements and mechanisms for ensuring their honorable compliance to such duties should be fairly similar.

It has always been my opinion, even while still a cadet at the USAFA, that the Academy had no need for either the honor system or the conduct adjudicatory process. There are no conduct offenses distinct to the academies. All the conduct offenses that take place at the academies can and do occur in the operational military, whether it be lying about accountability, stealing, cheating on tests (soldiers, sailors, and airmen alike take numerous tests during their job-specific training), beating someone up, harassing females, etc. There are no crimes or indiscretions committed by Academy cadets that do not take place in similar fashion in the operational military. Accordingly, I have always argued that the academies ought to be governed (and not just theoretically) by the same justice system; namely UCMJ. A study done at the Coast Guard Academy in 1989 determined that every offense against the academies' (USNA/USMA/USAFA) cadet regulations could be seen as an offense under UCMJ. Most conduct offenses that occur at the Academy could be charged under Article 133, conduct unbecoming an officer or Article 134, the General Article, as an offense prejudicial to good order and discipline.[32]

32 Ibid., 38 (1989 study done for Assistant Superintendent of the U.S. Coast Guard Academy).

Technically, the Academy has always operated under UCMJ; however, until recently, UCMJ jurisdiction was far overshadowed by the institution's conduct adjudicatory system. When a cadet assaulted or raped another cadet. the offender was usually punished under the school's conduct adjudicatory system instead of having the case properly investigated by professional investigators, going before a court-martial, and (if found guilty) locked up behind bars where criminals belong. These delinquent cadets unfortunately failed to meet an appropriate end (i.e., military prison) because Academy leadership neglected the legal obligation (according to UCMJ) to prosecute. The convolution of Academy disciplinary systems didn't help. If a cadet stole something, he or she could be charged and punished using the honor system, the conduct adjudicatory system, or the Uniform Code of Military Justice. The number of disciplinary systems actually impeded the proper enactment of justice; especially as there were no functional guidelines to determine which disciplinary system was supposed to deal with what offense.

When I was taking military strategic studies (MSS) as a freshman, we were taught the principles of war. The textbook taught that in order to properly carry out a military operation it is imperative to coordinate a unified effort to achieve strategic objectives, and that decision-making power should be limited to a few select individuals. The textbook described this element of war as the unity of command principle. This principle should be used to unify the three disciplinary systems at the Academy. There needs to be one unitary disciplinary system at the Academy that encompasses any and all infractions. Air Force administrators have taken steps in this direction by emphasizing UCMJ and attempting to "operationalize" the Academy and engender an Academy environment that more closely resembles the operational Air Force. However, there is still more to be done.

First, get rid of the cadet formulated-honor system. Teddy Roosevelt, considered by many to have been one of the greatest presidents in American history, outlawed honor systems at the academies during his presidency; we need to do it again. Today the honor system remains in full force. Although the Academy has introduced UCMJ nonjudicial punishment (NJP) such as letters of counseling (LOC), letters of admonishment (LOA), and letters of reprimand (LOR) in conjunction with its efforts to operationalize the archaic institution, relics from the former conduct adjudicatory system remain in place. I say again, do as President

Roosevelt once did and eliminate the dysfunctional honor system. Rid the Academy of whatever remains of the traditional conduct adjudicatory system, such as tours and confinements. Doing so will, in effect, bring everything under the jurisdiction of the UCMJ, as in almost every other element of the operational military.

Academies need a unity of disciplinary procedures in order to avoid inconsistent or erroneous punishments. All crimes and infractions at the academies should be dealt with under the Uniform Code of Military Justice, thus ensuring that cadets receive legitimate due-process protections and that punishments are fair and balanced and fit the crime or infraction. The objective should not be to ensure disciplinary consistency throughout the academies, but to ensure it throughout the military as a whole. Justice and equality go hand in hand, so in order to have justice there must be equality. An Academy cadet who is found guilty of a crime should be dealt the same exact punishment as would any commissioned officer or enlisted airman guilty of that crime, regardless of rank, job title, or duty station. Bringing the academies under the sole jurisdiction of the UCMJ will do great things for the proper enactment of justice at service academies, should someone with enough moral courage and high enough rank choose to do so.

Many would argue that UCMJ punishments are too harsh and that cadets are still young and rambunctious, that they don't need to have their careers ruined by heavy UCMJ punishments before they even graduate from the Academy. Despite the fact that anything less than exemplary conduct is unworthy of the commission in the first place, this is a dangerous argument, as it reduces cadets to less than adult respectability. People often act in a way congruent with the manner by which they are treated or expected to act. Many times when someone is expected to act inappropriately, that is what happens. Likewise, when a person is expected to espouse professionalism and respectability, he will usually do just that.

A perfect example of this phenomenon is a cycle that occurs within our education system. The oldest classes in middle schools or junior highs across the country are considered the mature ones by underclassmen as well as by teachers and school administrators. Generally speaking, these students act the part. They *try* to set a higher standard of conduct for the younger classes to follow. But, once they enter high school, they regress. High-school freshmen are considered immature, inexperienced, and incompetent, and even though just the year before it was a different story, they now behave erratically, brushing aside common sense much of the time. However, as this group moves up hierarchically, they become more and more collected, thoughtful, and respectable. Once these students reach their senior year they are expected to be exemplary individuals. They spend the whole year leading the student body, sports teams, school clubs, and other extracurricular activities; they apply to college, study hard, win awards and scholarships, give speeches, and inspire the underclassmen. When they graduate they are on top of the world and act accordingly. Then, as soon as they enter college, they go crazy. The stereotypical college freshman is considered to be an out-of-control, hard-core partier with little concern for caution or orderly conduct, even though just the year before the same person may have been a beacon of maturity and good conduct for everyone around them.

How does this happen? It's a condition propagated by nurture. When these students are expected to be mature they act maturely (more or less), and vice versa. Even though the students' behavior changes over the years in response to the various expectations placed on them, who they are on the inside remains the same. Their capabilities as human beings are not subject to changing environments.

Therefore, if Academy administrators want cadets to act like adults, they need to treat them like adults. Part of being treated like an adult is having adult-level consequences for one's actions. If a cadet hazes another cadet, do not have the hazer march around in a square for many hours at attention; instead, prosecute that cadet under UCMJ. When cadets realize there are real consequences to their actions and that they are expected to act like adults, they will ultimately do so. Adherence to a single disciplinary system will ensure equal justice for cadets across the Cadet Wing; cadets will begin to see fewer inconsistencies and erroneous decisions and will ultimately have more respect for Academy regulations, administrators, and each other. If left in its current problematic state, the Academy's array of disciplinary systems will only continue to exemplify complete perversion of what anyone would call justice or due process.

7

Impetus Climax

"There is something immoral about abandoning one's own judgment."

—John F. Kennedy

I spent Thanksgiving in a cabin with my brother in the Colorado Rockies. We didn't have enough money to fly home, so we paid some dues and went with the Academy ski club to Keystone where we did some snowboarding, football watching, and turkey eating. My brother and I wanted it to actually feel like Thanksgiving, so we bought a turkey, some Stove Top stuffing, cranberry sauce, pumpkin pie, instant mashed potatoes, and gravy. We even made green-bean casserole—a huge accomplishment for two male college freshmen. I still consider that Thanksgiving break with Chaz one of the best I've ever had. They say in order to fully appreciate the good in life one must experience the bad. The time I spent kicking back with my brother in that mountain cabin was just that much more enjoyable because of what my life was like during the academic year. This momentary departure from the insanity that had become my reality was short-lived. The clock turned midnight, and the fairy tale was over. As I returned to the Academy, I, along with my four-degree comrades, was only that much more disheartened by having to listen to the Christmas music upperclassmen were bellowing throughout the squadron; a subtle reminder that until that time, happiness was only an illusion.

The time between Thanksgiving and Christmas was more of the same for me: abuse, unwarranted Forms 10, and academic difficulties. The upperclassmen had even found a new way to harass me. My classmates and I had all created screen names in order to use AOL Instant Messenger (IM). We all knew each other's screen names and communicated freely. Instant Messenger proved to be quite advantageous because, one, the Academy had no regulations against it (that we knew of); and two, we could effectively communicate with each other without having to go to each other's rooms via the hallway where a four degree always risked being yelled at and thus significantly delayed. Almost all information passed between us went by means of IM or e-mail. Most of the time we messaged each other to organize group study sessions or make sure everyone knew about mandatory meetings or assignments, though IM was also used for other purposes.

For instance, later on in the year when even more three degrees in the squadron were getting in trouble for underage drinking, a couple of my female classmates used IM to inform people they trusted that they had locked themselves in their room as a safety measure. More than locking themselves in, they had locked out uncontrollable three degrees who were drunk and dangerous and attempting to gain access. These female classmates were obviously frightened by the siege and, as misfortune would have it, needed to use the restroom (standard physiological response to fear). After determining that an expeditious visit to the restroom was of the essence, they sent me an IM asking if I would be willing to escort them, still fearing that these upperclassmen were somewhere in the vicinity. Feeling obligated, I quickly responded in the affirmative and made my way over to their room. It took them a moment or two to open the door, and once they had, they pulled me into the room and shut and locked the door behind me. They explained to me that they had been in their room, door locked, for a number of hours listening to upperclassmen yell obscenities and threatening remarks at them through the door. They believed that these upperclassmen had finally left and explained that they felt bad asking me to take them to the bathroom but that they thought it was a good idea given the circumstances. After making a vain effort to calm them, I escorted them out the door. En route to the restroom we were unfortunately intercepted by the very same cadets of whom they had spoken. My female classmates continued on to their destination in spite of being ordered to stop. I was then trained for an indeterminate amount of time, by myself, out in the hallway while the girls remained in the restroom. The girls, realizing that these upperclassmen were probably not going to stop hazing me until they came out, boldly exited the bathroom and turned toward their room. As soon as they did so, the upperclassmen's focus immediately reverted back to them, that is, until I purposefully insulted one of the upperclassmen, subsequently redirecting the attention back to me long enough to allow my classmates to slip by and back to their room. Consequently, I spent another indeterminate amount of time subjected to even harsher training than before. At some point I was sent back to my room, and everyone called it a night.

Shortly afterward, though, most likely in anger about having been anonymously reported (my female classmates reported them) for underage drinking, they were able to ascertain my IM screen name and began harassing me anonymously for my participation in the whole situation. The messages they sent me by IM were incredibly offensive; even so, I never responded. I simply told AOL to block messages coming from their screen name, but that proved ineffective. When one screen name was blocked, they would just create another and continue the harassment. This went on for weeks until one night when I had had enough and wrote, "If you're such a hard-(expletive), how about we meet up and see if you can prove it." Even though that comment ended the IM harassment, I was still subjected to their extra attention during training sessions in the hallways and SAR.

About the only good thing that happened to me at that time was a wildfire in Nevada. Walking through the squadron one day, I noticed a flyer on the wall advertising the opportunity to work with some new horses the Academy had purchased. These horses had been herded by helicopter out of harm's way and onto the auction block, where the Academy purchased them for its equine program. The horses had been transported to Colorado Springs and boarded down at the Academy stables. Being a horse enthusiast, I decided to participate. I got in touch with the contact person for the program who, of course, inquired about my experience with horses. After a short conversation he enthusiastically invited me to come down. I coordinated a ride down to the stables and dashed out of the squadron with some borrowed jeans and boots.

This was the start of one of the only activities that kept me sane during my Academy career. The stables at the Academy were very well kept, and the employees were welcoming. I cannot describe how therapeutic it was for me to train these horses. Even though most people would not consider breaking horses serene, the process had an incredibly calming affect on me. Bringing the horses into the circular corral one by one, gaining a horse's trust, throwing a saddle on, attempting to ride and getting thrown off; I couldn't get enough of it. These horses took so much focus and patience that, fortunately, my mind lacked the space for thoughts about the Academy. I felt like one of those kids they send to a halfway ranch to work with horses in an effort to quell their inner turbulence. Working with these horses took me to a place where everything made sense. If I did things right with the horses, the consequences would attest to that fact, whereas at the Academy my performance made no difference. No matter what I did, I had been permanently labeled unacceptable; there simply was no changing that.

I had to keep my equine involvement covert, however, because I suspected that freshmen weren't technically allowed to participate. I had the suspicion because I was the only freshman and everyone, even the guy who I rode down with every time, evidently thought I was an upperclassman. I figured what they didn't know couldn't hurt them; I hadn't ever heard anyone say outright that four degrees weren't allowed, and the mental relief it provided me really wasn't worth jeopardizing by asking unnecessary questions.

Just before Christmas, the level of harassment at the Academy went down a notch as everyone prepared for demanding final exams. Finals at the Academy made up 25–30 percent of a cadet's final grade, so almost everyone took the mandatory preparation time very seriously. I studied until my brain hurt, day after day, not even eating for a good portion of the time. The already slightly pacified Academy climate became even more so as final exams were administered throughout Fairchild Hall.

Most cadets left for Christmas break within hours of completing their last final exam, not necessarily to spend more time with their families but to maximize their time away from the Academy. Once my brother had completed his last final, we headed up to Denver International Airport to catch our flight to Seattle. I actually felt proud walking through the airport wearing my uniform. I felt even better when, while considering what to purchase at a terminal restaurant, a woman approached, gave me five dollars, and thanked me for my service. To this day, I follow suit in remembrance of her kind gesture and the reassuring affect it had on me at the time. I make a point of thanking the great men and woman who defend freedom and ensure my way of life whenever I get the chance.

Christmas, much like Thanksgiving, was abnormally enjoyable, and for exactly the same reason. The only difference was that this time I knew just how unpleasant it was going to be returning to the Academy after the break and, to a degree, had that knowledge looming over me the entire break. Anyone who spends a considerable amount of time at the Academy begins to acclimatize to the malicious environment that exists there, to the extent that such an atmosphere begins to give off the impression of normality. When that individual leaves the Academy environment for a healthy setting, he or she cannot help noticing how screwed up the Academy environment really is.

When I first arrived home my mother immediately took me to the dentist, of all places, to have my teeth cleaned. I can still remember how shocked I was when the lady at the front desk smiled at me, welcomed me home, and asked me how I was doing. Those were the kindest words anyone had spoken to me in as long as I could remember. I was so shocked that I didn't even respond. Noticing my inability to speak, my mom answered for me, then I turned to her and asked, "Did you see how nice she was? That was really nice." Just like that, my mom knew I wasn't joking about how malevolent the climate was at the Academy. Just as astonishment had blocked my response to the lady at the front desk, my mom, taken aback by my demoralized state, couldn't answer.

Moments like that defined my Christmas break. Old friends found me distant and emotionless, hard to talk to. I found out later that most people, after speaking with me, approached my parents and asked if I was okay. My parents shrugged it off, believing what the AOG and parent association had told them—that the four-degree year would be difficult and that their cadets might be downcast, but they should just keep encouraging them, as after it was over it would all make sense and the cadet would see the experience as the greatest of his entire life. My parents believed this because they had no reason not to.

My parents organized the yearly Academy Ball to which all service academy cadets from the state of Washington were invited. It was held at McCord Air Force Base just outside Seattle. My brother and I brought prearranged dates and had an enjoyable evening of dining and dancing. That was the only date I ever went on while a cadet at the USAFA. I had my reasons for not dating at the Academy. I hadn't the time, transportation, or, more importantly, the desire to do so. Apart from Ring Dance, every other dance at the Academy is a joke. Dances at the Academy are called debutante dances, because some organization actually transports busloads of girls in formal attire to the turnaround outside Arnold Hall.

Cadets who choose to participate line up outside the buses and wait for the girls. The order in which the girls exit the bus determines who a cadet's date is for the evening. As the cadets and their dates enter the building, some of the cadets who have chosen not to participate sit idly by and make fun of the girls as they walk by, especially the less attractive ones.

In fact, most squadrons send around a collection bucket, and every cadet signed up for the dance puts money in it. A couple of the nonparticipating cadets are then chosen to attend the dance, survey all the cadets' dates, and determine who got stuck with the least attractive girl for the evening. That cadet wins all the money in the hat. But that's not even the most ridiculous part. The girls bussed in are predominantly of high-school age. Whoever organizes the dances apparently can't find girls of appropriate age to be dating college guys in the first place.

Back in Seattle I enjoyed the company of the young lady I brought to the Academy Ball and felt my parents had done a great job making it a special time for us, but I still couldn't loosen up. I really think part of the reason was an unconscious knowledge that if I did, going back to the Academy would be that much more difficult. I spent a few more days in the company of those I loved and cared for, then once again it was time to go back to the Academy. No matter how long you've been at the Academy, every time you return from a break it is an emotionally draining experience. It's not that you're leaving your loved ones; it's that you're reentering such an acrimonious place.

The next three months of my life would take me to the brink of insanity. I've heard that moments of irrationality equate to temporary psychosis. One definition for irrationality is the inability to think clearly because of shock or injury to the brain. By that definition, I probably didn't just come to the brink of insanity but actually fell over it briefly.

I was welcomed back to the Academy by an academic review committee (ARC) because of my academic performance during the previous semester. When I arrived at my room, I sat down and checked my e-mail. I had a message waiting for me detailing everything I needed to do to prepare for the ARC. I met with my AOC, cadet squadron chain of command, and my academic advisor and filled out a great deal of paperwork with each one. A couple of weeks later, I went before the board in a room in Fairchild Hall. I pled my case and told them exactly what had contributed to my previous semester's GPA—and they believed me. I told them about my relative weakness in mathematics and my insufficient preparation in that field prior to coming to the Academy. I had been forced by an early junior-high teacher to repeat pre-algebra even though I had passed the class with an A, because she felt I hadn't quite grasped the information. I remember thinking at the time, "I grasped it well enough to pass your class with an A!" Nevertheless, from that point on I was always a year behind my classmates in math. Whereas most cadets arrive at the Academy having already taken a full year of calculus, I had only reached the level of trigonometry.

I attempted to compensate for it by hiring a math genius friend of mine to tutor me in the school library for a couple of months before entering the Academy, but that didn't prove as effective as I had hoped. I also explained how difficult the upperclass cadets in my squadron were making it for me to study. I explained how my studies were being interrupted frequently by upperclassmen harassing me. The board voted to allow me to stay another semester, for which I was very grateful. I was placed on academic probation and ordered to serve weekend academic call to quarters (WACQ). I spent most every weekend at the Academy studying anyway, so it wasn't much of a change. More than that, though, even if I had wanted to leave the Academy, most weekends I could not have done so because of perpetual upperclassmen-mandated restrictions on four-degree liberties.

I was also ordered to participate in academic counseling with my chain of command. I understood that I was to meet with my cadet element leader and flight and squadron commanders and then submit the completed documentation of these meetings to my AOC. Apparently that was not the case, and after an e-mail and Form 10 from Major H, I started meeting with my AOC as well. Academic probation directives only required a person to attend academic counseling with the AOC on a monthly basis, but after a couple of meetings with Major H regarding probation counseling and other issues, he began calling me into his office regularly. I was in his office at least once or twice a week, sometimes daily. Major H, I believe, found our conversations intellectually intriguing and most likely enjoyed the effervescent and controversial environment I engendered in his normally lifeless office.

One might ask, "What was so controversial about academic probation counseling?" Nothing really. There's nothing intrinsically controversial about constructive counseling for the purpose of personal improvement, but in this case there was nothing constructive about it. Whenever we discussed the factors responsible for my inadequate GPA, the conversation would always turn to the legitimacy of the Fourth Class System. I would say something like, "Sir, I'm still finding it difficult to study when upperclassmen are constantly harassing me." Then he would start in on the purpose of the Fourth Class System, why harassment was necessary for me to become a good officer, and how I wasn't really being treated any different from anyone else. Disregarding the crazy-making—that is, his acting as if I weren't being subjected to any more hazing-like treatment than anyone else [a huge factor in textbook systemic, repetitive abuse]—I would counter with the list of reasons why the Fourth Class System was essentially worthless. And on and on it went.

These discussions were many and close together. We examined every aspect of the Fourth Class System, him attempting to persuade me of its utter necessity, me trying to bring to light the detrimental effects it had on cadets' moral foundations and leadership potential. My arguments repetitively dismantled those of Major H, not because of superior deliberation on my part, but because I was right. No matter how savvy the orators involved in a dispute, logic and reason will always wrest the truth out of the conflict.

I have been told I'm able to make the weaker argument the stronger, but in this case I didn't need to. I was speaking the truth, and the truth hurt, to the point that Major H, in a moment of exasperation, leaned forward in his chair, pounded the desk, and yelled, "Graney, you cannot be a good officer without having gone through the Fourth Class System!" His level of frustration was equaled by my perplexity. Major H had never gone through a Fourth Class System. He had graced some ROTC detachment with his presence, a program that includes nothing even remotely similar to the AFA's Fourth Class System.

I returned fire by saying "Sir, I don't understand how you can say that, as an officer having never gone through the Fourth Class System yourself."

He then shot back at me, "Graney, what the hell are you saying? Are you saying that I'm not a good officer? Is that what you're saying?"

I replied in my customarily ingenuous manner, "No, sir. I just question the necessity for the Academy's Fourth Class System, especially weighed against ROTC and OTS programs that produce perfectly sound officers without all the abuse."

Despite my efforts to assuage his anger and still speak the truth, he was enraged at this response and went on a five- to ten-minute verbal rampage about his Fourth Class experience and how difficult it had been and that I just didn't understand. He concluded by telling me that I lacked the mental capacity necessary to appreciate the Fourth Class experience. After the tongue-lashing we sat there looking at each other, neither of us any more convinced of the other's argument. S.L.A. Marshall says this about such argumentation:

> When a man argues violently, his purpose usually is not to serve wisdom but to prevail despite his lack of it.[33]

This was not my first experience with classic one-liners. One day while attempting to eat lunch at the training table. I experienced an abnormal amount of harassment from one cadet in particular. It had become commonplace for me to experience abnormal amounts of harassment, but compared to the usual this was even more abnormal. I sat through the entire meal listening to his provocative speech about my lack of value, not just to the Air Force but to mankind in general. He said, "Cadet Graney, you are the most worthless cadet I have ever known. You either do not possess, or lack the motivation necessary to show, any good quality whatsoever. You suck at everything here at the Academy; you suck at life. There isn't anything you do well. I just don't see how you could possibly benefit the United States Air Force; do you?" He took my lack of response as supporting evidence for his case. He then said, "Cadet Graney, not even you can tell me anything good about Cadet Graney. I just don't get it, I mean, not only are you totally worthless but you don't even care that you're worthless. Seriously, Graney, if I were you, I'd be crying right now."

I turned my head, stared him straight in the eye, and said, "Sir, I don't doubt that," then got up and started walking away. I was already late to class because of his little game going into proverbial double overtime.

As I walked away, he yelled at me from the table, "What the hell is that supposed to mean? Graney! Where are you going? I didn't tell you that you could leave." Few times in my life have I had the presence of mind to say something so spot-on. Like most people, I think of great things I could have said long after the moment has passed. This come-

33 Marshall, *The Armed Forces Officer*, 44.

back would go down not only on the Quote of the Day Board but as one of my favorite comebacks of all time.

As a result of our heated academic probation counseling debates over the Fourth Class System, Major H sent me to the cadet counseling and leadership development center, allegedly so they could correct my attitude concerning the Fourth Class System. Really it was meant to pencil whip me into ideological compliance by continuing to load my personnel file with negative documentation. I felt certain Major H had sent me to counseling hoping someone reviewing my file would wonder why I had needed to visit a mental-health professional and make negative assumptions as to my stability.

In due course the encounters I had with Academy counselors profoundly enhanced my understanding of human nature. Academy counselors acted as catalysts for me, unconsciously and unwillingly developing my intellectual maturity. I went into these discussions as a young adult with a sound mind capable of deep, analytical thought. I came away as something more. Before these counseling sessions I already had a solid moral footing, cultivated by delicate tutelage from my parents, religious leaders, teachers, and coaches throughout the years. But as a result of these counseling sessions, my intellectual prowess grew tremendously. I no longer felt the need to auto-subordinate my powers of discernment to age and experience. I came to fully understand that the value of an opinion is determined by the knowledge and experience upon which it is based. Whereas before, I would have attributed at least a degree of inherent worth to the perspective of individuals with age and experience, as a result of these counselors' mind-numbing reproaches, I no longer did so. I have always been the kind of person who only pays heed to that which upon reflection seems logical and reasonable to me. Because of the Academy counselors' unwillingness to use common sense when addressing the realities of the Fourth Class System, in my mind the time for second-guessing myself had come to an end.

Every time I visited the counseling center I filled out a questionnaire regarding my mental status. The questions ranged from how satisfied I was with my sex life to whether or not I felt like physically hurting someone. Whenever a competent person is thrown into a situation where incompetence is the expectation, there will always be friction. Attempt to explain to a professional basketball player how to dribble a ball and just see what he does. Attempt to determine what's mentally wrong with a mentally sound individual, then don't be surprised when the response is similar to what you might get by attempting to tell Pablo Picasso how to paint. I was in no need of mental doctoring. Yes, I was distressed, but my distress stemmed from the very system Academy counselors were trying to persuade me to believe in.

It's very much the same as trying to persuade the victim of a crime that the crime itself was carried out for the victim's benefit. No matter how convincing the argument, the victim knows better, because he or she feels the negative effects of the wrongdoing. If something has been stolen from the victim, no matter what is said to that person in defense of the thief's actions, the item is still gone. There is a natural cause and effect to everything in life; one cannot change that reality. One can attempt, and at times succeed, to distort another person's perception of reality; however, that which is true and that which is false cannot be altered by man's craftiness. No matter what the Academy counselors said to me in defense of the Fourth Class System, I could not justifiably believe a word they said, for not only did they present faulty arguments founded on half-truths and subjective evidence but, more significantly, I felt the negative impact the Fourth Class System had on my life. I regularly witnessed its negative effects on those around me, and I knew it was wrong.

The meetings I had with these counselors ended very similarly to those with Major H. Once they realized they could not distort my vivid perception of reality, they would resort to vain attempts to discredit me as a person and forget all about the tenets upon which my argument rested. They would say things like, "Cadet Graney, you're eighteen, maybe nineteen years old, just out of high school. What makes you think you know better than the one- and three-star generals that oversee this institution?" or "Cadet Graney, thirty-thousand-plus men and women have graduated from the Academy and are good officers. Why? Because of the Fourth Class System." Or, "You're just bitter and cynical. You don't have the mental prowess or the willpower to separate the good from the bad, so to you it's all bad."

The fact of the matter is, people are capable of subscribing to bad ideology at any age. Age is not the scale on which logic and reason are measured. Age alone does not morally or ethically justify one's words and deeds. That a person is older does not mean that person is wiser; age and wisdom are simply not inextricably connected. Reason, not my age, suggested that the one- and three-star generals were wrong about the Fourth

Class System. Furthermore, one cannot responsibly claim that every officer who graduates from an Academy is a good officer; the key figures implicated in the aftermath of the Iran-Contra scandal were all Academy grads. Nor can a person conclusively deduce that all those who are good officers are so because of the Fourth Class System. Finally, the power of accurate observation is often labeled cynicism by those who do not possess it, and most aspects of the four-degree system were all bad!

Essentially, these counselors attempted to silence my opposition, at first by challenging the tenets of my arguments, then, frustrated by their failure, resorted to attacking my credibility. One man in particular, whose quotes freshmen were ordered to memorize from the standard-issue *Contrails*, would have greatly disapproved of the latter part of such a course of action. John Stuart Mill would have vehemently disagreed with the majority-rules-morality ideology and the repress-the-dissenter methodology. Mill wrote in his work *On Liberty*;

> If all mankind minus one were of one opinion, and only one person were of the contrary opinion, mankind would be no more justified in silencing that one person than he, if he had the power, would be justified in silencing mankind.

I made the argument that to be continually yelled at in an offensive, demeaning manner for nine months straight was in no way productive for either the abused or the abuser. I think most people would agree. In defense of the practice, these Academy counselors argued that it was the *only* way to prepare a person for the stresses of battle. They would say, "If you can't handle a little yelling, how are you going to be able to handle the stresses of warfare?" They would always throw a low blow after that by saying, "I mean, seriously, Graney, maybe you ought to find a new occupation," as if they were tougher than I was because they didn't complain.

These counselors were unprofessional, intellectual weaklings. Later in the year, when an officer from the counseling center cavalierly sent an e-mail to the entire Cadet Wing containing the details of case files and personal information belonging to every cadet at the Academy who was or had been seen for mental-health issues, I began to understand how far their lack of professionalism went. I happened to be reading my e-mails at the precise moment that e-mail was sent and unknowingly read a number of individual cases thinking it was something I was required to read. After reading a couple, though, I realized something was very wrong. The e-mail contained names, class years, descriptions of their problems, events that had transpired (such as a case where a cadet was raped by his roommate), and more. The e-mail was retracted within fifteen minutes with a follow-on message stating that the content was not intended for the Cadet Wing and that any and all information contained in the message must not be discussed or passed along to anyone. Further instruction ordered the deletion of the e-mail from everyone's computer. I couldn't believe it. Who knows how many cadets reading that e-mail actually knew someone described in it? Worse yet, how incredibly devastating it must have been for the people being treated.

The real problem regarding my counseling sessions was twofold. First and foremost, most of the Academy counselors were Academy grads and passionately defended the Academy's way of doing things. Second, few of them had the proper training to be providing mental-health services in the first place. Many counselors' qualifications did not exceed a bachelor's degree in psychology, yet, as I'm sure many are aware, to be a licensed psychologist or psychiatrist in the normal world you must have much more than a bachelor's degree in psychology. In the name of fairness, the counselor who ultimately submitted my official counseling-center evaluation was a licensed mental-health practitioner with a PhD. Nonetheless, these counseling sessions were ridiculous. These counselors went to great lengths to try to alter my lucid grasp of the realities of the Fourth Class System. They turned what were supposed to be moments of constructive mentoring into interrogation sessions motivated by their resentment of someone who thought differently from the way they thought. It was ideological extremism, doctrinal terrorism for which I had very little tolerance.

When I think of the obstinacy of the Academy counselors, I'm reminded of a situation with my English teacher around the same time. While doing research for a history paper on Nazi Germany, in the Academy library I came across William L Shirer's book *The Rise and Fall of the Third Reich*. I meant to just scan through and use some material from the work to support my thesis, but after a few chapters I found the book compelling. After I read it in its entirety, I could not help thinking how similar some tenets of fascist ideology were to those of the Fourth Class System. I would never go so far as to say that the consequences of the Fourth Class System even remotely compare to the negative impact the

Third Reich had on the world—that would be absurd and incredibly irresponsible. Yet after close examination I found that much of Nazi Germany's mentality at the time, such as a distaste for distinction (anyone not of the Aryan race), selection of a person or group of people to oppress (Jews), a lack of compassion (especially regarding treatment of the physically and mentally handicapped), and harsh tyrannical rule (Hitler and the Gestapo) reminded me of certain aspects of the Academy's much smaller society. In Nazi Germany a person was viewed as acceptable if not Jewish or handicapped, while the general population lacked compassion and accepted dictatorial rule without question. At the Academy, a cadet was viewed as acceptable if not outwardly religious or female or physically or mentally lacking, while the general population disregarded normal human decency (by either accepting abuse as a legitimate form of training, actually carrying out the abuse, or both) and accepted without question all conventions of the Fourth Class System and Academy as a whole.

The assignment for the class taught by said English teacher was to write a five-page persuasive paper. I chose the topic that I felt the most passionate about at the time, the Fourth Class System. I went on to construct the best-written five-page paper of my life, attempting to persuade the reader that the Academy climate had become unrestrained and dangerous. I made the same comparisons previously mentioned.

Generally speaking, a stark contrast exists between a paper that should receive an A and a paper that should receive an F. I turned my paper in, more confident than ever before that it would receive a favorable grade, only to have it returned with an F at the top of the first page. I approached the teacher after class and inquired why he had given me such a low grade. He said, "Because it sucked. Do it again." After I asked him what I could do to improve the paper (I knew exactly why he had given me the grade) he said I might want to reconsider the content. I went back to my room and over the weekend wrote a paper attempting to persuade the reader that the Fourth Class System was for everyone's mutual benefit and leadership development and should be revered and adhered to at all times. It was a horrible paper. It was poorly constructed and of borderline passing quality for a college paper. I received an A.

Not only did teachers, who were generally Academy grads, enforce ideological compliance by punishing cadets for thinking outside the box, they even participated to some degree in targeting campaigns, and I'm not talking about the teachers who made their students do pushups in class for academic discrepancies. I'm referring to the willingness of some faculty members to turn out disciplinary Forms 10.

For example, three-degree trainers were obligated to ensure that their trainees' rooms were in order. On a weekly basis, three degrees would take the room-grade cards, handwritten to perfection by their Fourth Class trainees, and, after conducting a thorough inspection, would grade the room. The average of all the individual scores on a range of one to ten would determine whether a cadet passed or failed. Accordingly, at the beginning of one particular week, I wrote up a grade card and brought it to my trainer to initiate the weekly room inspection. Trainers wouldn't set a date and time to inspect a cadet's room until they had approved their trainee's grade card. My trainer made a habit of never accepting my first grade card and, on many occasions, refusing the second as well. This time was no different. He told me to redo the grade card I'd just spent an hour making. I spent another hour of academic call to quarters making another grade card. I brought the grade card to my trainer for the second time and was denied once again, this time with a smirk because we both knew there was nothing wrong with either the first or second cards. I went back to my room and forced myself to spend yet another hour making another. Every additional hour I spent writing grade cards to satisfy my conniving trainer's appetite for sick entertainment meant another hour I would have to stay up later to study. My trainer reluctantly accepted my grade card on the third attempt, scheduled the following evening for the inspection, and went to sleep while I stayed up for the next five hours hitting the books.

The next evening my trainer failed to show up. I set up another night for the room inspection to occur; once again he failed to show. Whether I completed a room inspection was of little concern to him, since he was not the one in danger of receiving demerits as punishment at close of business Friday for not having had the room inspected. This effort to waste my extremely precious time was just another way to harass me and intentionally facilitate my academic failure. I scheduled the inspection for early Friday morning. It started at 06:30 hours and concluded five minutes before my first class was scheduled to begin. Not only was I in danger of being late to my first-period class, I had also missed breakfast. This was fairly detrimental, as I was rarely allowed to eat at lunch on account of the relentless hostilities on the part of vindictive training-table upperclassmen. After my trainer had given me a failing grade on the room inspection and left the vicinity I quickly ran out of the squadron, bag in hand, and down the most convenient (and off limits to four degrees) stairwell right past an upperclassman who later gave me a Form 10 for doing so.

Every day at the Academy there is a uniform of the day (UOD). The UOD during my time for Monday through Thursday was dark-blue pants, baby-blue shirt and jacket depending on the weather. On Fridays, the UOD was our battle-dress uniform (BDU). Because this particular room inspection landed on a Friday, I was appropriately dressed in my BDUs. Nonetheless, after exiting the squadron and running out on the terrazzo I realized that either I had my days mixed up or the UOD had been changed, as I was one of the only cadets in BDUs. Apparently the UOD had been changed that morning via wingwide e-mail and an announcement over the intercom. I was not able, however, to read my e-mails because I was at attention in the middle of my room being inspected, nor could I hear the announcement over my trainer's shouting. At this point I had a decision to make. I could run back to my room, change uniforms, and arrive to class late but in the proper uniform, or I could make it to class on time but out of uniform. Either way I was in a tight spot and would have to explain myself.

I quickly deduced that, given the circumstances, my teacher would consider it more important to be on time to class, so I continued on to Fairchild Hall, but not entirely unobstructed. En route I was stopped by an upperclassman wanting to know if it was because of a medical condition that I was out of uniform. Injured cadets at the Academy could apply for a Form 18 from the doctor that allowed them to wear BDUs while recovering from their injuries. After I said no, he wrote down my name and promised me a Form 10. After this little encounter I made it to class just as it was beginning. At the Academy, cadets must rise and report in to the instructor in order for class to begin. I ran in the door as the class was reporting in. Seeing that I was out of uniform, my instructor heatedly ordered me to stay after class. I expected that. There was nothing unusual about an instructor ensuring adherence to Academy uniform standards. After class I approached my teacher and explained what had transpired that morning and the decision I had had to make, saying I had figured it was more important to be in class than in uniform. The dialogue went as follows:

Instructor: "You're telling me that every other cadet in the entire Cadet Wing can figure it out, can read their e-mails and listen to announcements, but you can't?"

C4C Graney "Ma'am, what I'm telling you is that because of the room inspection I was unable to check my e-mails or hear the announcement."

Instructor: "Are you the only fourth-class cadet at the Academy who gets his room inspected?"

C4C Graney: "No, ma'am, I'm just saying that I had an impossible situation this morning."

Instructor: "Well, you should have gone back to your room and changed."

C4C Graney: "Ma'am, again, if I had done so I would have been late to your class. The only reason I was on time today is because I was sprinting as fast as I could."

Instructor: "You could have run faster."

C4C Graney: "No, ma'am, I know for a fact that if I had gone back to my room and changed there would have been no possible way that I would have been on time to your class. I would have been late before I even finished changing."

Instructor: "Well, I don't know what you expect me to do. There's a reason we have standards, and when you don't abide by established regulations I have no choice but to give you a Form 10. You seriously need to put it together, Cadet Graney."

As result of this course of events, I was given three Forms 10: one for using the four-degree-prohibited stairwell and two for the same infraction of being out of uniform. Furthermore, even though there was absolutely nothing I could have done to avoid the situation, these Forms 10 were later used during squadron commander review boards and military review committee hearings as evidence of my poor conduct and lack of regard for Academy standards and regulations. The affront went like this:

> "You just don't care about regulations. You don't follow orders. You're disrespectful. For example, deliberately using a stairwell you know to be off limits to four degrees. Showing up to class out of uniform, and not just once. You were stopped on the terrazzo on another occasion for being out of uniform. You just don't care."

Another example was when my behavioral-science teacher punished me for being sick. The night before the seventeenth day before Recognition, the freshmen in my squadron participated in what was called a spirit mission to demonstrate our squadron pride. We were out running around trying to hang a Cadet Squadron 17 banner from the chapel until early in the morning. It was cold, and we slept very little that night. Someone might think that that was an objective choice we all made, but that wasn't the case. If we hadn't done something to celebrate CS-17, we would have been punished by disgruntled upperclassmen. Although the following morning consisted of an intense beat-down to commemorate the seventeenth day before Recognition, it would have been considerably worse if we hadn't done what we did the night before. Cadets who had once been part of CS-17 came to help our upperclassmen make it a beat-down to remember.

At one point, an upperclassman took me and a couple of my classmates outside to run around the terrazzo. It was early morning in the dead of winter, and we were not allowed to grab our jackets, even though we were sweating profusely from physical training. We ran around the terrazzo a couple of times, battling the below-freezing temperatures and swirling snow. Once we returned to the squadron my lungs were on fire, and I had a splitting headache. After some additional calisthenics we returned to our rooms. I wrapped myself up in a blanket but quickly developed a bad cough and the shakes. I couldn't stop shaking or coughing, and I decided it would be better if I rested instead of going to class and worsening my condition.

I sent an e-mail to my behavioral-science teacher to tell him I was sick. I used the first word that popped into my head to describe how I felt: "worthless" (people had been using that word around me rather frequently). I told the teacher I had been forced to run around the terrazzo in the cold by an upperclassman and consequently felt worthless. Apparently, my teacher considered my absence from class due to sickness inappropriate and gave me a Form 10. In his Form 10, delivered straight to my AOC, he wrote, "Graney didn't come to class because he said he felt 'worthless'; his own words." Evidently my instructor either believed that being sick was not an appropriate excuse for being absent from class, failed to put the word "worthless" in the context I meant it, simply felt obliged to participate in the targeting campaign against me, or perhaps all three. I find it hard to believe that in all the years he spent in school working towards his bachelor's degree, master's degree, and doctorate, he never missed class due to illness. Even if he hadn't, I find it very hard to believe that he would have felt remiss if he had. Nor do I find it plausible that after all those years of education he couldn't understand that (taken in context) my use of the word "worthless" in the e-mail meant that I wasn't feeling well. I believe the reality was that he wanted to act like a tough guy and give me demerits, which explains what I felt to be the snotty tone he took while writing up the form.

My instructor's decision to punish me for being sick had profound implications on my cadet career, far beyond what even his behavioral-science expertise could have projected. After I received the Form 10 from my instructor, Major H softly reprimanded the cadet who had taken us running in the bitter cold. This cadet then went and told all his friends that one of the freshmen he took outside had tried to get him in trouble by telling the AOC, and of course after I was fingered, without hesitation, as the person who told on him, I subsequently received even more intense harassment. Even though he was reprimanded for the action that caused my sickness, I was punished for the unavoidable and guiltless byproduct of the same action—my sickness—as well. I was actually punished more harshly than the perpetrator. Such action belies reason. Later, during those same SCRBs and MRCs mentioned earlier, board members, throwing logic and reason to the wind, would fabricate a pattern of misbehavior and poor performance based on such situations. Their thought process went something like this:

> Obviously there's a different reason for Cadet Graney's poor academic performance, and it's not what he's been telling us about all this supposed harassment. He doesn't even show up to class, and when he does he's in the wrong uniform.

What I found obvious was the complete and utter lack of willingness to accept reality on part of the board members making such assertions. I felt there was never any logical connection between what had *actually happened* and these individuals' interpretations of the facts.

From our first encounter with each other my freshman squadron AOC, Major H, and I maintained very little regard for one another. Major H seemed to me to have very little self-confidence. Consequently, I saw him as incapable of doing what he needed to do as the professional officer supervising my squadron. I couldn't stand his seeming inability to lead; he couldn't stand my unwillingness to buy into his ideology. We sustained a very low tolerance for each other, but whereas I believed I dealt with my distaste for him in a professional manner, he seemed unwilling to do the same for me. Whereas my trainer acted catalytically in my target development, Major H didn't act at all. His inaction enabled the upperclassmen to do what they wanted, unhindered. As the year progressed, his inaction transformed into action, with a hint of what I saw as malicious intent. He began to go beyond just allowing me to be abused and actually began taking steps to augment the abusive environment.

Thomas Jefferson is quoted as saying, "I have sworn upon the altar of God, eternal hostility against every form of tyranny over the mind of man." Major H's mantra could have been, "I have sworn upon the altar of the Fourth Class System, eternal hostility against every form of resistance against such." After our conversations regarding the Fourth Class System, he began to slander me in conversations with first- and second-class cadets, which only served to embolden them. Until this time my MTL truly didn't have any sort of ill-will toward me, though after continual prodding by Major H, in a matter of days he became hugely in favor of my outright removal from the Academy. Major H began increasing the recommended number of demerits on the Forms 10 I received. Ultimately, he even began giving me Forms 10 himself, although in a circuitous manner. Major H carried out his own pencil-whipping campaign against me by way of the MTL. The MTL essentially became his point man in this regard. All of a sudden I started receiving Forms 10, dirty looks, insulting comments, and threats regarding the future of my cadet career from the MTL.

For example, before we even arrived at the Academy we were instructed to bring with us a long list of items that would be needed in order to be granted a security clearance. Fingerprints, notarized police background check, and a number of other not so easily obtainable items. For that reason they asked us to gather them before coming to the Academy, as doing so would make it easier and more efficient for everyone. Accordingly, I showed up with the required documentation and kept it on my person until I surrendered it to my squadron cadre during one of the in-processing stages of BCT I. We were asked to gather all our security clearance paperwork in a manila envelope and place it in the appropriate file. I placed my envelope in the folder intended for all those individuals whose last name began with the letter G, then never saw it again.

In true AFA style, they lost all this documentation along with all the documentation for every other freshman in the squadron whose name began with a G. At the very moment that my MTL was going through the conversion process (leaving behind his old self who had no reasonable objection to Cadet Graney and becoming a new man in hostility conceived by third-party hatred), the Academy realized they didn't have my security paperwork. His first reaction was to claim in an e-mail that my "G" classmates and I were, as he put it, "way behind the power curve" with respect to completing our security paperwork. I e-mailed him back and told him that we had submitted our security paperwork during basic training like everyone else and that there must be some confusion. He responded by pretentiously repeating, word for word, what he had said in his previous e-mail. During the ordeal of resubmitting the security paperwork, my MTL made numerous accusatory statements claiming that I was taking too long to complete the paperwork, that I didn't respond in a timely manner to his e-mails, and that I even failed to walk down the hallway and speak with him. Ultimately, he voluntarily documented the entirety of our correspondence during this time in my personnel filel, in an effort to substantiate his allegations that I was at least unwilling to if not incapable of following orders in a timely manner; all of course without my knowledge.

I considered my MTL to be one of the dimmest-witted individuals I had ever known, but he wrote in my personnel file that I was "totally unimpressive" and that not only did I have character problems but that my character was "nonexistent." At least I wasn't (I'm still not) pathetic enough to hate someone merely because that person is hated by a colleague of mine. Moreover, he apparently never made the connection that (mysteriously) it was only those freshmen whose last names started with the letter "G" for whom no paperwork existed, and that it just might have been the Academy's own incompetence that lost the paperwork in the first place. Nor did he really comprehend the truly ruthless and relentless conditions under which we were operating as fourth-class cadets. The reason for his lack of comprehension was twofold. One, he was physically present in the squadron about as much as Major H; enough said. Many times throughout the security-clearance paperwork charade I went to his office during normal business hours to speak with him and was unable to do so because he had already gone home for the day. Two, because of, in my opinion, his insufficient intellect, he was never able to think outside his own experience. He never could understand why what he perceived to be simple tasks were so difficult for four degrees in the squadron to perform. What were indeed simple tasks in the normal world were not so simple for fourth-class cadets at this time, because we were subject to not only the ridiculous customary four-degree training regulations but an embellished form of such, called Forty Days.

The Forty Days training started on the fortieth day before Recognition weekend. Every day closer to Recognition meant just that much more intensified four-degree training. During this time, it was mandated that all fourth-classmen were to do lunges instead of walking throughout the hallways. Every time a freshman entered or exited a room or hallway, he or she was required to complete seventeen times two pushups in reverence for his or her beloved CS-17. Four degrees were expected to greet every upperclassman they passed along the way by rank followed by first, middle, and last name, as well as knowing that upperclassman's position within the squadron, declared major, and hometown. If a four-degree cadet could not remember any of this incredibly important officer-developing information, he or she was subjected to intense training for an indeterminate period.

I vividly remember how four-degree training passed the threshold from ridiculous to asinine on numerous occasions during this time. I remember, along with a few of my classmates, having to get my chin in to such an extreme that the upperclassman conducting the training had us leaning back at about a forty-five-degree angle toward the wall. He had us hold that position, not touching or leaning against the wall for relief, for a lengthy period. Holding such a position was without a doubt potentially harmful, but so was getting body-checked into the wall and pushed down the hallway shortly afterward by a separate upperclassman motivated by apparently uncontrollable hysteria over my four-degree performance.

It would be remiss of me to not mention as well the hundreds of knuckle pushups accompanied by more than 1000 regular pushups my roommate and I were required to do late one night when attempting to retire to our room after study in the library. On this specific night we were greeted by two upperclassmen as soon as we walked into the squadron. These upperclassmen decided we would do 2005 pushups in honor of our expected year of graduation. Somewhere along the line, one of our classmates stuck her head out of her door to see what was going on (we were creating quite a commotion, I'm sure) and was immediately seized upon by one of the upperclassmen conducting the pushups. He quickly ordered her out into the hallway where she was instructed to get into the Academy's version of the position of attention. While we continued to do pushups, he criticized her for not supporting her classmates by voluntarily participating in the pushup fiasco. She immediately started to cry. The upperclassman, obviously perturbed by her pathetic display of emotional stamina, decided to put new parameters on the current training session. He told her,

> "This is pitiful, how can you be crying, you haven't even done a single pushup. Here's what we're going to do. Cadet Graney and [my roommate] are going to do knuckle pushups until you stop crying."

My roommate and I looked at each other with a mutual understanding that this was not a good scenario for us (knuckle pushups on a tile floor) but obediently positioned ourselves up on our knuckles and began doing what was required of us. As soon as he had said this to her and we had commenced the knuckle pushups, she began to cry even harder. After about fifteen minutes of our classmate's exasperating crying and sobbing, the upperclassman couldn't take it any more and ordered her to leave. She went back to her room slightly dehydrated from crying, whereas we went back to our room (hours later) drained of water and blood from sweat and bleeding knuckles. Interestingly enough, this classmate of ours, the same one who faked passing out on a formation run in basic training, was at one point highlighted on the USAFA website talking about how much stronger she had become because of the Air Force Academy's stringent physical requirements.

Regardless, even to the most unobservant individual it would be clear that walking down the hallway during this time was not as simple a task for freshman cadets as my MTL claimed in my personnel file. Yet as historical precedent has proven many times over, to many people it's not necessarily the realities of the situation that matter, it's what is being said about such; their perception becomes their reality no matter how erroneous the framework. The reality was that every aspect of a four degree's existence during Forty Days was arduous, a reality that sharply contrasted with my MTL's ignorant take on the situation. My MTL's faulty perception was the result of what I perceived to be his mean-spirited bias, lack of intelligence, vain comprehension of his surroundings, and absence from the squadron at critical times of the day.

For my part, three specific activities or events that transpired during Forty Days have been forever burned into my memory, not just for the emotions provoked at the time but for the lessons learned as a result. The first of these is really a combination of two events, but together they fashioned a greater understanding of the consequences of ignoring one's conscience. During Forty Days, two of my classmates and I became close in our mutual disdain for the debauchery surrounding us. We often found ourselves discussing the absurdity of our present situation.

At the time I was still bound and determined to stay the course, to such an extent that I was actually willing to sacrifice a little sanity in order to accomplish the goal. I was so consumed by the thought of making it through Forty Days and Recognition weekend that I neglected to consider other important aspects of life, such as happiness. Our depreciated quality of life was a subject my two friends and I touched upon numerous times in our conversations, though none of us was then willing to do anything about it, because we were bound and determined to survive the four-degree experience. That was the case until about a week and a half before Recognition training, when my classmate and good friend abruptly decided to leave the Academy. He packed up all his belongings, signed the papers, and out-processed from the institution. It was a little disconcerting to see the four degrees in the squadron more concerned with grabbing what was left of his uniforms and belongings than with the fact that a person with whom they had all been through so much was leaving. I said very little throughout the process, but he knew his decision was a little heartrending for me. It wasn't his decision to leave that was distressing me, but simply the fact that he was leaving. He was a great friend, and I was sad to see him go.

Once he left, I thought about his decision for quite a while, never being able to fully understand why he would decide to leave so close to Recognition. After a great deal of consternation I finally realized he must have made the decision he did because he came to a point at which he was no longer willing to sacrifice his personal wellbeing or quality of life to accomplish the goal, especially considering that the value of said goal had been determined and assured to him by the very same people who, for the last nine months, had been purposefully jeopardizing his mental and physical welfare. I think he realized that often when someone attempts to tell another person what's best for that person, the respondent is being subjected to the unsolicited and arbitrary will of another. I think he decided that from that moment on he would choose his own destiny and he would decide what goals were worth attaining, what course of action was best for him. I think he realized that, in order to maintain his personal integrity, he would have to make decisions based on what *he* felt was the best course of action and not according to the potential social ramifications of such actions. I have since watched many people sacrifice adherence to their consciences in an attempt to create better social circumstances for themselves. I believe that every time a person subordinates his own judgment to a desired social outcome he loses a little bit of himself, damaging himself in the process.

Whereas the classmate previously mentioned epitomized how to take control of one's destiny and empower oneself, another classmate of mine exemplified the alternative. Around the time when our classmate left the Academy, this other classmate of mine tentatively decided to follow suit. He, too, packed his belongings and ran the necessary documents past the AOC. All he had left to do to out-process was sign on the dotted line. This classmate and I had talked at great length regarding his desire to leave the Academy, and apparently he had finally made up his mind to do so. Decisions of that magnitude are extremely difficult. To muster up the courage to make such a decision, even when the person *knows* he's doing what's best for him, takes a great deal of emotional strength. It was looking fairly certain that I was going to lose yet another close friend, until his dad, an Academy graduate, found out about it. His dad made one of the most intense coercive efforts I've ever witnessed. Not only did he tell his son that it would be a huge mistake to leave the Academy, but he also solicited the assistance of some friends of his from his Academy days. Over fifty of these old classmates e-mailed my friend attempting to persuade him to stay. Almost all the e-mails said something like, "Leaving the Academy would be the biggest mistake of your life. Don't leave. You don't know what's in store for you. It gets better. It's so worth it. Just stay. Don't leave." How could all these people who didn't even know him know what was best for him? Wouldn't it be more appropriate to say, "I stuck it out and I'm glad I did. I really feel that the full Academy experience has made me the man I am today," or something similar? Then at least they'd be talking about their own lives.

I believe people have stepped over the line when they directly or indirectly attempt to subordinate another's will to their own. These men belittled my classmate's decision-making capabilities. They attempted to force upon another man what they felt was best for him, disregarding his own thoughts, feelings, and beliefs. One of my former roommates championed a well-thought-out behavioral theory of his when he said, "People generally do not appreciate unsolicited advice." When people give unsolicited advice to another they are not just placing themselves on a superior plane but, in a way, insulting that person's intelligence and attacking his or her sovereignty of mind.

Unfortunately, my classmate caved in, did as his father and friends instructed, and stayed at the Academy. The consequences of his decision would haunt him, and in time they became more and more evident in his demeanor and his ideological adaptation. He was transformed from a man who didn't take anything from anyone to a person who subordinated his conviction to the collective will of the surrounding military body politic.

He found himself floating in an abyss of lost credibility with both his father and himself. He lost credibility with his father for attempting to leave the Academy and with himself for not actually doing so. Whether he was an outwardly or inwardly motivated person, he had lost credibility in both spheres of influence, and the loss was, as one might suspect, rather debilitating. When people succumb to arbitrary power, whether over mind or body, they weaken themselves and strengthen that which employs such power. My classmate's strong opposition to the Fourth Class System started to fade. He became more and more complacent, his arguments against the wrongs of the Fourth Class System becoming less and less enthusiastic. He began to accept the system and conform to it. He buckled psychologically in the face of what he evidently considered an indomitable force. He took one step forward by choosing to leave, then two large steps back when he subordinated his will to his father's and abandoned his own judgment.

Pierre Janet, the French psychiatrist who developed the concept of dissociation, placed an emphasis on the defense mechanism's utility in response to psychological trauma. As psychological trauma is understood to be emotional shock caused by an extremely distressing experience, not only did the situation that transpired between my classmate and his father constitute a traumatic experience, it would also, according to Janet's theory, lead someone to employ dissociation as a response. I believe Marlene Steinberg, a woman who incorporated eighteen years of research on the subject into her groundbreaking book *Stranger in the Mirror*, defines dissociation best. She gives us this description:

> Dissociation is an adaptive defense in response to high stress or trauma characterized by memory loss and a sense of disconnection from oneself or one's surroundings [34]

According to Steinberg, the individual separates particular thoughts and emotions from the rest of the psyche in order to cope with stress, trauma, or both. My classmate began to separate his negative feelings about the Fourth Class System from the rest of his psyche. This psychological modification was necessary in order for him to surrender his will to the collective.

In 1957, Leon Festinger introduced another useful concept in his book *A Theory of Cognitive Dissonance*. The theory is built around what Festinger called "cognitions." He defined cognition as any element of "knowledge, opinion, or belief about the environment, about oneself, or about one's behavior."[35] Festinger makes the argument that individuals strive toward consistency within themselves, consistency between what they know or believe and the actions they take as a result. He refers to any incongruities as "inconsistencies." He goes on to explain that this inconsistency can also be referred to as "dissonance." Therefore, cognitive dissonance can be described as an inconsistency between some element of knowledge, attitude, emotion, or belief and the corresponding behaviors. Festinger wrote,

> If two elements are dissonant with one another, the magnitude of the dissonance will be a function of the importance of the elements. The

34 Steinberg, *The Stranger in the Mirror:Dissociation—The Hidden Epidemic*, 1.

35 Leon Festinger, *A Theory of Cognitive Dissonance* (Evanston, IL: Row, Peterson, 1957), 3.

> more these elements are important to, or valued by, the person, the greater will be the magnitude of a dissonant relation between them.[36]

In my friend's case, the magnitude of the dissonance between the ideology of freshman indoctrination and his ideology as dictated by his own conscience was tremendous; hence the ensuing anxiety he experienced was quite severe.

The theory of cognitive dissonance maintains that contradicting cognitions serve as a driving force that compels the mind to acquire or invent new thoughts or beliefs or to modify existing beliefs, so as to reduce the amount of dissonance (conflict) between cognitions. Apparently my classmate arrived at a point where he felt it was imperative that he do something to reduce his anxiety level. The source of his agitation was most assuredly the cognitive dissonance he was experiencing, the most severe conflict being the inconsistency between what he truly felt about the Fourth Class System and the way he was *supposed* to feel about it, according to his father, friends, and Academy administrators.

Two decisions prefaced his decision to leave the Academy. First, he had to have decided that his impression of the Fourth Class System was valid and not going to change. Second, he must have decided that to carry on despite his intense distaste for the Fourth Class System would be unhealthy. These two realizations must have been the determining factors in his decision to leave the Academy. In order to reduce or eliminate the cognitive dissonance he was experiencing, he had to either leave the Academy or modify his existing beliefs concerning it. When he failed to follow through and leave the Academy, in effect he was left with one option—to somehow change the way he felt about the Fourth Class System. It shouldn't come as much of a surprise that that's exactly what he did.

After we became third-class cadets I vividly remember his describing a moment during which he had belittled a freshman cadet. What he had done wasn't even comparable to the abuses both he and I had endured as freshmen, but it was his nonadherence to what I understood to be a clearly established principle between us that distressed me; the principle never to use our training powers to humiliate or demean freshmen in the way that had been done to us. When I questioned him, he used the same

36 Ibid., 16.

logic as a defense for his actions that had been used by upperclassmen when we were freshmen. Initially it was a little bewildering, but after witnessing numerous such instances, I began to understand what was happening. This person for whom I cared deeply had seemingly collapsed, emotionally and intellectually.

Intramural rugby turned out to be another fascinating study in human behavior. After leaving the wrestling team I was required, like everyone else, to participate in an intramural sport after school. Because of the extreme level of frustration I felt at the time, the result of the nightmarish environment I was living in, I decided to play rugby as a means of letting off steam. My teammates and I hit the playing field like madmen on a mission to seek and destroy the competition, a group of disgruntled Academy cadets much like ourselves. These games were brutal. We were taught the basics of rugby, though most games more closely resembled a game of kill the carrier than organized rugby.

Most cadets' performance was determined by their level of frustration about their current state of affairs at the Academy. Accordingly, as one of the most disgruntled cadets out there (and rightly so), I excelled on the field. I was making more tackles than anyone else and scoring more tries than my teammates (a try is similar to a touchdown in football). My teammates vividly remember a game during which I reached a climax of impassioned ferocity. I had spent the entire day subjected to particularly aggravating harassment and came to the game more needful than ever of some rugby therapy. I came to play, as the adage goes, and consequently had one of my best games of the season. After I scored the third or fourth try, two upperclassmen with short-man's complex whom I would later refer to as the Napoleons started yelling at and cursing me as if I were doing something wrong. Their commentary just motivated me to hit them harder and score more tries, which ultimately heightened their hatred for me. I was bleeding intensity from every pore, and my teammates smelt it and as a result played that much better.

It wasn't superior athletic ability on my part that caused me to excel on the intramural rugby field. My intensity was caused by a genuine, deep-seated, abiding frustration that had discovered an avenue for release. My four-degree classmates were familiar with my intensity dating all the way back to basic training, but for many of my upperclass teammates my performance on the rugby field was rather mystifying. My reputation had been dragged through the mud for the entirety of the year, so many of these upperclass teammates of mine were torn by divergent forces as to how they regarded me. For instance, whereas I was accused of being pathetic and apathetic by malicious upperclassmen, my performance on the rugby field painted quite a different picture. When the time came for squadron evaluations, it wasn't coincidental that the only upperclassmen to give me a decent to superior evaluation were those who had seen me in action because they'd been cadre during basic training or teammates in intercollegiate wrestling or intramural rugby.

The predominance of my four-degree classmates gave me a decent evaluation because they knew me best. They had been through more with me than the upperclass cadets in the squadron and knew how I operated. The less exposure a cadet in the squadron had to me, the worse the evaluation. This was the case because the less exposure they had to me, the more they relied on what had been *said* about me. The merging of this experience with similar events has left a lasting impression on me. This experience reinforced my longstanding belief that one cannot simply deduce the value of an individual or group of individuals on the basis of hearsay. Some of the most important and inspiring individuals who have ever lived have also been some of the most despised and ridiculed. One must look at the facts. One must consider the evidence. One must come to one's own conclusions, conclusions founded on one's own understanding, observation, and experience. What a terrible mistake it is to come to a conclusion or moral determination about someone based solely on of the opinions of another.

The last experience of the three I have chosen to highlight is my first SCRB. I had been scheduled, unbeknown to me, for a SCRB, apparently because of the number of demerits I had accumulated along with my academic probation status. My SCRB was a kangaroo court, in essence; the very people largely responsible for my delinquent record were sitting on the board. It's much like appealing an undeserved parking ticket in court to the same officer who gave you the ticket because of a personal vendetta. Chances are such an appeal would be highly unsuccessful.

I was walking, or shall I say lungeing, out of the squadron on my way to a regularly scheduled function, when Major H caught me before I could make it out the door. With an air of hostility he informed me that I had a SCRB in five minutes. No one had notified me, by any means of communication, that such an event was scheduled to take place, so not only was I unprepared but I would not even have shown up. I ran, not lungeing (remember this was during Forty Days), back to my room, changed into my service dress, and with nervous anticipation made my way over to Major H's office where the SCRB was to take place. Squadron commander review boards are a time for the cadet squadron commander (squad comm) and other high-ranking cadets in the squad to come together, review a delinquent cadet's record, interview the cadet, and then formulate a recommendation to be submitted to the AOC for punitive action.

These wise and vastly experienced lawmen and jurists, averaging from twenty to twenty-one years of age, were all waiting for me impatiently. I could feel the animosity emanating from the room before I even made it to the door. As I reported in, I was a little entranced by the obnoxious looks on my fellow cadets' faces, a trance quickly broken by my squadron commander's vehement order to take a seat. The first act of the circus was a vicious rebuke from the squad comm regarding my military bearing and appearance. I immediately objected to his assessment, for there was nothing wrong with either my uniform or my military bearing. In fact, my uniform looked no different than it did every time I had visited the cadet counseling center. After two separate counseling sessions, counselors had specifically commented on my uniform, their comments being attached to evaluations of my overall psychological wellbeing and thus included in my personnel file:

> "C4C Graney was punctual, adequately dressed and groomed, and cooperative throughout the interview."
>
> "Cadet Graney appeared for his appointments on time and displayed a sharp military appearance." -Director of the Cadet Counseling Center-

Therefore, I felt confident I was correct in construing my squad comm's supposed disdain for my uniform to be, in reality, disdain for me as an individual. This did not come as a surprise but did forewarn me regarding what to expect for the remainder of the SCRB. Essentially, the board members took turns insulting me, the most agonizing affront coming from my squad comm. This cadet's commentary was not particularly aggravating because of its offensive nature, but because of where it was coming from. Listening to this individual accuse me of lacking responsibility and accountability was almost more than a sound mind like mine could handle. The hypocrisy was overwhelming. Remember, this was the individual who nearly killed himself with excessive drinking on his twenty-first birthday.

I was considered guilty before the board even began, so every effort to explain myself met with combative resistance. My visible irritation at their refusal to accept reality only exacerbated their indignity. My frustration reached its climax when my cadet squadron commander leaned forward in his chair and said, "Graney, not only do we think you're a worthless cadet, we think you're a worthless person." As I sat back and absorbed the insult, he continued his affront by means of a cynical rhetorical question regarding my alleged indifference to his opinion of my performance or worth as a human being. At that point I drew the line in the sand and informed the squad comm that I cared about his opinion regarding my overall performance and capability only for its impact on my performance evaluation, but that in no way would I ever allow an external influence to either increase or diminish the level of self-esteem I would naturally maintain. I held back from adding, "especially from someone who, at twenty-one years of age, is still immature and irresponsible enough to almost drink himself to death."

Some people would say that making such a statement was a mistake, that I should have attempted to be more diplomatic, apologetic, and conciliatory. I would argue that a more pacifist demeanor would indeed be advantageous in certain situations if, and only if, the potential existed for a divergent outcome. That being said, when a person is guilty until proven innocent and required to testify before a kangaroo court where there is absolutely no opportunity for impartiality of judgment, in actuality it doesn't matter what the victim of circumstance (in this case the individual on trial) does or says. Considering the situation, it would be unreasonable to expect that I had any real influence on the board's almost unanimous recommendation to have me involuntarily discharged immediately. Their main argument was that because of my allegedly unsatisfactory attitude, I was not only unfit to be an officer in the U.S. Air Force but I did not even deserve the opportunity to participate in Recognition training.

I had two ardent objections to their line of reasoning. First of all, my "attitude problem" was not really a problem at all. The negative sentiment I maintained regarding the Academy at that time was a very natural result of approximately nine months of severe harassment that encompassed all aspects of my life, for which many of my accusers were directly responsible. My second objection was that this opinion of theirs regarding my aptitude to serve as a commissioned officer in the Air Force had been formulated by individuals who had neither been commissioned officers in the Air Force nor served any active duty time as enlisted personnel. The value of their opinions regarding my aptitude to be an officer was intrinsically worthless, because they had neither practical knowledge nor experience to make such a determination. What we had was a bunch of prejudiced *amateurs* deciding whether or not I had the potential to succeed *professionally*; something of a paradox I would say.

Nonetheless, my understanding of the injustice of the experience was only enhanced by a later visit from the only board member who did not vote for my removal from the institution. After the SCRB concluded and I had returned to my room, this upperclass cadet came by to briefly discuss some of her thoughts concerning the proceedings. Although she apologized for her classmates' vindictive behavior, her real concern had nothing to do with my welfare. It was obvious to me that she was deeply concerned over her reputation amongst her classmates, the root of this consternation being that, by supporting me, she had potentially jeopardized her own good standing in the squadron. She had dangerously stitched together her supercadet status with my not so prominent reputation, a maneuver that turned out to be fairly worrisome for her from the get-go. Her counsel in regard to my future performance was no doubt an endeavor motivated almost entirely by self-interest. I'm sure she was hoping that by giving me some animated encouragement she could help me perform better (according to the upperclassmen's standard of better performance), consequently maintaining her solid reputation. Therefore, after insightfully deciphering her true intentions, I accepted her admonition to perform for the remainder of Forty Days as well as Recognition, for what it was worth, and carried on.

I include this experience because of the momentous realization I had subsequent to this experience. I had been told on more than one occasion that the first year at the Academy was a game and that a person must simply play the game to survive. I refused to play the game, as I hadn't gone to the Academy to play games. I went to the Academy to prepare for a professional career as an active-duty military officer. If I had been interested in playing games, i.e., grab-assing and slap-jacking around, the military would not have been my first option. Nothing about the Academy experience had ever been a game. Every action my classmates and I carried out had real-time, real-life consequences that reverberated well into the near and distant future. That particular SCRB fused together this erroneous notion that we were all playing games with the real-life consequences of my superiors' malicious behavior. Their bad sportsmanship, so to speak, was now critically jeopardizing my Academy and Air Force career.

This was the most concentrated assault on my prospective career I had experienced up to this point. The injustice of the experience had an astounding affect on me, in that my appreciation for justice and equality became all the more intense. A former political-science professor of mine, also an attorney by profession, told me in class one day that many lawyers think of themselves as great prosecutors until they end up on the other side of justice, i.e., accused of a crime; then all of a sudden they become staunch defense advocates. To a degree this is what happened to me. Although I never thought of myself as a great prosecutor, of course, I suddenly became even more concerned with the proper enactment of justice. This experience evoked from within me a deep and abiding desire to ensure that the people, institutions, and organizations with which I involve myself maintain a high standard of justice and equity. People, not some inhuman conglomeration of detached power structures, are responsible for the enactment of justice. Therefore, because of this experience and the fact that all injustice can be attributed to the respective human element involved, I have since made a habit of tenaciously counteracting the influence of unjust people. I believe, with many others, that injustice prevails when good men and women do nothing; therefore I chose to act.

Even as emotionally charged as these experiences were, ultimately they would pale in comparison to that which was yet to come—Recognition, the three-day culmination of close to nine months of abuse. The emotionally provocative experience that was Recognition 2002 would challenge my presence of mind, intestinal fortitude, and moral understanding like no other experience before. It would require one of the most concerted intellectual and physical efforts of my life just to maintain the edge, i.e., my emotional stability.

8

Recognition

"When you're going through hell, keep going."
—Sir Winston Churchill

Recognition was one of the most arduous experiences of my life. Before Recognition even started, I had been told by numerous individuals that they were going to effectively end my life before Recognition was all said and done. The upperclassmen had been talking up Recognition for the duration of the year, and never with more intensity than the week before it was scheduled to take place. The entirety of the Cadet Wing floundered around in an abyss of nervous anticipation: upperclassmen eager to lay the hurt on, freshmen preparing for anything, and Academy administrators more than eager to view the spectacle. Recognition was the end-all—the haymaker of beat-downs, the training session of training sessions.

Even though we had been yelled and screamed at for nine months, there was something strangely imposing about the prospect of going through Recognition training. I don't know if it was all the superfluous threats against my life or the fact that it was no doubt the climax of what had already been exorbitant training. Whatever it was, it was unquestionably the only thing on everyone's minds the week prior to its commencement.

Recognition was set to begin immediately following our last-period class, or at 15:30 hours, on Thursday, 14 March 2002. We had been instructed to meet in a specific classroom in Fairchild Hall to await the arrival of our squadron upperclassmen. I decided on this particular Thursday that it would be prudent not to bring my computer to class. The wisdom of that decision was only verified by the illegal actions of a select unidentified group of individuals I will address later. Students and instructors alike put on a façade of academic interest throughout the day, though very little actual learning occurred that day. The closer Recognition drew to us, the more anxiety we all felt. One might argue that for some the anticipation was worse than the actual event. In support of such a thesis, one could present as evidence the numerous cadets observed throwing up in the restroom and the plethora of extemporaneous injury claims that were conveniently filed just before training was set to begin. One could also discuss the pale, bloodless complexions of the majority of cadets, the distant, troubled look in their eyes, and their overly pensive or worried demeanor throughout the day.

When my last class of the day came to an end, the instructor bid us farewell and good luck with a look on his face that eerily reminded me of the look I had received from the lieutenant colonel Academy graduate the morning of the first day of Basic Cadet Training. I immediately registered that as a bad sign; an explicit foreshadowing of unpleasant things to come. The fact that most nonmilitary personnel were required to leave the Academy at this time and not come back until Recognition training ended merely fostered the aura of trepidation. I met up with my classmates in the designated room, and together we awaited the arrival of our upperclassmen. A strange silence dominated the room, a silence haphazardly broken by the earsplitting noise of one squadron after another being swiftly ushered away to begin one of the longest weekends of their lives.

As we sat in the room, my classmates and I were inadvertently regressing back to basic training where we would hasten to a location or event only to wait, upon arrival, for long periods of time for something to happen—the hurry up and wait phenomenon all over again. Along with relishing the good old days, my classmates and I were also reverting back to our respective states of nature. The strong among us were unconsciously preparing themselves to perform, the weak to merely survive. The most interesting aspect of times like these is that, among the individuals involved, there's relatively no question about who the strong and weak members of the party are. My mother always used to say, "Difficulty does not build character as much as it reveals character." This was another moment of unavoidable character revelation.

Nevertheless, the time came when preparation met opportunity, and nine months of anticipation on the part of the upperclassmen was violently unleashed. The onslaught began as our upperclassmen arrived at the rally point and burst into the room screaming out orders and insults. We were told to secure our laptops in the room's storage space, supposedly to be personally retrieved at the conclusion of the weekend. That was the last time my unfortunate classmates who had brought their laptops to class that day would ever see those computers again.

My classmates and I made our way, arms interlocked according to instruction, through a gauntlet of screaming upperclassmen to the snowy parade field where the squadron cadet-training officer had chosen to begin the festivities. A long game of the Academy's version of ping-pong ensued, with my roommate and me as the key players. Academy ping-pong consisted of running back and forth between two locations, at which select upperclassmen were strategically positioned to officiate the volley. The first set of cadre abruptly yelled "Ping!" thus initiating what turned out to be a two- to three-hour session of running back and forth and hundreds of up-downs in the snow all along the way to the sound of whistles, yelling cadre, and the shouts "Ping!"and "Pong!" What happened next would only be the first of a long series of training violations that would occur over the weekend.

Before Recognition even started, the cadet in charge of planning and coordinating Recognition 2002, who also happened to be my squadron element leader, sent out an MFR detailing the rules of engagement (ROE) to be strictly enforced throughout the weekend. The first line of the MFR went as follows:

> 1. Squadron commanders will ensure that all upperclass cadets read and comply with this directive, as well as Air Force Cadet Wing Instruction (AFCWI) 36-3004, Military Training Standards, and AFCWI 36-2909, Conduct Standards, regarding definitions of hazing and professional conduct.[37]

---

37 Cadet Captain Vaughn Brazil, *Recognition 2002:Concept of Operations* (USAFA, CO: United States Air Force Academy, 10 March 2002), 9.

Author's Note: This document was for "Internal Use Only" but a copy of the directive may be obtained from the USAFA; however, the requestor must submit a Freedom of Information Act Request (FOIA).

As evidenced by the upperclassmen's behavior throughout the year, these individuals maintained very little respect for training or conduct standards. The reference AFCWI 36-2909 clearly defined the way we had been trained for the entirety of the year as hazing. Even though that was the case and everyone knew it, they still put on a façade of professionalism in the official arena, full of empty promises and deceptive intentions.

As the sun set and the temperature dropped, the cadre decided to relocate. We quickly made our way back to the squadron across the cold, dark Academy grounds, even though upperclassmen had been directed not to do any running outside after dark. Although our present situation (exhausted and cold, rather chaotically running through the darkness) painted a dreary picture, most of us were more concerned with what awaited us upon arrival back at the squadron area.

Our consternation was well founded, in that as soon as we entered the squadron area all hell broke loose. Upperclassmen were running us around in every direction, screaming out orders and leading calisthenics in the dimly lit hallways. In accordance with the long-established modus operandi, I was quickly ushered away to a room carefully prepared to resemble, as much as possible, a heavy-metal rock concert gone wrong. I was immediately surrounded by overly excited cadre dressed in very nonmilitary garb, i.e., bandanas on their heads, shirts with condescending phrases written on them, etc. I spent the next three or four hours in that room predominantly by myself (without any freshmen classmates). The lights were turned off except for the strobe light, which, after hours of exposure, just about fried my brain. The heavy-metal music was so loud that I could hardly hear what the numerous upperclassmen were screaming at me from an inch or two away.

More training violations were being broken in this room than I could ever remember. I was singled out from my classmates, the training was purely negative, inappropriate language was used, the lights were out, there was pushing and shoving, and proper supervision was nonexistent. I spent almost the entire time blindly jumping up and down from the floor to the top of a bed frame with some periodic sessions of pushups and up-downs to mix things up a bit. I had some very interesting things said to me in that room, things that would make most people question their degree of safety. Up to that point, however, I had never been the victim of any purposefully injurious physical contact and therefore had little reason to fear, supposing that past behavior functions as an accurate indication of what to expect regarding future behavior.

This seemingly endless training session eventually came to a close only because of the evening meal, for which attendance was mandatory. According to custom, after my special training session, I was reunited with my classmates, and together we marched at the quickstep over to Mitchell Hall, where all kinds of strange things were in store for us. The same upperclassmen who had spent the majority of the day screaming in my face were right there anxiously awaiting my arrival at the squadron training table. Although the venue and main event had changed a few times over the course of the day, the personnel had not. Essentially I just moved from one training session to the next with my rather large entourage of personal trainers eager to make every aspect of Recognition as unpleasant as possible for me.

After a delightful three-course meal consisting of sizable portions of personal attacks, threats, intimidation, and not much food (another training violation), the Cadet Wing was brought to a standstill in order to listen to an announcement from the cadet wing commander (wing cc) up on the staff tower. The cadet commander was quietly observing the Cadet Wing, much as a great general would look out over his troops before going into battle—composure's true description. Just when I thought I'd seen and heard everything, he told us all with a straight face that the Academy was under attack by terrorists. He gave us an intricate status report concerning the Academy's effort to ward off the strong terrorist offensive raging on and around the north perimeter of the Academy compound. He assured us that Academy personnel and security forces were doing everything in their power to secure a perimeter around the cadet area, while it was imperative that we all know and internalize the gravity of our situation. After I absorbed what had been said, a feeling of surrealism came over me. I knew that we weren't being attacked by terrorists. I began to wonder if there was anyone in the building who actually believed that. I also wondered whether *he* actually thought we would believe that. It was as if someone had made a sequel to H. G. Wells's *The War of the Worlds* tailored specifically for us.

Even though there was absolutely nothing humorous about my situation at the time, I couldn't help finding the notion wildly amusing, especially when after a lengthy and rather cumbersome account of our precarious defensive posture he abruptly shouted, at the top of his lungs, that there were bombs on the terrazzo and for everyone to clear the building at once. He ordered us to reassemble at Arnold Hall, where it would be "safer." At Arnold Hall we were to be given an intelligence brief concerning our next move as a Cadet Wing in response to the alleged terrorist threat and the rules of engagement.

My next thought was, *Supposedly the terrorists are bombing the terrazzo.* Of course, it would only make sense to run out on and across the besieged terrazzo to get to another building, a building situated even closer to the alleged terrorists' position out on the north perimeter of the Academy grounds. Sure enough, moments later we all found ourselves running across the terrazzo on our way to Arnold Hall. Thankfully, we all made it to Arnold Hall without losing a single cadet on our daring terrazzo crossing.

Upon arrival at Arnold Hall, the inevitable chant, "Zero five, full of pride," began to ring out among the Class of 2005 assembled in the theater. While we were belligerently chanting our compulsory slogan, the wing commander came running out onto the stage wearing a flak jacket and carrying a pilot helmet. He ran up and down the aisles a couple of times like a madman, then made his way back up onto the stage. As soon as he returned to the stage, upperclassmen commenced a steady infiltration of the theater. Evidently they had been brought in for crowd control, because as soon as they entered the room their attention was directed toward a cadet who, amidst all the noise and chaos, had said something to his neighbor. Multiple upperclassmen closed in on his position and enthusiastically took us all on an instructional field trip through the dictionary of explicit vocabulary. The field trip was cut short when the wing cc arrived on location. The wing cc toned it down to a certain degree, then struck up a personal dialogue with the cadet concerning his motivation to be an Air Force officer and whether he understood what pride stood for. As soon as he asked the cadet on an individual basis what pride stood for, we all collectively answered, "Sir, the answer is professionalism, respect, integrity, endurance." Our halfhearted rendition of the phrase must have offended our fearless leader, because he interrupted us by fanatically yelling, "Shut the hell up, I didn't ask you!"

After shutting us up, he returned to his personal dialogue with the target freshman. He brought the discussion to a close by saying, "Boy, you're lucky you have classmates," then made his way back up onto the stage. Feeling empowered by the reestablishment of his authoritarian rule over the fourth-classmen, he abruptly turned, pointed at the audience, and threatened us with the now-immortalized quote, "You'd rather scratch a bobcat's ass with sandpaper than piss me off." Numerous cadets immediately burst into muffled laughter, and just like that the wing cc was running back into the audience yelling at the top of his lungs along with every upperclassman in the room. The inevitable result was a massive training session that eventually came to an end late into the night after having carried over into our respective squadron areas.

I couldn't help being amused by the fact that our mobilization and deployment in response to the "terrorist threat" consisted of the same sort of high-intensity hazing-like treatment that had been our Academy experience since 28 June 2001. Bringing the entire Class of 2005 to the point of complete physical exhaustion just didn't seem to be the most effective way to position ourselves for victory against a determined enemy.

The end of the first day of Recognition came only after an impassioned rebuke of our initial performance, followed by sincere promises to the effect that if we maintained the current level of intensity we were not going to make it to the end of the weekend. Thoroughly exhausted, we retreated to our rooms; hearts still racing and BDUs dripping. Once returning to our rooms we had a decision to make; whether to sleep in our BDUs and therefore make our BCT-style wakeup, which we knew was coming, a little easier, or change into something comfortable and get a better night's sleep. We decided to change into some shorts and passed out, but the mind is a crazy thing, because although our alarm clocks had been confiscated by upperclassmen, approximately an hour before the cadre came banging on doors, my roommate and I both simultaneously woke, changed into our BDUs, and fell back to sleep without saying a word. That's when you know you've been truly institutionalized.

Zero five hundred hours came early, and amongst a considerable amount of noise and commotion the second day of Recognition training commenced. We were met in the hallway by a whole host of reenergized upperclass cadets burning with a desire to get the party started. They started the party right where we had left off the night before; in the front-leaning rest. After an abnormally intense half-hour beat-down, we made our way across the terrazzo through the chilly winter morning air on our way to Mitchell Hall for breakfast. Despite not even being able to taste what I was eating, I forced some food down amidst a firestorm of derogatory commentary. After the morning meal madness had concluded, as a squadron we made our way down to the center gym at the Academy sports complex to participate in some group training. The course, as we came to find out, was intended to resemble the BCT II assault course. Unsurprisingly, this quasi-assault course consisted of hours of high-knees, sprints, low-crawling, and an unexpected yet special appearance by Assault Course Meathead. We went 100 miles per hour for the duration of the assault course and didn't really slow down until we returned to our seats in Mitchell Hall for lunch. The only thing different between the morning meal and noon meal was the information we received concerning the alleged terrorist attack. With a somber look on his face, our "rather scratch a bobcat's ass" cadet wing commander announced that the alleged terrorists were gaining a foothold and that our initial counteroffensive had proven relatively ineffective. Even amidst the internal turmoil that can come with the fear of death, we found a way to carry on and swiftly made our way back to the squadron for some squadron discretionary time training.

Upon our arrival at the squadron area, a training activity called heaven and hell ensued, a high-intensity training session that would span another three to four hours. Heaven and hell was an interesting arrangement encompassing all six levels of a nearby stairwell. Upperclassmen were strategically positioned on all six levels according to their fondness for training freshmen. The upperclassmen exuding the greatest amount of hostility for freshmen congregated at the bottom of the stairwell, which was referred to as hell during the training scenario. One could probably deduce that there was some intense training going on in hell, and naturally that's where I spent the large part of my time. The idea behind this genius objective-based training was that, by performing well (according to the cadre), a cadet could advance up the stairwell where training was less severe, thus theoretically rewarding performance and giving freshmen something to strive for. The ultimate objective was to arrive at the top of the stairwell, or heaven, where there was a complete absence of physical training, only pleasant rewards such as juice and cookies. My classmates and I were first evenly dispersed among the six training levels; then pandemonium broke out. Following an hour or two of some of the most intense training of my Academy career within the confines of hell, the hell cadre decided to initiate an Academy ping-pong rematch, only this time it would be vertical as opposed to horizontal. Accordingly, I spent the remainder of the training session sprinting up and down the stairwell and jumping over bodies while having the words "Ping!" and "Pong!" portentously yelled into my face at the top and bottom of the stairwell.

Two factors contributed to my perpetual detention at the bottom of the stairwell. First, I was (and had been for the duration of the year) the primary target for the majority of the most antagonistic upperclass trainers in the squadron. Second, I had intentionally stirred the bees' nest by answering every request to recite four-degree knowledge by providing no more information than that which POWs are authorized to divulge to enemy interrogators. I only gave my name, rank, service number, and date of birth. Even knowing my history of abuse through training, there are still some who would say, "Of course you're going to get trained harder if you do things to intentionally provoke them. How stupid is that?" But my behavior in this instance was not reflective of my behavior throughout the year, and I got the extra attention anyway. This was the second to last day that I was going to be subjected to this treatment, and as far as I was concerned they could all go to Hades. I had spent nearly a year of my life operating in an extremely hostile environment propagated by individuals bent on my emotional ruin. Even so, I had emerged victorious. I had maintained my integrity and self-determination, and I was still at the Academy. I felt empowered. This was quintessential triumphant defiance and well worth it. My rebellious posture was my living, breathing tribute to William Ernest Henley, whose poem *Invictus* had served as my personal creed during this most unforgiving time:

Out of the night that covers me,
Black as the Pit from pole to pole,
I thank whatever gods may be
For my unconquerable soul.

In the fell clutch of circumstance
I have not winced nor cried aloud.
Under the bludgeonings of chance
My head is bloody, but unbowed.

Beyond this place of wrath and tears
Looms but the Horror of the shade,
And yet the menace of the years
Finds, and shall find, me unafraid.

It matters not how strait the gate,
How charged with punishments the scroll,
I am the master of my fate:
I am the captain of my soul.

Although this poem may seem overly dramatic to some, the comparative drama that was my four-degree year surely justified such a mantra.

Cadre brought heaven and hell to a close just in time for us to make it over to Arnold Hall for the start of the widely anticipated wing knowledge-bowl championship. The only difference between this knowledge bowl and past knowledge bowls was that the two squadrons involved were freakishly knowledgeable with respect to relatively insignificant Air Force–AFA information and were competing in front of the entire Cadet Wing. For freshmen who took the Fourth Class System seriously, it was awe-inspiring to see neither squadron miss more than a few questions throughout the entire competition. For cadets who understood the inconsequentiality of both knowledge bowls and the system at large, the competition served as comic relief; at least we didn't have to participate.

At one point (knowledge-bowl halftime) it was determined by cadet leadership that four degrees should be afforded the opportunity to use the restroom. Like cattle going to water, we made our way in droves to the building's restroom facilities. I can remember wondering at the time about the sexual orientation of select upperclass cadets who apparently found it necessary to observe us while in the act of urination. Such an unbecoming personal invasion led me to cast an accusatory glance at the cadre along with my classmate at an adjacent restroom fixture, actions the self-appointed restroom cadre must have considered belligerent and in need of merciless repression. While assembling to leave, one of my classmates muttered, "You guys ready?" Without the slightest hesitation the restroom cadet commander blew up on us because of our disobedience (we had broken the no-talking-in-bathrooms-for-four-degrees rule). He wrote down our names and vowed that he would make us pay for our noncompliance to stated AFCWI. We looked at him in disbelief, though by this time there was very little that we were incapable or unwilling to believe with respect to AFA cadet behavior. We chalked up the experience as another example of how degenerate some of our fellow cadets had become and returned to the auditorium. Nevertheless, the fact that we were able to dissociate ourselves from the obnoxious memory and move on was largely immaterial. This upperclass cadet wasn't in the business of forgiving and forgetting, no matter how insignificant the deed, and his actions would generate real consequences that would manifest themselves via course cadre the following morning at a wingwide training activity, after this upperclassman had the chance to write and send his draconian e-mail detailing our allegedly inexcusable restroom behavior to the entire corps of Recognition 2001 and CS-17 training staffs.

The squadron with the greater number of Fourth Class System sympathizers won the knowledge bowl and expeditiously relocated to Mitchell Hall for a dinner that began a series of events I could never have envisioned taking place at the Academy. They say the eyes are the windows to the soul, and there was a haunted look in the upperclassmen's eyes. They looked as if they were remembering how they, too, had experienced what they were about to put us through. It was a little unnerving. Just as I was coming to this realization, our cadet wing commander told us we were going to be sent on a very special mission in the coming hours. He counseled us to remember what we were fighting for. I stared curiously at the staff tower until ordered to form up outside the building.

We returned to our dimly lit squadron area. As soon as we made it through the door we were split up into groups of two and three with two to three cadre assigned to supervise our progress through what I later learned were called theme rooms. The theme rooms were supposedly designed as a mock deployment against the mock terrorists on the northern perimeter of the Academy compound. My hazing-hardened roommate and I were directed to the briefing room, a cadet dormitory poorly designed to look like an operational Air Force briefing room. Once we were seated, the briefing began. We were told we were going to be flying a dangerous sortie consisting of an air-to-surface missile attack on the terrorist position. We were provided with the word of the day in case we were shot down and needed an aerial rescue. The rescue party would request that we identify ourselves by asking for the word of the day via radio correspondence. Only after we had correctly repeated the word of the day would the rescue-chopper pilots calculate our position and extract us from hostile territory.

Immediately following the briefing, we were directed to sit in chairs intended to resemble the cockpit of a fighter plane. After buckling the chin straps of our pilot helmets, we readied ourselves for "takeoff." Not even having been instructed as to what enemy positions to take out or even where the enemy positions were, we found ourselves looking at a video presentation of some intense aerial combat. Apparently the terrorists were better equipped than our intel guys in the briefing room had estimated, in that (if we were to suppose that the F-15E *Strike Eagle* flying around on the screen was us) we weren't engaged in an air-to-surface missile attack but a treacherous dogfight with multiple Russian MIG-29s! While we were watching the video projection, upperclassmen were erratically emerging from behind a makeshift blind on the other side of the room and throwing random objects at us with considerable velocity, apparently to simulate being shot at. Evidently the barrage of random projectiles thrown in our direction, i.e., MIG-29 cannonfire, was too much for our penetrable "aircraft" to handle, and we quickly self-destructed. While my aircraft was breaking apart on screen, the upperclassman who had been violently shaking my cockpit throughout the dogfight (which obviously greatly impeded my ability to fly the plane and led to disastrous results) decided we needed to eject, an action he carried out on my behalf by throwing the chair and me forward into the bed in front of us (or maybe it was a high-altitude weather balloon or even the partially detached canopy of the aircraft, like what happened to Goose in *Top Gun*).

Once I had been ejected from my plane, a green laundry bag was placed on my head. With the bag securely fastened, I was swiftly ushered away to another room in the squadron where some kind, yet elusive Samaritan removed the bag from my head and directed me where to go. The room I found myself in was designed to resemble some sort of jungle environment, though to me the camouflage-draped maze of tables, beds, and chairs felt more like a haunted house than a jungle, especially when upperclassmen strategically hiding in various locations in the room abruptly jumped out at me along my evasive journey to safety, i.e., friendly territory (wherever that was).

Apparently, although unbeknownst to any of us, all my classmates and I had been captured by the enemy through some crazy scheme the terrorists had conjured up to trick us into divulging the highly sensitive word of the day. Once captured, we were all made to lie down on the floor, hands behind our green-bag–covered heads. While we were piled on top of each other, upperclassmen, by way of a nearby stereo system, blasted strange music incorporating the sound of helicopters in the distance with an occasional interlude of gunfire, all the while shooting us with water guns and spray bottles. It was a very awkward moment but still no comparison to hygiene time, which would come later.

After a considerable length of time in the awkward stack, upperclassmen began taking us out of the room one at a time and sending us into the next phase of the saga. I was one of the first to be taken out of the room, but I didn't get far. I went straight from lying face down in the discomfiting helicopter room to kneeling in the middle of the hallway. The hard-line terrorist forced me to kneel down on the tile floor, hands behind my back, while yelling at me in French. The fact that she spoke to me in French was not only entertaining but revealing, as I knew of only one female cadet in my squadron who could have spoken French with such proficiency—a first-class cadet living across the hallway from me who had studied at l'École de l'air (The French Air Force Academy) as an exchange student during a previous semester. Once I determined it was she (I still had the bag over my head), the same cadet who had attempted earlier in the year to stop my drunken trainer's attack on me late one Saturday night, I realized why she had taken me. This being the interrogation phase of the dramatization, she had probably put one and two together (one being my history of mistreatment, two being the precarious nature of the current situation) and realized the potential danger of allowing me to be interrogated by any number of her classmates. So, although the time I spent on my knees being yelled at, shot by her water gun, and periodically pushed around wasn't all that enjoyable, chances were she had done me a favor by keeping me from becoming another statistic in some dark room behind closed doors. It's amazing what we can appreciate when put in proper perspective.

Eventually, I was ordered to rise from my knees. After much-needed, life-carrying blood had returned to my lower extremities, I was directed toward the last theme room of the night, where I was faced with a puzzling barrage of conflicting instruction coming from my classmates on one hand and an upperclassman on the other. The theme of this final room was trust. With the bag still in place over my head, my classmates tried to verbally guide me through a predetermined task while a nearby upperclassman attempted to thwart those efforts by yelling contradictory instructions in my ear. Interestingly enough, following my classmates' directives as opposed to those of the upperclass cadet fundamentally contradicted the whole idea behind a year's worth of training. I can remember being told on numerous occasions that it wasn't my job to think, that I was being trained to follow orders unconditionally with no regard to the insignificance or triviality of the task. The now-infamous line, once repeated like a broken record at the Academy, was this:

> Graney, if you're told to blow up a school full of kids, you have neither the time nor the prerogative to question or even consider the moral justification of such an action; you must simply follow orders.

I was never quite comfortable with that idea. Personally, I find the notion of surrendering one's inalienable right of self-determination to anyone or anything to be entirely abhorrent. It is not a soldier's duty, and UCMJ would agree with me, to blindly follow orders. It is the soldier's duty to follow legal orders, and legal orders alone. It is of the utmost importance that soldiers do not carry out illegal orders, not only to protect those who could be harmed by their illegal actions, but in the interest of self-preservation as well. If a soldier does not want to be subject to courts-martial and potentially end up in the Castle (United States Disciplinary Barracks, Leavenworth, Kansas), it would always be in his or her best interest to take a quick moment to determine the legality of the orders given.

My argument against blind followership even while at the Academy consisted of three words: My Lai massacre. On 16 March 1968, at the height of the Vietnam War, soldiers of Charlie Company, 1st Battalion, 20th Infantry Regiment, 11th Brigade, Americal Division, ruthlessly murdered about 500 (504 by many estimates) noncombatants, many of them women, children, and the elderly in My Lai, Quang Ngai Province, South Vietnam. The excuse given afterward by many of these soldiers was that they were merely following orders, as if by following orders they somehow exonerated themselves of any responsibility.[38] In fact, the sixth article of the Code of Conduct by which all service members are obliged to live states:

> I will never forget that I am an American, fighting for freedom, *responsible for my actions*, and dedicated to the principles which made my

38 James S. Olsen and Randy Roberts, *My Lai: A Brief History with Documents* (New York: St. Martin's Press, 1998), 22–23.

> country free. I will trust in my God and the United States of America.[39]

According to the Code of Conduct, each soldier is responsible for his or her actions. No one will ever convince me that it is acceptable for a mature, intellectually and emotionally sound individual to surrender his or her judgment to the will of another.

Either way, the futility of following the upperclassman's orders soon became evident, and I realized that it was probably a team-building exercise. With my classmates' assistance I quickly performed the task at hand, which led to the removal of the bag over my head and the conclusion of our dangerous mock sortie, evasion, capture, interrogation, and escape from terra incognita. After the last two freshmen had made their way into the room and performed the same task, we were told to return to our rooms to await further instruction. If I had known what our upperclassmen had in store for us next, I probably would have taken this time to lock the door and hide under my desk in the fetal position.

Further instruction came in the form of a swift command to change into our shower gear, BCT style, and form up in the hallway. As we assembled along the wall near the bathroom, upperclassmen were walking up and down the ranks endeavoring to frighten us with inflationary threats and promises concerning the difficulty of what they were now calling the shower course. I remember thinking, shower course? They can't be serious. If we're to be trained in the bathroom wearing nothing but our bathrobes or even less, their professional depravity, which has been my four-degree experience, has unquestionably reached its zenith.

The typical apprehensiveness associated with the unknown weighed heavily on our minds as we entered the bathroom. Once inside, we found ourselves passing through a dense fog of steam, assumedly on our way toward the so-called trees of life (multiple showerheads on a single beam). As soon as we arrived at the shower area and had disrobed for showering, the lights and music came on. With the song "YMCA" bellowing through the bathroom, upperclassmen appeared out of nowhere wearing a wide array of women's clothing including both swimwear (bikinis) and lingerie (thongs, push-up bras, and teddies). One upperclassman had on only a pilot helmet with the air tube connected to his penis.

---

39 United States Air Force Academy Cadet Handbook, *Contrails*, 185.

As I stood there paralyzed from shock, thoughts raced across my mind. I couldn't help finding the scene before my eyes paradoxical. The same cadets who had spent the entire year chastising my professionalism, military decorum, and sense of propriety were now dancing in front of me wearing women's lingerie. The same individuals who were theoretically responsible for my professional, intellectual, and spiritual development were now groping each other while jokingly acting out sexual maneuvers and positions. The exotic dancers shaking it in front of me were the same individuals who had decided I should be removed from the Academy, that I was inept enough with respect to the four Academy pillars (academic, military, physical, spiritual) to necessitate denying me the privilege of participating in Recognition training. Apparently it was a privilege to witness a bunch of grown men dancing up on each other in women's lingerie! I was dumbfounded. I remember thinking at the time, How could anyone possibly expect me take these guys seriously? My estimation that the shower course could develop into the most professionally depraved experience of my Academy career could not have been more on point.

After this outrageous Chippendales-style performance came to a close, we were ordered to run through the showers by these same cadre, who were now wielding megaphones and whistles and donning snorkeling equipment. We hesitantly ran through the showers, which had all been turned on either as cold or hot as possible. After burning and freezing our bodies' largest organ for an undetermined period of time, we were ordered to return to our rooms. While passing through the narcissistic group of upperclass artistes on the way out, some of my classmates actually managed to muster up a smile. I think they did so because they knew the upperclassmen would appreciate the gesture, much as a comedian enjoys a few laughs from a tough crowd after a bad show. I found nothing even remotely humorous about the experience; nor did the majority of my smiling classmates, by their own later admission. It is my belief that they pretended amusement, as well as acting if everything was agreeable, for appeasement purposes only. I believe that what I perceived as these classmates' duplicitous façade was the result of a protracted and pathetic obligatory feeling on their part that it was somehow unconditionally necessary to please upperclassmen. I believe that what I perceive as these classmates' fraudulent appreciation for the shower course was the result of their year-long effort to unquestioningly and unconditionally do and think as the upperclassmen desired in order to survive.

My negative reaction to the ordeal that was the shower course was most likely interpreted by upperclassmen to be additional evidence of my substandard attitude. But I was not the only one to visibly manifest my aversion for the experience. Many of the more militarily experienced classmates of mine felt completely disgusted and debased by the incident. A few days later, my brother related the reaction of his close friend and roommate, who had served in the operational Air Force for a number of years before coming to the Academy. After participating in their squadron's version of the shower course and having returned to their rooms, this man said, "I don't even feel like I'm in the Air Force any more."

My roommate and I returned to our room, shared a moment of concentrated silence, and then abruptly passed out. A deep sleep ensued, one of the best nights of sleep I've ever had, as I was utterly exhausted physically and emotionally. Even so, if I had known what was in store for me the following day, I'm sure I would not have slept so soundly. To this day I have never experienced a more emotionally charged or physically taxing twenty-four hours than that last day of Recognition 2002.

My roommate and I woke up to the sound of a great many footsteps walking toward our room. At 05:00 hours on the last day of Recognition that could only mean one thing. We quickly jumped out of bed, dressed in dry BDUs, slipped our feet into boots still sweaty from the previous day's training, and prepared ourselves for anything. As soon as the cadre had reached our alcove, they unleashed a fury of fist-pounding the likes of which our door had never felt. We made our way out into the hallway through an abnormally energetic group of cadre to become the focus of attention for the next hour or so. I don't know if it was that I was tired from a day and a half of grueling physical training or that the training was more intense on that specific morning (maybe a combination of both), but I just about collapsed from fatigue near the forty-five minute mark. Luckily, the calisthenics ended and we went to breakfast. Breakfast was more of the same: incessant yelling, not much eating, and ridiculous reports concerning the terrorists' position on the perimeter of the Academy grounds.

We returned to our squadron just in time for one last BCT-style room and uniform inspection. We attempted to put our room in SAMI order as far as possible, but were cut short by a speedy infiltration of upperclassmen, a disproportionate number of cadre (the regulars, of course) eager to get the party started. They entered the room in a blaze of rage, thrashing anything and everything in their path. They threw every article of clothing and personal effects across the room. They turned our beds over and threw them against the wall, kicked chairs over, and turned tables and desks upside down. At the end of the "inspection" I can't remember any item still being in its original location. It was quite the scene, items flying, extraordinary insults, exuberant calisthenics.

This room inspection, however, was somewhat different from those of the past, as cadre were miraculously finding all kinds of contraband that neither my roommate nor I had ever seen. Evidently, while we were at breakfast, someone had planted contraband such as women's underwear, *Playboy* videos, cigars, beer bottles, etc., in various places throughout our room. The upperclassmen tearing our room apart "discovered" these items and vehemently chastised us for having them in our possession. One upperclassman even took it as far as to authoritatively label us "sick bastards," furthermore diagnosing us as "sexually frustrated" and "depraved." They expressed their opinions as if it were fact that we needed to "get laid" and give up on the toys. It was immediately apparent that this was just another upperclass antic similar to the shower course. This experience ultimately had the same affect on me as the shower course, in that it just reinforced my lack of respect for my immediate superiors and their below-average level of maturity and professionalism.

Once our rooms had all been thoroughly wrecked we were ordered to form up in the hallway with our mouthguards and web-belts. As soon as we were all together, the upperclassmen marched us down to the cadet field house at the double time for what I consider the most notorious training session of my Academy career. Sweepstakes (also known as crossroads) was the name of the course. We had been hearing rumors for quite a while that sweepstakes would be the worst training session of our Recognition experience, and that the almost exclusively black, intercollegiate athlete cadre operating the course would make every effort to run us into the ground; especially the freshmen African-American cadets among us.

There was no official race requirement to participate as sweepstakes-course cadre, of course, but there was definitely an underlying expectation that nonblack upperclassmen were not to serve in that capacity. Supporting evidence concerning the existence of an unofficial policy of racial exclusion could be the fact that all but a few of the entire course cadre were black, as well as the almost universal understanding among cadets that sweepstakes-course cadre positions were for black cadets. I couldn't help but think how backward the whole idea was.

We silently ran through the underground tunnels that connected the cadet gymnasium and the cadet field house. The silence was broken at the other end by the deafening roar of seven squadrons of fourth-classmen yelling and being yelled at. We emerged from the comparatively peaceful tunnel into an extremely hostile environment. As soon as our squadron had made it to our designated station and had formed up, I was approached by Cadet 2nd Class J.

I do not know why he chose to victimize me that day; however, there are some compelling theories. It could have been the fact that one of my black roommates who played on the basketball team with Cadet J considered me a quasi-racist because I had mentioned to him my distaste, irrespective of the races concerned, for entities that use race as a criterion for inclusion, entities that fervently exclude or strongly dissuade certain people from participating merely because of race. Being a member of a few organizations fitting the profile, my roommate didn't care for that stance of mine and could very well have communicated as much to his teammate, Cadet J, at practice or in the locker room and unwarrantedly and counterintuitively infuriated him as well. Evidence to this theory could be the wide array of accusations Cadet J would make while assaulting me concerning my alleged indifference or dislike for black people.

Another possibility as to why Cadet J chose to be an assailant for the day could have had to do with the e-mail sent the day before to all squadron and Recognition 2002 training personnel from the vengeful restroom cadre mentioned earlier. Before every station we were sent to during sweepstakes training, course cadre announced (reading from the printed e-mail) that they were looking for Cadet Graney and two of my classmates. It is very likely that Cadet J memorized the names off the e-mail and eagerly sought us out. I could simply have been the first to be identified out of the three.

The other possibility is that my AOC may have put a plug in to course cadre concerning his desire to see me get hit hard on the last day of freshman training. I felt certain he despised me, as did his loyal MTL. I do not consider it farfetched, based on his pre- and post-Recognition behavior and attitude concerning my situation, that he was not just capable but readily willing to do something of that nature. His supervisory position over sweepstakes training would have given him easy access to course cadre.

Either way, as soon as Cadet J arrived on the scene he began to forcefully poke me in the eyes, nose, and mouth while threatening me with all the unpleasant things he was going to do to me. He told me he was going to break my nose just as he had broken those of the last five four degrees that gave him "attitude." He was in and out of my face like someone indecisively contemplating a physical altercation when all of a sudden he grabbed my arm and ordered me to follow him. I followed him through a maze of four-degree training toward the corner of the building. I only realized where he was taking me once we had reached the target destination. I was perplexed to find myself entering the building's restroom facility. At the time I could not think of a legitimate reason why he would have chosen to take me to the restroom (there wasn't any); nonetheless, there I was, standing at attention while he frantically searched the urinals and stalls to determine whether or not we were alone. Finding an occupied stall, he realized we were indeed not alone and came storming back over to me. As he passed by me he stated acrimoniously, "We can't do it here," and sharply motioned for me to exit the restroom behind him. Obviously, whatever it was that he wanted to do to me in the restroom, he wanted to do it unobserved. It goes without saying that he wanted to isolate us in order to negate the danger to his career that a witness to the implementation of his malicious designs would pose. I realized what was happening as I walked out of the restroom and, of course, was somewhat unnerved by the whole scenario. Who's to know what his true intentions were, what he was planning on doing in the restroom had we been alone in there?

After exiting the restroom, we sprinted back to our original location near the rest of my classmates, where he commenced the most aggressive and inappropriate training session (if it can even be called that) of my Academy career. I was ordered (or maybe I should say threatened) to do pushups for the next ten to fifteen minutes. Throughout the specified time period Cadet J, apparently disregarding any sense of decency whatsoever, carried out one of the most deplorable verbal assaults I've ever been subjected to or even personally witnessed for that matter. His training style was to do a couple of pushups every now and then while carrying on his monologue of hateful accusations and insults focusing, albeit not exclusively, on a sexual relationship with my mother and my alleged racist persona. "You're a mother-****ing racist, Graney," were his exact words.

The pushup session came to an end only when my arms ceased to function, for after two days of intensive physical training, small amounts of food, and insufficient rest, my body was beginning to show serious signs of fatigue. Although the pushups stopped coming, the order for them to be performed remained. The fact that I had stopped even in the face of his vehement orders to the contrary enraged Cadet J, and he became even more hostile. He rebuked me for what he saw as my unwillingness to follow orders, screaming things like, "I'm going to ****ing kill you, Graney! What the hell is wrong with you, Graney? Don't like taking orders from a black man? Is that your problem? You don't like taking orders from a black man, do you? Do the ****ing pushup, you God-**** mother ****er!"

I tried to do another pushup instead of merely holding the pushup position as I had resorted to moments before and at once lost control of my arms. With my arms limp and unable to even sustain my body weight any longer, I collapsed to the floor. As I hit the ground, Cadet J quickly went from a supervisory to a participatory leadership posture. Instead of just watching pushups and yelling, now he was *doing* pushups and yelling. Over and over again he called for more pushups, though my arms wouldn't perform. I managed to position myself in the front-leaning rest once again; however, the longer I maintained that position but did not do "the ****ing pushup," the more exasperated Cadet J became. Once he realized that no amount or severity of insults was going to get me to do a pushup I was physically unable to perform, he allowed himself to resort to physical violence.

Apparently, the proximity of his head to mine made a head-butt irresistible, a temptation too strong for Cadet J to resist. He forcefully drove his forehead directly into the left side of my head near the temple, causing a sharp pain to reverberate through my entire body. This initial head-butt from Cadet J was much like the infamous head-butt the Washington state high-school wrestler gave the referee officiating his match in mid-January of 1996. I vividly remember the incident, because I'm also a product of Washington state wrestling. Along with seeing the video of the head-butt on both local and national television numerous times, our junior-high wrestling team (along with many other teams in the state, I'm sure) received preemptive counseling concerning good sportsmanship to prevent the same thing from happening at any of our matches. Immediately after losing the match, this wrestler stood up, charged his opponent, then viciously head-butted the referee who was attempting to control the situation and knocked him out cold. This referee was struck in the side of the head much as I was, but fortunately I didn't lose consciousness, although I was left feeling lightheaded, with my ears ringing and a slight stream of blood coming from a laceration on my head.

I reacted more complacently than most self-respecting young men do to physical assault, in that instead of fighting back, I merely shot a distasteful (and slightly incredulous) glance in his direction. I think Cadet J interpreted my reaction as not just unremitting insubordination (four degrees were not to even look at upperclassmen while being trained, much less do it in frustration) but as an affront to his superiority as a human being as well. Unsurprisingly, he immediately head-butted me again. This time, instead of striking and withdrawing, he maintained pressure on my face long after impact, pushing my head to the side until my cheek touched my deltoid. Even with my face buried in my shoulder he continued to scream obscenities in my ear and push into me with his battering ram of a forehead, until I fell on my side.

When I fell on my side, it seemed that Cadet J smelt blood (as they say in boxing). He ordered me to my feet, and the attack continued. After having been head-butted twice I was experiencing some problems with balance and coordination, so that standing at attention Academy style as Cadet J had ordered just wasn't happening. Cadet J apparently considered my unstable posture, hate-filled gaze, and cantankerous demeanor unacceptably provocative and intolerable. Cadet J viewed it as further evidence of my "attitude problem," necessitating modification by additional physical violence. He threw and connected with a right jab, knocking me back a couple of steps. He then made the punch into a combo by quickly following it with an aggressive body check. Cadet J's body check was accompanied by some hysterical commentary. In all sincerity, he kept repeating the same provocative question-statement combination over and over: "Graney, you want to hit me, don't you? You want to ****ing hit me, don't you? You know you want to. Well, then, do it mother****er. Hit me ******! Graney, ****ing hit me, tough guy!"

I'm not going to lie; I really did want to hit him. In fact, never in my life have I wanted to hit someone more. But I knew that to have done so would have meant immediate expulsion and stringent 24/7 Air Force security-forces supervision until my departure from the Academy. That's not what I think would have happened, that is what *I know* would have happened. That being the case, along with the fact that I actually wanted to graduate from the Academy, I chose not to retaliate.

Although Cadet J was only interested in training or attacking me, there were a few classmates of mine who courageously took it upon themselves to intervene (as much as four degrees could at the time) when they caught wind of what was going on. These classmates, who were nearby, had noticed my head being thrown to the side by Cadet J's initial head-butt directly following the many threats to my physical safety that anyone within a twenty-yard radius would have heard just as clearly as I. These classmates ran over and assumed the pushup position by my side as a gesture of support. Cadet J, infuriated by the interruption, began screaming at them to leave from the moment they arrived, to no avail. His orders ignored, Cadet J strategically positioned himself between my classmates and me, restricting their vision and thus their overall involvement. It was at this moment that Cadet J head-butted and battering-rammed me to the ground.

As we all came to our feet after this second head-butt, Cadet J vehemently repeated the order for my classmates to leave, claiming that the issue was only between the two of us. These classmates stubbornly continued to disobey (as they had been indoctrinated to do, not leaving a classmate alone during training sessions), and although their support was appreciated, it was also very short-lived. These classmates, on account of their nerves, left moments later when Cadet J's heightened exasperation ultimately frightened them off. However premature their departure, they should have at least witnessed Cadet J punch me in the chest and push me back while ordering me to "****ing hit" him. Unfortunately, each of them would later fall far short of providing an accurate account of the incident as it truly came about.

The fact that I chose not to retaliate only emboldened Cadet J, though after more than half an hour of energy-draining fanaticism, even Cadet J was ready to bring the fiasco to a close. He concluded the aggravated assault by insulting my intelligence, then sent me to the next station, a station where the rest of my squadron had been for quite a while. My arrival was met with a great deal of anticipation by station cadre who, in spite of my best effort to clandestinely infiltrate the training activity long underway, immediately called me out. I was sent to the middle of a circular, makeshift pugil-stick arena to face my good friend and classmate Cadet R, who just happened to be a prominent linebacker on the football team. Pugil-stick competitions consisted of hitting each other with pugil sticks until a point was scored. Only the strikes we were taught to use in combat scored points, such as the butt-smash. Cadre threw the pugil stick to the ground in front of my feet as a gesture of animosity, and the match began. While picking up the pugil stick I inconspicuously attempted to tell my classmate to go easy on my head as it wasn't doing so hot, but amid the noise and chaos there was no way for him to hear me, and as soon as the cadre blew the whistle to begin I took a shot right in the side of my face that dropped me to the ground. The chances of winning a pugil-stick bout against Cadet R even under normal circumstances were never very good (no matter who you were), let alone with a concussion. The last time I had taken up arms (pugil sticks) against Cadet R was in BCT II, at which time I think he may have given me a hairline fracture of my thumb. Either way, after the relatively mild shot to my head (relative to the kind of blow he was capable of delivering) I dropped to the ground, wincing in pain, hands grasping my injured head. While course cadre laughed at my pathetic performance (in their eyes indicative of my military ineptitude), my classmates stood by bewildered.

This was something my colleagues were not used to seeing. Those classmates of mine who were capable of thinking outside their own experience recognized that I drew more negative attention than any other four degree in the squadron. They knew I had been subjected to a truly disproportionate amount of hazing-like treatment throughout the year, and yet they had never seen me waver physically or emotionally. I don't mean to say that I never reached the point of muscular failure, only that my classmates never saw it. I never cried, nor did I wear my emotions on my sleeve. To see my unrestrained manifestation of physical pain as I lay on the ground and to see me so flustered—after an entire year of emotional restraint—must have been rather startling. Although I was not broken, I was definitely discomposed, and it was obvious.

If my visibly shaken demeanor didn't give away that I was exceedingly upset, my subsequent actions might have. Although I should have gone to the hospital, I picked myself up off the ground, my head throbbing, and made my way to the second half of the training station. The training activity taking place there was something I happened to be rather good at: hitting football body bags (six years of competitive tackle football does that to a person). Course cadre had instructed my classmates to take it easy on the guys holding the body bags, to simply sprint to the bag, slow up, then quickly strike the bag. The action the upperclassmen were describing, whether or not they knew it, was a stalk block, the kind of block a football receiver would attempt on a defensive back during a running play. However, when my classmates slowed their momentum to stalk-block the bags, the cadre holding the bags repeatedly charged the approaching four degrees and hit them so hard that they completely redirected their momentum, most of my classmates flying through the air and landing hard on their backs or sides. Obviously this was just another opportunity for upperclassmen to get their jollies at the expense of freshman cadets.

When it was my turn to hit the bags, I don't think there was any doubt in my mind which one of us was going to end up on his back. I ran at the bag and, taking the exploitive upperclassman by surprise (I didn't slow down as my classmates had done), powerfully rocked him back about ten feet. Speaking of football, in reality it was closer to fifteen feet if you count the backward rolls he did and not just the distance he flew through the air. They wanted us to hit three bags altogether, and even though the second bag-holder had just seen what had happened to his colleague, there was little he could do to prevent a similar result. After seeing his colleagues flattened, the third bag-holder attempted to sidestep my arrival, I suspect because he was thinking that I would end up on my face in the absence of something to hit. He was probably quoting *Top Gun* in his head, just as he'd been doing since he was a freshman in BCT. He might have been rehashing Maverick's line to Goose when the two are being pursued by an enemy aircraft: "Don't worry, Goose, I'll hit the brakes and he'll fly right by!" Whereas the tricky maneuver works for Mav and Goose in the movie, it didn't work for this upperclassman. My football know-how clicked in, and instead of flying right by I stopped on a dime, ripped the bag from his hands, and threw it off into the distance. Although my beleaguered classmates appreciated the encounter, upperclassmen obviously did not. I spent the rest of my time at that station doing up-downs.

When it came time to rotate stations, I actually went with my squadron this time. Upon our arrival, an upperclassman reading from a familiar printed-out e-mail asked for Cadet Graney and two of my classmates. My two classmates and I spent the rest of our time at that station doing pull-ups, at first unassisted, then later assisted. I did pull-ups until I couldn't even hang on the bar any more. My hands slipped off the bar, and I fell awkwardly onto my head and shoulder when the person holding my feet failed to let go as I began to fall. I fell from the bar almost as soon as the station rotation bell sounded. I gathered myself up off the ground once again and continued on to the next station with my classmates. Apart from watching the African-American course cadre rip into the African-American freshmen in our squadron, all we did at the next station was run back and forth between lines (in sports they call it running lines). Chances were the black upperclassmen felt it necessary to come down hard on the black freshmen in our squadron for the same reason I was trained harder in basic training by the upperclassmen with whom I went to church with and future teammates on the wrestling squad. Apparently there existed some inherent attraction toward training one's teammates and those of the same race or religion.

Nonetheless, after more than two hours of strenuous physical training (and an assault and battery), sweepstakes (or crossroads) finally came to a close. When the final bell rang, we were expeditiously gathered together by our squadron upperclassmen in order to vacate the premises as soon as possible. We were already late to the distribution point where we were to pick up our box lunches; any later and we'd have had no lunch at all, something that concerned our squadron upperclassmen more than it did us, as extreme physical activity often depletes one's appetite. However, despite the urgency, my assailant, Cadet J, was able to approach me again while I stood in formation with my classmates waiting for the order to move out.

Instead of seeking me out for additional training, Cadet J said he merely wanted to talk. He told me at the time that he wanted to talk "man to man" in order to "clear things up" between us. In essence, he told me that he wouldn't have had to do what he did had I not given him "attitude." He then explained why it was necessary for him to be so rough. His reasoning was that guys like me don't understand anything other than brute force, that it takes sheer brutality to get through to guys like me. I found his one-sided conversation decisively Machiavellian and entirely deviant, not only for the rationale behind his argument but for the very fact that he found it necessary to talk to me about his actions in the first place. Generally speaking, upperclassmen were far from apologetic regarding any inconvenience or wrongdoing they perpetrated, especially if the aggrieved party was a freshman cadet. However, I think even Cadet J realized that he might have stretched his training license a bit too far. Realizing the potential consequences of his actions regarding both his Academy and Air Force careers, he must have felt compelled to make an attempt at patching things up as much as possible between us, or, in other words, attempt to manage the crisis (crisis management) as something of a first-ditch preventive measure.

Well, time waits for no man, nor does it backtrack and provide second chances to those unfortunate souls who fail to consider their actions beforehand, thereby affording them the opportunity to correct past indiscretions. History, not David W. Graney, became Cadet J's most dogged adversary. Cadet J could not change what he had done, nor could he afford a criminal indictment. Therefore, in true mafioso style, he attempted to manipulate, intimidate, and thus coerce me away from reporting the crime. I believe Cadet J's one and only intention was to silence any opposition that I might have put up to his criminal behavior; to somehow silence the voice of incrimination by employing the aforementioned scare tactics engineered to roll me up and tie me off.

Although Cadet J's delusional treatise was quite thought-provoking, like many bad things it had to come to an end. Cadet J was forced by circumstance to abruptly discontinue his ranting when my squadron finally began moving toward the exit. As I marched away with my classmates, Cadet J put his final touch on the exposition by, as I see it, deceitfully complimenting me on a "job well done," then surreptitiously disappeared into the background.

Entering the same tunnel whence we had originally come, we left behind the madness that was sweepstakes once and for all. After a short yet strangely therapeutic stint below ground in the coveted silence of the tunnel, we emerged to find ourselves in the cadet gymnasium, the place where our sack lunches were to be collected. We were ordered to sit against a wall and await the return of our upperclassmen. I couldn't help but notice the kind of looks I was receiving from my classmates. All seemed to be rather spellbound by the uncharacteristically browbeaten and despondent comportment of the usually emotionally indomitable C4C Graney. It was likely obvious to most that, although I was physically present, my mind was somewhere else. My classmates had never seen me like that before, either: complete intellectual isolation, entirely deflated, severely discouraged. They had watched as I had uncompromisingly endured a year's worth of an unequivocally disproportionate amount of abuse, excessive according to any reasonable person's standards.

Moreover, just the day before they had witnessed my energetic defiance during the heaven and hell training. Furthermore, that same morning not too far removed, many of my classmates had watched as I unreservedly leveled a couple of upperclassmen holding football body bags. To see me finally reach what could be considered a breaking point must have been rather intriguing for my classmates, even more so for the upperclassmen when they returned with our box lunches.

It's been said that everyone likes to see the strong man stumble, and for many upperclassmen in my squadron this was one moment they'd been waiting for since my entry into Cadet Squadron 17. It had been the upperclassmen's rather explicit desire for much of the year to see me break, a sight they felt they were closer to seeing now than ever before. Feeling that I knew quite well where these upperclassmen's heads were, when approached by the third-class cadet who had videotaped sweepstakes and asked how I was doing, I chose not to humor him with a response. Although at the time I had no motivation to communicate with anyone, my decision to withhold a response to his seemingly two-faced question was quite deliberate. I think it was at that moment that I realized my colleagues not only greatly anticipated my mental collapse but truly believed, once and for all, that such an event was actually about to transpire.

I think it was this belated realization in conjunction with my "never go quietly into the night" attitude that gave me the strength to mount yet another emotional defensive. The very idea of losing control of myself and allowing these upperclassmen the long-sought and elusive satisfaction of seeing me break was probably the *only* thing that prevented me from doing so. The thought of their taking pleasure from my pain was so unappealing that, even though no visible change in my demeanor could be detected, I had already emotionally regrouped, thereby empowering myself to handle the next onslaught with dignity, no matter what that might be.

The next onslaught was referred to as the buddy down course. After lunch, we marched through the snow to the bottom of a sparsely wooded hill leading up to the gymnasium where the course was to begin. Upon arrival we were greeted by a course attaché whose job was to give us the prebrief. The briefing that we received went something like this:

> All right, guys, here are some paintball guns. What you're going to do is try and get to the top of the hill without getting shot. The only thing is, though, there's a lot more of them than you, so keep your head down. Yeah, and if you do get shot being a dumbass, you have to go to what we call hell, and, trust me, you do not want to go there. So don't get shot.

The briefing we received here was quite different from the briefing we were supposed to have received:

> Listen up, ladies and gentlemen. The situation on the war front has become extremely intense. We have received word that there have been a number of pilots who were performing CAS shot down in an enemy-intensified area. The area is highly protected, and the recovery of these pilots is mandatory if we hope to win this war. Your mission is to rescue these downed pilots as quickly as possible with as few casualties as possible. Unfortunately, our resources have been cut and we only have a limited number of weapons to issue you for your protection and there are only two medical kits available. If there aren't any questions, you will have 15 minutes to plan your course of action and then we will be dropping you into the area. Good luck and Godspeed.[40]

Although it would have been humorous at best to have received the latter briefing, at least we would have had an idea as to what we were supposed to do with the five paintball guns and two medical stretchers given us. Nonetheless, one would assume that, given the circumstances, it would have been wise to assign the limited number of paintball guns to the squadron members with the most paintball experience, or the persons most suited to lead an assault on an elevated position.

Although the stated rationale did factor into the equation, the decision as to who would brandish the paintball guns was rather a simple passionate game of hot potato. The guys who ended up with one of the five guns (for our entire squadron of approximately thirty freshman cadets) were those who put up the least resistance to being assigned a weapon. My classmates were smart enough to know that whatever was going to be shooting back at us as we attempted to take the hill would most likely first take aim at those among us who had the ability to shoot back, in

---

40 C/Capt Vaughn Brazil, *Recognition 2002: Concept of Operations*, 28.

other words, those carrying paintball guns. Everyone also knew that if we happened to be shot we would have to go to the place they called hell where we supposedly didn't want to go. It was for that reason that most of my classmates did not want a paintball gun.

Suffering and recovering from a severe concussion at the time, I was one of the incoherent people, so to speak, in my squadron who put forth very little resistance. Accordingly, upon commencing operation by running up the hill and trying not to get shot, I was one of those unfortunate individuals standing in front wielding a paintball gun. I knew my fate, as did my classmates, long before any paintballs were fired. I knew very well that in the not too distant future I was going to get lit up like the ill-fated cowboys at the O.K. Corral. It didn't take long. Just seconds after we started up the hill, the whole forest came alive with gunfire. I fired off a couple of rounds in the general direction of the firing and dove into some underbrush. As I sat there, dozens of paintballs whizzing by my head, I watched as the trees around me turned pretty shades of fluorescent red, yellow, blue, and green. It could have been amusing if I didn't know from previous experience the kind of welts paintballs can leave on your body. I wasn't going anywhere for the time being.

I stayed put until a classmate of mine, who also happened to be on the Academy paintball team and was wielding a paintball gun, made his way up the hill to a tree near my position. He put aside his surprise at the fact that I hadn't been shot yet in order to formulate a makeshift plan to move us further up the hill. We both knew that no plan would be good enough to defeat the kind of firepower we were up against. I found out later that we were outgunned about ten to one throughout the engagement. Furthermore, while our enemies had unlimited ammunition, we had been given fifteen apiece, hardly the quantity necessary to take out the number of upperclassmen that lay before us, even with that many extremely well-aimed or lucky shots.

In spite of our rather futile position, we devised a plan consisting of slight position changes in the direction of the enemy simultaneous with a diminutive amount of cover fire. Knowing that both of us were going to get blown away regardless, I decided to move first, but instead of the small movement we had planned, I stood and ran straight up the hill, gun ablaze, shooting everything that didn't look like a tree; dead animal, or smaller vegetation—upperclassmen and all. Even after running out of ammo I just kept running, hands in the air, similar to the way Elias comes out of the southeast Asian jungle in the movie *Platoon*. As I ran, the enemy paintballs hit hard and frequently. Although it was quite obvious I had been shot multiple times, course cadre just kept shooting (something greatly discouraged within the paintball community). I started making my way toward hell, having been shot somewhere around twenty times in the face and chest and about five more times in the back while exiting the course.

With paint adorning my brightly colored BDUs, I walked blindly past my classmates (I had paint all over my mask), who had dug in at least fifty yards behind where the previously mentioned firefight had occurred. I found it very discouraging that most of my classmates hadn't moved more than ten yards from where the course attaché had given us our initial briefing. Apart from noticing the fruits of their "as long as I'm good" approach to the training activity, their body language as I passed by communicated even greater selfishness. The way they looked me up and down said only one thing: "Yeah, that's why I didn't want a paintball gun."

Feeling a little abandoned by my classmates and not really knowing where this notorious hell was, I asked some random upperclassman standing nearby for some assistance. When I asked him where I was supposed to go, he replied emphatically, "Go to hell, and get your knees up!" before pointing me in the right direction. After jogging down a service road for a time I finally saw what was unmistakably the target destination. Even if there hadn't been a little sign reading HELL to give it away, the large pit full of mud and snow with two obnoxious-looking upperclassmen ready and standing by could have just as well told me.

Much to my chagrin, the two obnoxious upperclassmen manning the station happened to be the Napoleons. These were the short-man-syndrome guys who had developed a deep and abiding hatred for me because of the ferocity with which I tackled them during a knock-down, drag-out, intramural rugby game a couple of weeks before. Not only did I have it coming, but at the time I was the *only one* who had it coming. Apparently, I was the first and only freshman who was shot up to that point, making me hell's first visitor. Just as I was coming to grips with my unfortunate circumstance, the Napoleons saw me coming. As I approached the place where dead paintball players go, these two recognized their first victim—me. Eager to get the party started, they came out to greet me long before I even arrived, in order to give me a proper hell course cadre-style welcome. Their first words were something like this: "Well, would you look at that. I can hardly believe it. The little piece of **** himself. GET YOUR FACE IN THE ****ING MUD, GRANEY!!!"

Thus commenced about a 45-minute beat-down consisting mainly of up-downs and push-ups. If I hadn't been in such a bad mood from the morning's festivities, even I probably could have found a degree of humor in the things they said during our time together in hell. There's just something funny about a couple of short-man-syndrome guys trying to make up for the self-respect they lost on the rugby field by pulling rank and verbally harassing the guy who so squarely took it from them.

After about ten minutes of personal time with the Napoleons, just before the mud on my face became so thick as to render me unrecognizable, another cadet came running up the road to perdition. This cadet, apparently the second casualty of the supposed downed-pilot rescue operation, was a sight for sore eyes; not just because he could possibly share with me the brunt of the Napoleons' verbal harassment, but because it was my brother Chaz. My brother was fully aware of the humiliation I had wrought upon the Napoleons on the rugby field. Accordingly, the look on his face when he realized what was going on was priceless. In the midst of an up-down, I shot a "Can you believe this?" look at my brother, who returned with a look saying, "Wow! What are the odds?"

The Napoleons, who were unaware of my brother's existence, simply could not contain themselves when he showed up. They were like kids in a candy shop, they were so excited. My brother's arrival did not have the desired effect, in that the Napoleons simply upped their game and became that much more abrasive and hostile. So even though there was now someone to share my harassment, there was also more harassment to go around.

After another thirty-plus minutes of rolling around in the mud together, with new paintball-dead people arriving all the time, our squadron cadre finally showed up to take us back to Vandenberg Hall. I found it rather comical that as our squadron formed up, I was so caked with mud that the CS-17 upperclassmen responsible for gathering us all together kept screaming, "Where's Graney?" even as I was standing right in front of them. When I sounded off to inform them of my presence, one upperclassman asked with a disgusted look on his face, "Graney, what the hell happened to you?" Apparently, it was a rhetorical question, for when I started to answer he quickly said, "What the ****, Graney? I didn't ask you to say anything!" Still hovering close by were the Napoleons, who couldn't help hearing my upperclassman's comment and follow suit with some remarks of their own: "Nice doing business with you, Graney. You suck at life. Kill yourself."

That "business" having been cleared up, we made our way back to the squadron at the double time. Upon arrival we spent very little time in the squadron, just enough time to change into better-smelling uniforms and prepare for the run to The Rock. The Rock is a giant redrock formation north of the Academy that can be seen from miles away, which used to symbolize the beginning of the end of Recognition. Before Recognition had even begun, Academy tradition required that we, CS-17 Class of 2005, paint a stone that would be hidden by CS-17 upperclassmen at The Rock. Toward the end of Recognition we were to run as a Cadet Wing to The Rock, find our painted stone on or around the premises and bring it back home to the Academy where it would be proudly displayed with all the other squadron rocks.

When we were told that the time had come to run to The Rock, shock waves of excitement radiated through the Academy's freshman population. The slightly premature sense of accomplishment that we all felt at this time managed to overshadow the physical exhaustion that up to this point had weighed so heavily on our willpower. The run to The Rock was to the class of 2005 like the opportunity to train two Graneys at the same time was to the Napoleons.

Most formation runs lacked luster; not this one. This run marked the end of nine months of perpetual verbal and episodic physical abuse. The run to The Rock, although relatively uneventful, was quite amusing; not so much because of the scenery or even the significance of the event but for the commentary. Upperclassmen, realizing their reign of terror was coming to an end, turned up the heat, whereas freshmen, equally aware of that fact, started chanting, "Can't stop the clock. Can't stop the clock." Classmates of mine who had spent the entire year flying under the radar began saying things they would never have said even a few hours before.

For instance, when my AOC, Major H (who was required to run with us and was apparently very much out of shape), began huffing and puffing no more than fifteen minutes into the run, certain classmates of mine provocatively rehashed some of the insulting comments he had previously made to them concerning *their* physical abilities. I had to laugh, reminded of what Major H had said when he placed me on athletic probation for failing the running portion of the initial spring-semester physical-fitness test (PFT) by half a second.

Other than when I tore all the ligaments in my ankle rock climbing, or when I had water on the knee from a junior-high football game, I've never had a problem running in my life. During that entire year at the Academy I had never fallen out of any training activity. I failed the earlier run, while nearly maxing every other component of the test, because I was suffering from exposure after that forced early-morning run around the icy terrazzo through a freezing Colorado winter snowstorm as part of CS-17 training-day festivities that took place just days before the administration of the PFT.

Nonetheless, as he placed me on athletic probation he said, "Graney, I'm just not sure you have the physical capability to be an Air Force officer." Those words kept flashing across my mind as Major H fell further and further behind until he vanished from sight. I found it outrageous that the same guy who just weeks before had had the gall to tell me, a Division I intercollegiate wrestler and lifetime athlete, that I lacked the physical capability to be an Air Force officer, evidently lacked the physical stamina to last more than fifteen minutes into a rather lackadaisical formation run. These are the experiences cadets are drawing upon when they write captions next to their senior pictures in the AFA yearbook like, "The best thing I've learned from officers at the Academy is what not to do." Nothing could better sum up the lessons I learned from Major H's leadership and experience.

When we arrived minus our AOC at The Rock, we commenced the search for our squadron rock. Not too long after, we had found our rock and were laboring to figure out a way to transport it back to the Academy. Normally, squadron members would just take turns carrying it back to the Academy, but we lacked that option because our rock was much larger than any of the other squadron rocks and could not be carried by any fewer than four people at a time. Why, one might ask, would these freshmen intentionally complicate their lives in such a way? The answer can be found by means of an amateur, but I think accurate, psychoanalysis of the more insecure freshmen brains in the squadron. We struggled mightily with this oversized rock, taking it no more than 200 yards before it was loaded onto the bed of some random truck to be driven back to the Academy, because of a few overzealous squadron freshmen entirely consumed by their desire to prove themselves worthy in the eyes of the upperclassmen to be at the Academy; worthy to be recognized as part of the Cadet Wing.

These are the same cadets (the survivors) who would lick upperclassmen's boots on command, empty a pitcher of juice over their heads, ascend a lunchroom table to sing and dance nursery rhymes before thousands of cadets, the same cadets who would, without hesitation, sacrifice any degree of self-respect to please the upperclass cadets in their lives. These classmates of mine wanted to have the biggest rock, not for the accolades that would be conferred upon them from other squadrons, but to gain that which I feel they most dearly coveted, the approval of our CS-17 upperclassmen. I found the very notion to be utterly pathetic, and even though I was one of the dissenters, with respect to the rock chosen, I ended up being one of the four who carried or dragged the rock those 200 yards to the truck.

After arriving back at the Academy, we stood at attention through a rather long and drawn-out flag ceremony; long because of a speech about our promising future as recognized members of the Cadet Wing, which few cadets wanted to hear. The uniform discontinuance of a fifteen-minute-long concluding salute marked the end of the ceremony, after which we quickly made our way back to the squadron for the official Recognition ceremony. Once we had all changed into our Class A uniforms, the ceremony was set to begin.

Very seldom over the course of my life have I taken pleasure from someone else's pain, much less actually been justified in doing so. The CS-17 Recognition ceremony was one of those extremely uncommon occurrences of which I speak. My continued presence at the Academy was very disturbing for a number of CS-17 upperclassmen; let alone my official recognition as a member of the Cadet Wing. I'm not a malicious person myself; therefore I can only empathize with the kind of pain and suffering they must have experienced watching me go through the Recognition ceremony. Moreover, the sadistic, self-imposed nature of their anguish left me feeling wholly vindicated in taking pleasure from their pain throughout the ceremony.

The Recognition ceremony reminded me of something from a bad movie about fraternal rights of passage, tradition, ritual, and secret societies of which the members are all hush-hush about their dealings, comings, and goings. To each his own, as they say, but my choice is not to indulge in excessive secrecy through membership in cloak-and-dagger societies that consider themselves superior or abnormally enlightened and thus entitled to insider knowledge, power, and privilege inaccessible to everyone else.

Nevertheless, after changing into my service dress, I finally had the chance to sit down; an opportunity I took full advantage of. It was only then, sitting there watching the room stare back at me, that I realized there was something different about my surroundings. When I had left my room earlier in the day, it was in complete disarray from an upperclassmen tirade; now it was in perfect order. After ruling out the cleaning fairies, the only other viable explanation was that upperclassmen had come and cleaned the room as a kind gesture of sorts while we were running to and from The Rock. Even though it was indeed a generous move on part of the upperclassmen, I could only consider it window dressing for an entire year of mistreatment. As we all know, some things cause irreparable damage, and nine months of abuse undoubtedly qualifies as one of those things. Cleaning our rooms was like placing a Band-Aid on a severed limb.

Either way, we were ordered to vacate our rooms, march to a room at the end of the hallway, and await further instruction. Further instruction never came, though out of the blue someone from the other end of the hallway started bellowing out our names one by one. After each name the speaker would hesitate, then declare the cadet to be either "Accepted!" or "Denied!" depending on whether the said cadet was still at the Academy. I found the melodrama rather amusing, in part because after denying Recognition status to our departed classmates, someone would violently slam a door to symbolize being shut out or something. One by one, my classmates disappeared into the hallway until eventually my name was called. The speaker yelled, "Cadet Fourth Class David W. Graney!" then, after a protracted silence, as if still debating my fate, pronounced me, "Accepted!" Following the example of my classmates I walked out into the dark hallway still a little confused as to what I was supposed to do. Finding myself alone in the hallway with no direction, I simply turned and started walking towards the mysterious voice that had spoken to me from somewhere in the darkness ahead.

Not long after I had begun my journey into the darkness, I realized I was in fact not alone in the hallway. The upperclassmen had hidden themselves in alcoves along the hallway where they waited and watched my passing. While making my way through the hallway I felt as though

I was walking through a gauntlet. With upperclassmen on both sides and some unsettling experiences behind me, I couldn't help feeling a little uneasy. My heightened sense of awareness at the time enabled me to hear rather clearly the condescending remarks being thrown in my direction, things like "Leave, Graney," and "You don't deserve to be here," as well as some choice expletives. Although disturbing in that this was supposed to be a special moment for fourth-classmen, the ceremony of ceremonies to honor our achievement, I had heard it all before.

Notwithstanding, though most of the commentary flanking me from both sides was undeniably negative, some of it was not. I was surprised both to hear some encouraging remarks from congenial voices and to see a few upperclassmen actually saluting me as well! Upon my arrival at the end of the hallway I was greeted by my AOC, MTL, and cadet squadron commander, all of whom were unfriendly enough. The apparent agony associated with having to recognize C4C Graney was visibly unbearable for the three of them. Each seemed to hate me in his own special way for whatever demented reasons. Therefore, shaking my hand and saying nothing more than "Congratulations" must have required an incredible amount of personal restraint on their parts; and to be honest, it would be remiss of me if I failed to mention that, to a degree, I was impressed with such composure.

Immediately following the last handshake I was ushered down to the SAR for the pinning-on portion of the ceremony. As I entered the room I saw those classmates who had gone before me standing on the perimeter of the room, all silently facing the wall. After positioning myself in order next to the classmate who had gone before me, I remember thinking as I stared at the wall in front of me, Okay, this is a little weird. Just keep your head down, Dave, and it will all be over soon.

Even after all my classmates had arrived on the scene, it seemed as though we had waited forever for something to happen. Just when my classmates' muffled grumbling grew to audible disgruntlement, upperclassmen started pouring into the room. Not long after they had all assembled behind us, some heartfelt congratulatory remarks were shared, after which we were asked to turn and face them. At this point, upperclassmen were free to personally commend the fourth-class cadets whose four-degree performance they felt deserved a personal commendation. The mark of a recognized cadet at the Academy is a prop-and-wings pin on the flight cap; therefore, along with commending these four degrees' performance, upperclassmen pinned a prop-and-wings on their uniforms signifying their official acceptance into the Cadet Wing.

Supposedly, the harder a four degree worked during the year, the more prop-and-wings he or she would receive from upperclassmen at the conclusion of Recognition weekend. Coming away from the pinning-on ceremony with the most prop-and-wings was considered by many cadets an honor second to none. Accordingly, those classmates of mine who received the greatest number of prop-and-wings were absolutely thrilled beyond comparison. With all due respect to their sense of accomplishment, in reality, the pinning-on ceremony was nothing more than a popularity contest.

The best-liked freshmen in the eyes of the upperclassmen received the most prop-and-wings. For instance, the same girl who had faked passing out during a BCT II formation run by slowly falling to the ground and then awkwardly rolling into a drainage ditch, the same girl whose incessant crying resulted in my having to do fifteen minutes of bloody one-handed knuckle pushups, the same girl who seldom completed a training session (much less without entirely breaking down both emotionally and physically) received more prop-and-wings than almost every other freshman in the squadron. This cadet received more prop-and-wings than many of her far more deserving classmates who, unquestionably, greatly outperformed her on a continual basis from the day our Academy experience began—and for no other reason than that upperclassmen liked her more. That being so, one could probably guess how many prop-and-wings I received, though it was honestly more than I had expected. I received eight prop-and-wings, most of them a result of my Recognition performance.

Words can't describe my surprise upon hearing what one of these cadets in particular had to say to me: "Graney, I've never seen anybody do what you did during Recognition. I've never seen anybody get worked as bad as you did and still find a way to come out on top. I don't really care if all these other ****bags think you're worthless. Everyone has haters. I just want you to know that there's no doubt in my mind you're going to be doing big things with your life. Good job, Graney."

I was speechless. Encouragement in general at this time was something of a foreign concept for me, especially from an upperclassman. This upperclassman's comment brought back a long-absent, almost-forgotten source of power—second-party reinforcement.

The conclusion of the Recognition ceremony marked the end of an era and the beginning of another. As recognized cadets, the Fourth Class System and all its accoutrements no longer applied to us. Ending our unhealthy relationship with the Fourth Class System meant a much greater degree of personal liberty. Therefore, we quickly posed for some pictures, then put our new level of autonomy to the test. After pictures we walked tentatively alongside CS-17 upperclassmen to dinner, our feeling of trepidation a consequence of having not yet fully internalized our new freedoms, and much to our surprise, we enjoyed a lively and pleasant conversation all the way to Mitchell Hall. The surreal feeling we all experienced at the time could not have been far different from the sensation a person might undergo upon watching the lamb and the lion walk together in paradise.

Dinner was equally shocking because of the subdued, almost peaceful atmosphere within the dining facility. The noise level must have gone down by at least fifty decibels from what we were all used to, thus making dinner yet another pleasant experience. We sat and talked with upperclassmen over a delicious meal as if we were all friendly acquaintances. Although most upperclassmen still wanted nothing to do with me, apparently a number of them had somewhat expunged the record of any bad blood.

Toward the end of the meal Mitchell Hall staff brought out a special treat: platters of ice cream stacked high and wide. As we enjoyed our dessert, upperclassmen played a video presentation depicting our road to Recognition complete with pictures from BCT I and II, the Acceptance Day parade, both wing round robins, and Recognition 2002. One of the pictures showed four degrees being shot at on the buddy down course, which reminded me that we were supposedly still under attack by terrorists. I guess the terrorists must have packed up and gone home, since never again was there any mention of terrorist attacks on the perimeter of the Academy.

That evening, freshmen were invited to a celebratory gathering in Arnold Hall to commemorate the occasion. The party, although well intentioned, was too much for me at the time, having been assaulted and battered just hours before. I made an awkward appearance (awkward enough to make some of my friends worry), then went back to my room. I was so shell-shocked (the law refers to it as duress) by the day's events that I desperately needed some alone time to collect my thoughts. According to custom, I sat down in my chair, propped my feet up on my desk, and stared out the window, contemplating my four-degree experience until the morning light. Although exhausted in every way, I felt no drowsiness at all as I rehashed nearly every demented experience of my freshman year, specifically my most recent victimization.

As the sun came up my eyelids went down. I woke about fifteen hours later to the sound of drunken cadets yelling outside my window. Rising to my feet, I was so delirious that I thought it was still Saturday night, the last day of Recognition. After some bumbling about in my room, I realized it was in fact Sunday night and that I had promised to call my dad with news of my Recognition experience. I grabbed a calling card and hurried down the hallway to the squadron phone booth to place the call. The phone rang only one time before my dad picked up; he had been hovering near the phone, anxiously awaiting my call.

"Graneys," he said, guessing already that I was on the other end.

"Hey, Dad, it's Dave," I said rather despondently; my unusually apathetic tone of voice startling him into saying, "Is everything all right, David? How was Recognition?"

"No, Recognition was worthless," I said, not even really wanting to talk about it, even though that was the predetermined topic of conversation.

As I said earlier, my parents (because of what they had been told by the AOG) were expecting a complete reversal concerning my attitude towards the Fourth Class System. They had been told that after Recognition, their cadet (in their case *cadets*) would be very excited and appreciative of their four-degree experience, that it would all make sense to them, that they would suddenly understand why they had been required to go through so much.

That being the case, my gloomy response was of course totally unexpected and thus of concern. My dad then asked, "Why, Dave? Did something happen?" to which I responded simply, "Yeah. I got beat up."

9

The Triumph of Experience over Expectation

"In Israel we consider pessimists to be merely optimists with a little life experience"

—Ehud Barak, Israeli defense minister, former prime minister[41]

Ehud Barak and I must be kindred spirits. Anyone who's willing to look at life with an objective eye has at least one thing in common with me—the understanding that life isn't all peaches and cream. Let's call a spade a spade; there are bad people in the world who do bad things. It is my belief that people who, repeatedly and without reservation, participate in immoral or illegal behavior, throwing any sense of propriety to the wind, can be considered bad people. Whose sense of propriety? Who determines what's right and wrong, moral and immoral? Who are you to label someone a bad person? These are all common queries intended to question the justification of making such determinations, most often championed by people who lack the courage to take a stand on *anything*, let alone morality. Irrespective of all the philosophical arguments against having a backbone and standing for something, I believe in moral resolve, as do many of the people who profess otherwise. I believe some things are right, and some things are just flat-out wrong.

---

41 Ehud Barak, *The Middle East: Today and Tomorrow*. (World Leaders Forum, Obert C. and Grace A. Tanner Humanities Center, Kingsbury Hall, University of Utah, February 14, 2007), citation from author's notes.

If I were a betting man I'd say Mr. Barak has been called a pessimist more than once in his lifetime, probably by the same sort of people who deny there's right and wrong in the world. I'm not saying there is no such thing as excessive negativity. I'm merely reiterating my previously stated personal conviction that accurate observation should not be mistaken for cynicism. In the course of one's life, experience teaches that which often cannot be learned any other way. It also provides the groundwork for a realistic perspective on life. Acquiring an education can take a person a long way, and, generally speaking, it is in everyone's best interest to get one. However, there is no replacement for life experience. Although a person can teach from experience, experience itself cannot be taught. That which I experienced following Recognition weekend served as a real-life lesson in behavioral science. I came to see, better than ever, the extent to which people are willing to go in order to carry out their designs, as well as (despite what anybody says) the fact that, although perception can often parallel reality, there certainly is no inherent connection between the two.

For instance, I operated the entire year under the assumption that the four-degree experience, albeit distinct, was at least *somewhat* consistent from squadron to squadron. That assumption came crashing down upon my return to school, hearing my classmates talk about their Recognition experiences. My behavioral-science class was especially enlightening, in that the teacher set aside the majority of the time period for the purpose of showing and telling about the interesting experiences we had had over the weekend. One by one, my classmates fired off such comments as, "Oh, it was special."

Apparently I was the only cadet with anything concrete to show, i.e., the bulging laceration on my head where I was head-butted. If I had showed that, not many words would have been needed to describe my Recognition experience. However, I saved them the trouble and merely said something along the lines of, "I don't mean to be anticlimactic or anything, but to be honest with you, I really didn't enjoy my Recognition experience." You could have heard a pin drop as my classmates waited to see how our teacher would respond to the truthful statement I believe they were all too afraid to make themselves.

After an awkward, melodramatic pause my instructor managed to say, "Really? And why is that, Graney?" In order to alleviate the uneasy feeling in the air I responded quickly by saying, "Well, I got beat up by an upperclassmen at one of the courses." Without hesitation, my teacher snapped back at me, "What do you mean, you got beat up?" Although I felt my words were falling on deaf ears, he had asked me a question, so I responded, "I'm saying I was physically assaulted. Does that make sense?"

Before the instructor could even utter a word, one of my contemporaries from across the room blurted out, "No, that doesn't make sense. People don't get assaulted at the Academy. That just doesn't happen here."

Having been accused of lying rather explicitly by my classmate, something I don't take lightly, I quickly fired back, "Are you calling me a liar?" Ignoring proper decorum, he responded, "You're calling yourself a liar." Although rather bamboozled by the implicit stupidity of the comment, I did understand the message he was trying to convey, hence my response, "No, my friend, I'm not, you are. You're calling me a liar, and you don't have a clue what happened to me this weekend, so how about you keep your mouth shut."

As I stood up to leave, frustrated beyond words, my instructor snapped, "Graney, if you walk out that door, you'll have a Form 10 waiting for you in your room before you can even get there." Although raging with anger, I didn't want an additional Form 10, so I sat back down and silently awaited the end of the class period.

While venting to my brother on the way to lunch about what had happened in class, we passed Cadet W and company (my brother's perpetual antagonists) coming the other way. Cadet W waited until we had passed to say, "Faggots, kill yourselves." Both of us turned around to see the back of his head. He had already turned and was walking away as if nothing had happened. The incident merely fuelled the unquenchable fire burning within me at the time. We might have been newly recognized cadets, but that wasn't going to stop Cadet W from pursuing his year-long personal vendetta by taking every opportunity to badger, slander, and plot against us.

The day's bombardment didn't end there. Every day something happened at the Academy that would blow my mind; as a result we were never in need of good story material. Not only did I have a great deal to vent about, but so did my roommate. After class, we went down to the weight room to let off some steam, and after hearing the breakdown of my day, he said, "Bro, you think that's bad? At least you didn't get your laptop stolen." He went on to explain that all our classmates who left their computers in Fairchild Hall (per upperclassmen instruction) prior to Recognition weekend had been robbed, all their laptops stolen right out of the closet in which they had been "secured." Apparently when my classmates went to retrieve their government-issued laptops from Fairchild, the laptops were gone; all fourteen of them.

The Academy supposedly conducted a thorough investigation, though for a number of reasons I have a hard time believing that. In addition to the fact that most nonmilitary personnel had been ordered to vacate the Academy premises before Recognition even began, only upperclass cadets would have known when and where those laptops were to be deposited. In light of the facts, I find it highly unlikely that cadets were not responsible for the theft. That being the case, it should not have been that difficult to discover the criminal plot formulated and carried out by cadets with limited resources and connections with the outside world, given that we were dealing with Academy investigators at least partially willing to do their jobs. In fact, the 10th Security Forces Squadron investigation was so poorly conducted that the case was eventually turned over to the Colorado Springs Police Department to see if they could figure anything out.

Nonetheless, because the Academy once again failed to properly investigate criminal activity, the thieves were never apprehended, and in the year 2002, somebody (most likely American taxpayers) contributed well over $14,000 to buy each of my four- degree colleagues a brand-new laptop. After the incident, a concerned parent wrote to the Academy over the matter, only to receive this in response from General Dallager, then Academy superintendent:

> In reference to the 14+ stolen computers, according to 10th Security Forces Squadron (10 SFS), there have been reports of computers left in academic classrooms, open storage areas (designed for books), and many other unsecured areas where they could easily be taken by anyone. Unfortunately, many times cadets have not taken the time to permanently mark the computers or write down the serial number so they can be positively identified. The Office of Special Investigations (OSI) and 10 SFS have been tackling this problem to address this issue with commanders. Previous Recognition weekends did have laptop comput-

ers reported stolen, mostly from Fairchild Hall. Most were left over the weekend as the cadets were pulled out of class.[42]

This response indicates, to me at least, that Academy leadership really didn't much care that these laptops had been stolen. First of all, laptops left in "academic classrooms, open storage areas, and many other unsecured areas" could not have been stolen by "anyone." Generally speaking, any person found within the classroom areas of Fairchild Hall during school hours would have fit into one of three categories: cadet, instructor, or janitorial staff. The Academy's janitorial staff consisted almost exclusively of individuals with mild to severe mental handicaps. People with significant mental handicaps do not devise intricate plans to steal computers. That leaves us with two groups of people, cadets and instructors. Most would agree that it's rather unlikely that a moderately well-paid instructor would jeopardize his or her future career by stealing cadet computers. Not to mention that it would be rather conspicuous to have an instructor fishing around in the open cupboards in the hallways and then walking away with a cadet-issued computer bag in hand (or fourteen of them for that matter). That leaves us with cadets, allegedly underpaid, often disheveled, and always disgruntled.

Second of all, the statement, "previous Recognition weekends did have laptop computers reported stolen, mostly from Fairchild Hall," appears to be either an effort to say, "Hey, this is not just my problem, this was going on even before I arrived here," or downright stupidity (my class was the first class to be issued laptop computers). Either way, both rationalizations are unacceptable, as they indicate a largely unconcerned command structure. Cadets were almost incontestably the ones stealing computers, and the Academy's response was apathetic at best.

Nevertheless, about halfway into our workout in the AFA's nonintercollegiate athlete weight room where I learned of the stolen computers, a classmate approached me with a message from the squadron. She struggled to catch her breath in order to tell me that the AOC wanted to talk to me as soon as possible, as if I hadn't already had enough drama for one day. Looking at the clock, I was surprised that Major H was even still around. It was just past four, and he hadn't gone home yet, which explained the urgency (Major H had a distaste for a full day's work). I

42 John R. Dallager (then lieutenant general), letter to the Graneys, 21 April 2003.

made haste back to the squadron, changed into my uniform, and then reported to Major H's office, where I found him staring anxiously out his window.

Without acknowledging my presence he said, "Cadet Graney, your dad called to say you were assaulted during sweepstakes. Do you really think you were assaulted?"

At this time in my life, barely nineteen years old, I was not well versed in legal terminology; however, I did recognize what had happened to me as an assault. Therefore I responded, "Yes, sir, I do." I hesitated for a moment, then asked, "Why? Would you call it something else?"

He wasted no time in responding, "I don't know. I wasn't there."

He must have thought I was as stupid as I am American, in that I *knew* he was there. *He was the supervising AOC for the course and had been watching as I was tossed around by Cadet J*! I knew that because I saw him numerous times standing on the sidelines, so to speak, observing sweepstakes training. I had also actually made eye contact with him haphazardly *while* being assaulted. There was no way on God's green earth that he didn't witness the assault, much less that he wasn't even there.

After realizing Major H was actually being serious, I was at a loss for words. It was one thing for him to have told a story over the phone to my dad, who was 1,394 miles away; it was another thing to tell that same lie to a person who knew he had been present during the assault. For him to think that he could actually get away with telling me that he wasn't there was nothing less than astounding. When I finally got hold of myself I asked, "Sir, what do you mean, you weren't there?"

He finally turned away from the window to say, "Graney, I don't know what you're having such a hard time with, but I didn't call you into my office to argue with you. I called you in here because your dad said you were assaulted. So what happened?"

I responded to his patronizing question with a statement and questions of my own. "This is unbelievable. I just can't believe that you can sit there, sir, and tell me you weren't there when both you and I know you were. How can you do that? How can you deliberately lie straight into the face of a person who you know *knows* you're lying?" Not even caring to grace him with the opportunity to respond, I stood up to leave. He barked an order at me to sit down, though before he could even complete the command I interrupted him to say, "You know, sir, I had a low opinion of you to begin with, but seriously, what little respect I had for you is gone." I walked out of his office more upset than I had ever been in my life.

Without changing out of my uniform, I went back down to the weight room to resume where I had left off. I spent the next six or seven hours trying to work off my frustration by way of every conceivable exercise a person can do in a gym, the maddening display only coming to an end by way of an impatient gym-facility employee eager to close shop and go home.

Although the workout did indeed help, momentarily, to alleviate some stress, for the remainder of the week I was plagued by the memory of my AOC's blatant fraudulence. Even though I had never accumulated much respect for him in the first place, I began to severely question Major H's legitimacy, questioning his motives on an unprecedented scale. I remember thinking, *If he's capable of such brazen dishonesty, what else is he capable of?* I reconsidered the meaning behind all the things he had said to me in the past; reevaluating each prior conception of mine about Major H that, evidently, had been conceived in ignorance. So intent was I about accurately reconfiguring my perception of Major H that even when Cadet W (for the second time that week) told me to kill myself while exiting cadet issue I didn't really notice.

The conversation that occurred in Major H's office that day (18 March 2002) served as a moment of truth not just for me but for Major H as well. Whereas I was compelled to reevaluate my AOC's character, I believe Major H was obliged to reevaluate and reposition himself regarding his long-time goal of seeing me disenrolled from the Academy. It seemed that instead of desiring my permanent departure from the institution solely on account of his hatred for me, now Major H wanted me gone because of the potential threat I posed to his career. If there were to be an investigation into my assault, it would reveal that he had lied to both my parents and me concerning his whereabouts during the incident, not to mention that it was his negligence that had allowed the assault to happen in the first place.

Before leaving for California at the end of the week, I was informed of two things. Following a wingwide spring-break safety briefing on how to avoid coming back to the Academy in a body bag, Major H caught up to me in the crowd and requested that I accompany him back to his office. Upon our arrival he informed me that he was going to set up a conflict-resolution meeting between Cadet J and me, set to take place sometime after the break, no further details available. That being the case, I excused myself only to be intercepted by an upperclassman in the hallway bearing news of an SCRB that I had also been scheduled for after the break. I was quite aware of the fact that neither of these experiences would be pleasant, and maybe that explains why I drove so fast, almost recklessly, all the way to Huntington Beach, CA, and so slowly on the way back.

Spring break served three purposes. One, I was able to enjoy my youth a little, surfing and playing beach volleyball with the ladies at the pier, golfing with my great-uncle, snowboarding with the boys at Sundance, UT, and visiting with my parents who traveled all the way to the Rocky Mountains to see me. Second, I was able to think about something other than my distressing situation back at school, and lastly, the important realization (for both my parents and me) of how emotionally distraught I had really become after a year's worth of verbal and occasional physical abuse as a freshman cadet at the Academy.

During the visit with my parents, not only did I unintentionally scare the hell out of my sister's boyfriend over dinner, but I also attended Sunday services at the nearest church we could find. I hadn't brought a dress shirt and tie with me on spring break because I hadn't planned to go to church that week. Even so, when I arrived at the chapel without a tie I immediately caught my mother's attention. Already in a bad mood, she inadvertently stretched her motherly prerogative a bit too far when counseling me about what was and wasn't appropriate church attire. After her comment "I can't believe you would come to church with no tie on. I raised you better than that," I completely lost it.

After I walked downstairs and found myself alone, everything came flooding out, a year's worth of bottled-up frustration that I could no longer hold in. It wasn't that my mother's commentary was particularly abrasive; nor was it in any way her fault. The emotional meltdown arose from my extraordinary level of distress preexistent before her comment was even made. I was at the end of my rope, and my mother said the wrong thing at the wrong time. The Academy had finally visibly shaken me. Not only had I been verbally mistreated for the duration of the year, but no more than a week before I had also been the victim of a relatively vicious physical assault. Just as a perpetual state of battle awareness erodes emotional stability, so does the actual consummation of the threats to one's personal safety responsible for such hypervigilance in the first place.

Feeling as though she might have made a mistake, my mother came in search of me. After one look at me she realized she had grossly underestimated the severity of the abuse I had been subjected to. She knew that straight away because she knew her son. The son she knew hadn't shed a tear in years, so seeing me crouched in a corner with tears running down my face she knew that something was badly amiss. She knew that there was obviously more to the story, that her son's four-degree experience had been far from what she had been led to believe by the AOG and the AFA Parents' Association.

Although embarrassing to say the least, those tears were strangely therapeutic for me. Afterward, I felt as though a huge weight had been lifted off my shoulders, enabling me to more fully enjoy the rest of my time with my family and friends.

Just before my brother, friend, and I left to return to the Academy, we decided to go to the lake. While we were skipping rocks from the shore (a Graney family tradition), my dad stressed the importance of reporting Cadet J's assault. I heard him, but obviously I wasn't listening as well as I should have, for only months later did I finally report the assault. In my own defense, my delay in reporting the assault, that is, to law enforcement, was due more to the Academy's confusing, dysfunctional conglomeration of disciplinary systems than to unwillingness on my part to talk. At the time, when my dad spoke of reporting the assault to law enforcement, I hadn't the slightest clue what that even entailed. The security forces (Air Force law enforcement) were an unknown entity to me, unfamiliar even to a majority of the Cadet Wing. What I knew (what *everyone* knew) was the squadron/training wing chain of command, for it had governed every aspect of our lives since day one, and for most of us, including me, anything else was misunderstood if not entirely unheard of. In addition to this typical misunderstanding and lack of knowledge as to both the whereabouts and function of the 10th Security Forces, I questioned the usefulness of even reporting the assault at all because of the way the situation had been handled by my squadron leadership when the issue was raised the first time.

In any event, some would say that it's unacceptable to report an assault months after it occurred, that such a delay merely indicates the accuser's lack of credibility. Both I and the United States legal code would strongly disagree. The UCMJ statute of limitations for assault and battery is five years. That means that former legislatures and judge advocates, responsible for having enacted the laws by which military members live today, regarded assault and battery as a significant enough crime to justify allowing the victim up to five years to report the incident to proper authorities. Therefore, the only unacceptable action on anyone's part relative to the March 16, 2002, assault and battery of which I was the victim was the assailant's, Cadet J, for committing the crime in the first place.

However true that may be, convincing the parties involved of that fact proved impossible. The conflict-resolution meeting between Cadet J and me was scheduled to take place at the end of the week following spring break. The only snag was that the negligent first-class cadet-training officer who would be facilitating the showdown failed to inform me of the time and place of the meeting until a couple of hours before it was scheduled to begin. Furthermore, the means by which he conferred the information was an e-mail sent to my Academy e-mail address, which I didn't read as I was studying in the library at the time.

When I returned to my room, I had two e-mails in my inbox waiting for me: one telling me about the meeting scheduled to begin a couple of hours before, and the other a stiff rebuke from the same training officer for not having shown up. How dare I! Especially when, because of his own negligence, I hadn't been informed in a reasonable amount of time that a meeting was scheduled in the first place; and shame on me for having been away from my computer for so long, studying in the library.

Nonetheless, another meeting was scheduled, this time a few days in advance. I showed up to the meeting and found the belligerent party, my training officer, and my element leader pleasantly chatting while waiting for my arrival. As soon as I walked in the atmosphere changed completely, much like when a fan of the away team unknowingly sits down in the home-team bleachers.

Without saying a word, I sat down, and the meeting began. The training officer started by saying something like, "Well, I think we all know why we're here, so let's get this thing over with. I'm going to have you both tell your sides of the story, then we'll go from there. Graney, you start."

Not wanting to be there any more than anyone else did, I gave a one- to two-minute recap of the assault as I remembered it, though before I could even finish Cadet J interrupted to say, "That's a **** lie."

I stopped and asked if I could finish, to which he replied, "Yeah, whatever, go ahead and finish your lies." This caused me to hesitate for a moment in that, as I said before, I really don't appreciate being called a liar.

Nevertheless, I wrapped up my side of the story, and before the training officer could give Cadet J the floor he had already taken it. He proceeded to tell of how I had come to his station and given him "attitude" and not "followed orders." He told of how he hadn't done anything that he didn't have to do, that he *had to do* what he did because of the "attitude" I had given him. Finally, after claiming that I actually head-butted *him*, he concluded by saying, "Look, we was both out of control. We both went too far and things happened. We both learned from this experience, and I've apologized for what I did. I haven't heard any apologies from him, how come he don't apologize?"

Following my superior's example, I did not wait for the mediator to turn the floor over to me either. With a flare of rage I shot back, "Well, sir, *as your victim* I have nothing to apologize for; and whether or not you want to believe it, not only have you falsified the facts of the matter, but *you* are the perpetrator, not me. I didn't head-butt you, give you attitude, or exhibit disorderly conduct in any way. I have absolutely *nothing* to apologize to you for, but you know that."

Before Cadet J could fire back at me, he was cut off by my element leader. "Now, hold on, Graney, you're no more justified in accusing him of assault than he is to accuse you. Trying to put the blame on each other isn't going to solve anything. As far as I'm concerned, you're both at fault and need to apologize to each other and move on. Now I've heard Cadet J apologize already, so suppose you be a man about this, Graney, and do the same."

I was speechless. Here I was, the victim of a vicious physical assault, being told that I needed to "be a man" and *apologize* for my own victimization! Was this actually supposed to be effective conflict resolution? In utter disbelief I sat and stared at the floor for a moment before responding, "Lowering yourself to the level of cowardice necessary to apologize for your own victimization has nothing to do with being a man. Here I am, battling three-on-one odds, one madman and two criminal sympathizers, being told that it's *my fault* that *I was assaulted,* and not only that but that I should actually *apologize* to the very man who assaulted me! This is so sick and twisted it's making me nauseous. I do agree with you on one point, though, the fact that our little meeting here isn't going to solve anything."

Having heard enough, the training officer spouted off. "Graney, no one cares what you think. You've been a ****up this entire year, so why should we believe your story over that of Cadet J? I mean, who do you think you are? You don't even act like you're addressing a superior. What do you think, you're God or something?"

Without hesitation I responded, "It's unfortunate that you feel it appropriate to turn this into another demented four-degree training session, but to answer your ignorant question, no, I don't think I'm God. I know you don't care what I think, but to be quite honest with you, I don't give a **** what you think, either. You have been a pathetic example of leadership this entire year, starting from when you got your jollies by opening our mail and reading personal letters during basic training. What makes you think I should care about what *you* have to say?"

Before he could respond, Cadet J seized the moment by saying, "This is the kind of **** I'm talking about! This is why—"

Before he could get any further I cut him off by shouting, "This is why what? This is why what, Cadet J? This is why you had to head-butt me, or punch me, or call me a mother-***ing racist? You're out of control, bro. I don't know what the hell is going on inside your head, but if this were the real Air Force you'd be in jail right now for assault and battery, making little rocks out of big rocks. You're **** insane!"

Infuriated, Cadet J stood up and provocatively squared off to me, his desire to augment his dossier with a repeat offense only matched by my determination to end this chronic victimization. Therefore, before he could take a step toward me I was already standing on the other side of the room waiting for him. Both mediators immediately intervened, and amidst a great deal of yelling and screaming managed to usher us all back into our seats.

A long and awkward silence ensued as the mediators considered their next move, as all the while Cadet J and I exchanged hate-filled glances from across the room. Aware that their vision of our coming together, apologizing, hugging, and making up was merely an illusion, they turned to crisis management. Instead of asking for any more input from us two belligerents, they simply ascended their collective soapbox and gave Cadet J and me a spiel about being on the same team, forgiving and forgetting, and ultimately moving on. They finished up their inappropriate sermon on love and forgiveness with some such asinine comment as "Whatever happened happened; and it's in the past. No one can change what happened in the past, so we all need to act like men, get over it, and leave it alone."

That was easy for them to say; they hadn't been assaulted and battered. More than that, however, this was not a simple case of kiss and make up; this was a felony-level crime for which people go to jail. They were actually trying to tell me that it would be manly of me to turn a blind eye to my own victimization, to pursue the matter no further and simply move on. This was just another example of the Academy's minimalism and containment philosophy taking priority over confrontation and correction. Instead of going through the hassle of duly punishing the guilty party, it was their policy to just silence the victim by crushing him into submission.

I was so disgusted with their condescending and purposefully manipulative banter that I stopped paying attention. I mentally removed myself from the situation, although while my mind was somewhere else the meeting came to an end. I was ordered to shake hands and leave it at that. I shook hands only because I had been ordered to do so and left the room without saying another word.

Apparently, it was reported back to Major H that the matter had been resolved and that all parties involved were satisfied with the outcome of the conflict-resolution meeting, for when I went into his office to provide mandatory feedback concerning the event he started out by asking me, "Well, sounds like everything's been taken care of, eh, Graney?"

Somehow or another, Major H had been grossly ill advised by at least one if not both of the conflict-resolution mediators. Things had not been taken care of by any stretch of the imagination, although, according to the young men mediating the meeting, not only had the accounts been settled, but they were settled largely in my favor. In a summary MFR, written at the behest of the 10th CS/SCSF conducting the follow-on criminal investigation, the cadet training officer made these interesting observations:

> We had each individual state his view of the events that took place. Neither changed his story, but both admitted that they were angry and went too far. The physical claims remained "he said/she said," so we moved past that. It was clear that Cadet J did use inappropriate language, so it would have been possible to issue a Form 10 on those grounds, but I specifically asked Graney how he wanted that handled.

> Graney said that he felt his concerns had been addressed and he did not want to get anyone in trouble. Since Graney was partially at fault for the incident and I wanted to solve this problem at the lowest possible level, that worked. I once again made sure that Graney was satisfied with this resolution, had them shake hands and that was it. It was my opinion that they both left having learned where the other was coming from and on amicable terms. The next day I informed Major H that the situation was resolved and that both parties were satisfied with the outcome.

He must not have been in the same meeting I was in! Call me crazy, but at least I wouldn't write that two people who were yelling and screaming, almost at each other's throats, were on amicable terms. Nor would I purposefully distort the facts or outright lie in an MFR for Air Force *security forces* conducting a *criminal investigation.* Maybe he had killed one too many brain cells that night he almost drank himself to death alongside his buddy the squadron commander, but to lie as he did under oath, in a sworn statement, was playing with fire, that fire being perjury and obstruction of justice.

However, as a professional pyrotechnician's tradecraft serves to minimize the inherent danger of playing with tangible fire, Academy administrators made playing with this intangible fire (high crimes and misdemeanors) just short of risk free due to their incessant dereliction of duty. This training officer knew full well that an institution often unwilling to prosecute even the more violent criminals (assailants and sexual predators) was clearly not going to come after him for making an inaccurate statement here and there within a sworn statement, especially in a he said/she said situation. There simply was no deterrent to dissuade him from using the meeting and subsequent MFR as another opportunity to slander my name and reputation.

My man-child AOC had read a similar MFR written and submitted to him the very next day by the same training officer. Major H referred to this MFR as we went back and forth for close to an hour as to the details of the conflict-resolution meeting and the assault itself. However, as we should all know, not all sources are equally reliable. This training officer submitted an MFR with erroneous information to Major H, leaving me the unpleasant task of debunking the multitude of lies it contained.

I argued with Major H until I was blue in the face. I started by responding to his assertion that things had been taken care of. I explained to him that things had indeed *not* been taken care of, despite the training officer's claims to the contrary. Later I broke down the illogic (to say the least) behind the accusation that I was somehow partially at fault for my own victimization. I argued the irresponsibility of tasking an inexperienced 21-year-old college-student cadet to investigate a felony assault in the first place; as if he could actually perform at the same level as professionally trained criminal investigators. I argued how nonsensical it was for a first-class cadet to ask a fourth-class cadet how *he* wanted the situation handled (e.g., issuance of a Form 10, nonjudicial punishment, court-martial) with the upperclass perpetrator sitting right next to him, supposing, of course, that he actually asked me that in the first place during my externally motivated daydream.

Evidently the cadet-training officer wasn't the only one lacking important leadership qualities. Shortly after I had made this last argument, my AOC asked me, "Well, Graney, what *do* you want? What do you want *me* to do?" If I hadn't already witnessed the kind of lackluster performance Major H was capable of, this comment would have been rather startling. What did this comment say about Major H? Here we had a field-grade officer in the United States Air Force asking a USAFA freshman cadet, barely nineteen years old, what he wanted his commanding officer to do in response to a reported assault and battery. It was truly unbelievable. S.L.A. Marshall would have been very upset with this sort of dereliction of duty:

> It is the task of the *officer* to see that all is right, and *to take the trouble necessary to make certain of it* ... It is always the duty of an officer to intervene for the protection of his people against *any manifest injustice*; whatever its source.[43]

At this point I sat back and considered my options. At this stage in my Academy career I had very little understanding of how the UCMJ system operated. I didn't even know that the 10th CS/SCSF existed, let alone where their office was. I had been accused of my own victimization by the training officer, my element leader, and my attacker himself. Furthermore, the man responsible for my welfare, Major H, had been

---

43 Marshall, *The Armed Forces Officer*, 151, 176.

and still was one of my most determined adversaries and had already flagrantly lied to my face concerning his whereabouts during the attack. At the time I felt there was little hope, if any, for justice to be served; I was in checkmate.

Accordingly, I responded to Major H with something like, "It's blatantly obvious that no one cares what happens to me at this school, even when I'm physically assaulted, so to be honest with you, I don't know. I don't know what to do or what should be done."

Major H responded contemptibly, "Graney, I'm not going to do anything about this unless you want me to."

Setting caution aside, I immediately put the record straight., "Well, sir, I sincerely doubt you'd do anything about this even if I *did* want you to. We both know that you don't give a **** what happens to me. I mean, that's been pretty well-established by the way you've personally treated me this entire year, not to mention how you've allowed me to be treated by the upperclassmen in this squadron and others. You sit here and act like we're on the same team, but I know better. I know we're not on the same team."

Major H then sat forward in his chair, slammed his hand on the desk, and told me to leave. This was when I really started wondering if the Air Force, not just the Air Force Academy, was for me. I began to think, Am I going to have to deal with this kind of nonsense my entire career? Is this how the operational Air Force functions as well? Later that evening these questions led me to approach a four-degree classmate and friend who had served five years in the operational Air Force before entering the Academy. We talked at great length over a number of issues, all having to do with my prospective career with the Air Force. He reassured me that the operational Air Force was nothing like the Air Force Academy; that the USAFA in no way mimicked the "real" Air Force. He told me that although I was considered one of the most underperforming, undeserving, and incapable freshmen in the squadron, he would rather have served under a person like me than any other cadet in our squadron because of the kind of person I was. He told me the reason I had been targeted for the duration of the year for extra harassment, hazing, and abuse was jealousy more than anything else. He introduced me to a quote from a speech by Teddy Roosevelt delivered at the Sorbonne in Paris, France, April 23, 1910. It has been my favorite quote ever since:

> It is not the critic who counts; not the man who points out how the strong man stumbles, or where the doer of deeds could have done them better. The credit belongs to the man who is actually in the arena, whose face is marred by dust and sweat and blood; who strives valiantly; who errs, who comes short again and again, because there is no effort without error and shortcoming; but who does actually strive to do the deeds; who knows great enthusiasms, the great devotions; who spends himself in a worthy cause; who at the best knows in the end the triumph of high achievement, and who at the worst, if he fails, at least fails while daring greatly, so that his place shall never be with those cold and timid souls who neither know victory nor defeat.

After I read the quote my friend said, "Graney, you're that man in the arena, and people want to see you fail. These upperclassmen who hate you know that you possess moral conviction, a level of confidence and personal integrity that they do not, and that bothers them. Don't worry about what they say. No matter what happens, you'll do fine."

Then he pulled out his staff-sergeant insignia, which he had kept from his enlisted days, and gave them to me as a gift. He told me that in the Air Force, enlisted men and women sometimes give their old rank insignia to a person who they think has done an exceptional job representing themselves, the service, and the country. He told me that he had been watching me the entire year and couldn't help being impressed with the way I handled myself despite the harsh treatment. He told me I deserved some recognition, and as no one else was willing to "show me love," he was taking it upon himself to bestow the accolades.

My friend would never know the impact his generous words had on me at the time. He graciously played the role of the Good Samaritan when I needed it most, allowing me to regroup and attempt to chart a new course at the Academy. I had weathered the four-degree storm and was looking forward to getting my life at the Academy back on track.

My renewed conviction's first crucible turned out to be my *second* squadron commander review board. Knowing what I was in for, I meticulously prepared and perfected a defensive argument with a conciliatory undertone. Although I was much better prepared for this second SCRB than the first, so were the board members, who happened to be the same individuals as before. Whereas I planned to defend myself more effectively before what I knew to be an incredibly biased review board, I was certain the board members assiduously plotted against me with even greater zeal, increasing their ammunition with all the things they hadn't thought to say on the last go-round. Unfortunately, my preparation came to naught, as it became readily apparent I had absolutely no chance of success.

My favorite example of closet lunacy displayed during this kangaroo court rematch came from my very own element leader, newly invigorated from his participatory role in the recent conflict-resolution meeting. During my first SCRB, I had claimed that my so-called attitude (more like *perception* of the Academy) would improve once I was no longer subjected to the absurdities of the Fourth Class System. However, when I made that statement, I wasn't planning to fall victim to assault and battery; nor could I have guessed the flagrant dishonesty I would encounter from Major H. Finally, I would never have imagined that I would be accused of partial culpability for my own victimization.

In an effort to highlight my allegedly bad attitude, my element leader made this statement: "Graney, you said your attitude was going to improve after Recognition. I don't know about any of you all [addressing his colleagues], but I don't see nothing other than the same old ****."

I took a second to absorb the blow, then responded with something like, "Sir, I don't know exactly what it is that you would be referring to when you say same old ****, but to be honest with you, *why would I* hold the Academy in greater esteem? It's not like I wasn't physically assaulted or anything, wasn't lied to by my AOC, then later wasn't blamed for it. I don't know how I could *possibly* have a better attitude without being entirely delusional! Getting head-butted and punched, lied to, and blamed for one's own victimization, these things don't tend to inspire a positive mental attitude, especially with respect to the institution *responsible* for such debauchery."

At this point it spiraled into a competition between board members and Major H for an opportunity to speak. All at once Major H was squirrelly telling me he had never lied to me, while my element leader was saying that I hadn't been assaulted or victimized by anyone, that it was in actuality, an excuse for my own poor performance. The cadet squadron commander was telling me to stop slouching, that this was no casual meeting; and numerous other cadets on the board eagerly put in their two cents' worth of verbal garbage as well. It was chaotic at best; all I could think about was how ridiculous this whole scene would look to an outside observer. Here you had a bunch of college kids in this guise of military professionalism (using serious insider acronyms such as SCRB, dressed in military uniforms—ranks, titles, etc.) yelling at each other mostly about utter nonsense. Imagine how much more outrageous it would seem to an outside observer if he knew that just weeks before, many of these same people had danced in front of me in women's lingerie in the dormitory showers. I couldn't help being reminded of William Golding's novel *Lord of the Flies*. In the book, only the boy holding the conch was allowed to speak during a debate. I just kept thinking, Where's the conch? We need a conch.

As I said nothing in opposition to the remainder of their inflammatory appraisal of my worth as a human being, the upperclassmen seemed to feel they had successfully crushed me into capitulation and that any additional commentary would be nothing more than beating a dead horse. Therefore, apparently feeling that their work was done and proud of it, they brought the meeting to a close. But just before doing so the squadron commander asked one last question: "Graney, what reason, if any, can you give me for your being allowed to remain a cadet?" After an extensive, unbroken silence, I leaned forward and said, "You know what *I* want to know? I want to know what's the point in even asking that question, when we all know that no matter how I respond, you're going to recommend disenrollment anyway."

With that, the meeting came to a close. It probably takes more time for a Maserati 3200 GT to go from zero to sixty than it took for these board members to unanimously recommend disenrollment. Some might say I was idiotic to make such a defeatist statement just before the SCRB concluded, although realistically, attempting to win over these clowns would have been no less foolish than to ask the sun not to go down or rivers to run uphill. Just as before, I was guilty before the SCRB even began, the meeting itself merely serving protocol.

What may have taken a bit more time was the formulation of all the lies included in the summary MFR. At the time, I wasn't allowed to see what the cadet squadron commander wrote; however, a Freedom of Information Act request long after the fact has provided me that opportunity. After reading what was written in this 18 April 2002 MRF, it pains me to say that almost every statement attributed to me during this second SCRB (and the first, for that matter) was an invention of my squadron commander's mind. For me, a cadet trying to achieve his dream of graduating from the Academy, the statements my squadron commander claimed I made during these review boards were horribly damaging, the most injurious of his lies being his claim that I had said, "I want to leave [the Academy]" five times during the second SCRB, followed closely by the false accusation that I said, "I can handle my probations, but I don't seem to have the drive to do so."

I believe my cadet squadron commander wrote that I had said these things knowing that any leadership entity higher up the chain of command reading it would be much more inclined to discharge me from the Academy. It was enormously malicious and effective, in that it had exactly the desired effect. Without hesitation, Major H concurred with the SCRB recommendation, though I'm sure that doesn't come as much of a surprise. Where these lies would really take a toll was at the training-wing level months down the road.

The final stage of my Academy career was nothing short of a bona fide Sisyphean challenge. Whereas Sisyphus, in Greek mythology, was punished in the underworld with the task of repeatedly rolling a huge stone to the top of a steep hill only to have it roll back down again and again and again into eternity, my task was to stay out of trouble and get off probation, only to have something (more often someone) perpetually foiling my efforts.

After Major H concurred with the SCRB's recommendation and produced what must have been one of the most negative commander evaluations on record, I was immediately scheduled for a so-called soft-look MRC. Soft-look MRCs were conducted at the group level; therefore, I was sent to meet with the group commander posthaste. Unfortunately for me, the group commander was not just higher up the chain of command but Major H's neighbor and barbeque buddy as well. Accordingly, my reputation preceded me, in that the group commander knew of my existence long before I ever stepped into his office. Most likely having been unofficially briefed (off the record) by an incensed Major H concerning my allegedly way-below-average performance, the group commander merely reiterated many of the same issues that had already been exhaustively hashed out at the squadron level.

Although I had heard it all before, there were a couple of things that came as a surprise. One was the group commander's dispassionate tone of voice; for I had become accustomed to discussing these issues amidst a great deal of hostility. The other surprise came in the form of a question.

The group commander asked me, "Graney, how are you going to be able to train next year if you're so adamantly opposed to the Fourth Class System?" It was at this moment that I felt sure he had been in cahoots with Major H, as the AOC had asked me that exact same question verbatim. Major H also told me, as if it was a foregone conclusion, that I was going to be "the worst three-degree trainer at the Academy," because, he said, "It's always the guys who get it the worst that become the worst trainers."

I found his statement to be both an insult to my conviction as well as wildly ironic, in that he had been one of the many to resolutely stand by the enduring claim that I had been treated no differently than any other four degree in the squadron and that my feeling of victimization was merely a product of my imagination and bad attitude.

Nevertheless, I answered the group commander's question as best I could: "Sir, I'll train exactly the way training is to be conducted according to the Academy Training Philosophy handbook, which doesn't entail any of the inappropriate training activities to which I object."

With a blank expression on his face, the group commander changed the subject.

Unwilling to recommend disenrollment, the group commander decided upon six months' aptitude-conduct probation with the following stipulation:

> Any discipline trouble (e.g., Form 10) of any kind will result in an immediate hard look MRC with the recommendation for disenrollment.

Although an extremely inauspicious stipulation, it was the condition I was given. Managing to carry on six months at the Academy without receiving a single Form 10 would have been quite challenging for even the most beloved USAFA cadet, let alone for a cadet plagued by a reputation like mine. Considering the circumstances, the probability of my making it six months unmolested by those who, in the past, had so liberally sprinkled my personnel file with negative documentation was unlikely at best.

Nonetheless, however insurmountable the task or disconcerting the prospect, it was my only chance to remain a cadet at the Academy. My options at the time were simple: sink or swim. I chose to swim. I dutifully agreed to the terms of the probation and returned to my squadron.

After a quick debriefing with Major H, I went straight to work. As a result of approximately twenty-five Forms 10, I had accumulated more than 120 hours of confinements and about a dozen tours that would need to be served before I could ever be taken off probation. One confinement consisted of remaining in one's room with the door open in service dress, studying either school material or military knowledge for one to two hours, a process always closely monitored by Cadet Wing training staff to assure compliance. Any breach in protocol, e.g., getting up to use the restroom, immediately invalidated the confinement. One tour consisted of marching around in a square wearing the USAFA Class A uniform, rifle over the shoulder, for an hour straight. Tours, unlike confinements, could only be done on weekends, thus effectively laying to rest any modicum of a social life the cadet might have had.

I painstakingly served all twelve tours and 120 confinements required of me in just three weeks' time. It was unquestionably one of the more tormenting experiences of my life. The frustration of having to march around in a square for hours on end while being spied upon by the binocular-wielding training-group commander, Colonel Slavec, from her office window across the terrazzo was substantial to say the least. Agitating as it was in and of itself, the fact that I truly did not deserve such punishment made it all the worse.

However, I paid my debt to society, as they say, and moved on; but not before a significant altercation with the one and only Cadet W. Toward the end of my two-week sentence (120 confinements and twelve tours felt much like a prison term), I received an e-mail from my brother describing just one more in a series of rude and provocative statements coming from Cadet W. Up to this point I had chosen to ignore this lowlife, but two weeks of confinements and tours had forced me to my wit's end.

My brother and I had attempted, on more than one occasion, to have the harassment dealt with through proper channels—a formal complaint in the form of an MFR to the CS-16 AOC—and had not only seen nothing done about it, but ended up being chastised for even bringing it up. The system having already failed us (my brother and me), and really not wanting to continue being harassed by this degenerate any longer, I took matters into my own hands. I sent Cadet W a rather abrasive e-mail in hopes of warding off any further harassment. What I said to Cadet W wasn't flattering, but it also wasn't nearly as obscene and mean-spirited as the verbal garbage that had been incessantly spewing out of his mouth for almost an entire year by then.

Although my e-mail had the desired effect, in that I never saw or heard from him again, it also had a considerable undesirable effect. In keeping with his characteristically underhanded way of doing things, he immediately forwarded the e-mail to his good ol' boy of an AOC, whom I considered incompetent and ineffectual, with an allegation of gross insubordination proudly tacked on. The CS-16 AOC then passed along the forwarded e-mail to my AOC, Major H, with a little snide remark, "There you go!" and nothing else. I can only speculate what Major H's reaction was upon reading the e-mail, although, the euphoria in his eye when he came to my room to lecture me concerning the matter was unmistakable.

This was just what he needed to put the nail in my coffin. He gleefully wrote up the Form 10 that would later send me to a hard-look MRC, which was essentially an appellate committee having final jurisdiction over the recommendations of group commanders, squadron AOCs, and SCRB members. Major H issued the most severe punishment possible, a Class D hit containing the maximum number of demerits and confinements allowable on a single Form 10.

I did, however, like every other cadet, have the opportunity to challenge the Form 10 by way of an MFR, an opportunity of which I took full advantage. I knew that when I wrote my dissenting opinion it wouldn't change anything (and it never did), but I wrote the MFR anyway for general principle. A reader familiar with the film *Braveheart* will especially appreciate this analogy. The movie is set in Scotland around the turn of the fourteenth century during a period of English occupation. A scene toward the beginning depicts a council meeting wherein a group of Scotsmen are deliberating over what to do in response to a recent English ambush and massacre of many of their countrymen. The character playing William Wallace's father proposes fighting back against the English, only to be vigorously opposed by another man at the meeting. The voice of opposition argues that the English are too strong, they can't be defeated. Wallace senior looks at his countrymen and says authoritatively, "We don't have to beat them, we just have to fight them."

I try not to get my information from movies, although, I do believe in giving credit where credit is due. I believe that there are times in our lives when succeeding by winning is less important than the effort itself. Even though I knew nothing would accrue to my favor from fighting the Form 10, in the long run it was better to have tried and failed than to have not tried at all. I tested the mettle of Major H by writing the following rebuke:

> On May 27, 2002, I sent an e-mail to C2C W in CS-16. The content of the e-mail message was intentionally insulting. I know that it is inappropriate to send messages such as this to anyone with which you hold a professional relationship. If Cadet W would have had a professional relationship with me, the e-mail message would not have been sent. Cadet W violated any professional relationship he might have had with me through the incredible number of demeaning experiences to which he subjected my brother and I throughout the entire four degree year. A professional relationship, according to the Academy Training Philosophy, is built on mutual respect. This does not mean that the subordinate obeys and respects the superior while the superior demeans the subordinate. Demeaning anyone is not only unprofessional but cruel, and when this happens, any sort of professional relationship, tangible or intangible, has been jeopardized and most likely ruined altogether.

I then went on to describe the many unprofessional statements that Cadet W had made, such as, "Maybe we should make Graney go up to the staff tower and tell everyone how small his dick is," or "Kill yourself, faggot," or "Graney, you are such a worthless piece of ****." I went on to say:

> The bottom line is that Cadet W has said more gross and unprofessional things to both my brother and me than I would ever dream of saying to anyone holding a professional relationship with me. I could imagine myself accepting the punishment outlined on this Form 10 maybe if Cadet W received forty tours, forty demerits etc.for every time *he* violated the mutual respect clause of which the Academy Training Philosophy speaks. The fact of the matter is he won't, because that would be more demerits and tours than would be possible to give someone at the Academy and leave them with a chance to stay.
>
> And yes, all these issues that I have brought up in this MFR were explained in detail to proper authority (CS-16 AOC) at the time of

> the incident(s), and nothing happened. Not only did nothing happen but Charles was mocked by Cadet W for bringing these issues to the AOC and called a "pussy," *in Cadet W's own professional vernacular.* No punishments, whatsoever, were given out even after all that.

I was hoping that citing a higher authority, the Academy Training Philosophy, would give even greater legitimacy to my argument; however, my Academy leadership's reaction to my MFR reiterated to me that I was alone in my reverence for the ATP, completely alone. I concluded the MFR with this:

> Despite my reputation, I can see (better than most people here) when something is not right. The way in which my brother was treated in his squadron by not only Cadet W but the majority of CS-16 upperclassmen (who had allowed themselves to be swayed by Cadet W's perpetual slanderous banter behind Charles' back) was irrefutably wrong. Charles took these issues to his AOC only to be chastised, insulted and denied due justice. As a frustrated brother, I took matters into my own hands and it was, perhaps, not the wisest choice.
>
> The issues I brought up with respect to the relationship between Charles and Cadet W are a mere fraction of what happened. Cadet W is not a professional military member by any standard, and for me to be punished in any other way than a warning stating that I should probably avoid sending e-mails like the one I did is ridiculous. In any event, a second-class cadet should be held to a higher standard than a fourth-class cadet. Cadet W received no punishments whatsoever with respect to his mistreatment of my brother. It would be an incredible breach of integrity within the system as well as complete and total hypocrisy for me to be punished for this infraction any other way than how Cadet W has been punished for his numerous indiscretions.

As I stated, not only was my brother chastised, insulted, and denied due justice, but his pathetic excuse for an AOC even recommended in an MFR concerning my brother's situation that Chaz be sent before a wing honor board for even making the claims at all, in his own words: "… the only response appropriate is a Wing Honor Board for lying."

Although extremely upsetting, the most disturbing aspect regarding this whole situation was not the fact that my Academy career was now in jeopardy because of Major H's decision (despite my compelling opposition) to issue the Form 10 anyway; it was the shameless double standard embodied by the Academy leadership involved. It's just as my brother wrote at the time:

> This represents a gross double standard. Cadet W is allowed to say and do whatever he wants entirely unabated, whereas the one time my brother makes the mistake of sending an offensive e-mail the book is thrown at him full force. Why is something like that [the e-mail message] seen as such an important issue, but the fact that I was physically assaulted, continually hazed and harassed by three different upperclassmen (one of which was my brother's e-mail's recipient) is seen as so insignificant?

The CS-16 AOC's allegation of some sort of dishonesty on my brother's part was astonishingly disjointed and inequitable. Although it may be an effective measure in a court of law, challenging the victim's credibility does not unequivocally divest one of culpability. More than that, though, any reasonable soul reading the MFRs written by the three upperclassmen of whom my brother speaks in relation to the lunch-table incident would realize that at least two,if not all, of them provided false testimony regarding their involvement. That would have been obvious to an intellectually sound, unbiased individual, because all three of them provided significantly different versions of the same event. If the CS-16 AOC had been mindful of his duty as a commissioned officer in the United States Air Force, he would not have accused my brother of lying.

Worse yet, in due course Cadet W admitted to my brother that both he and his colleagues had lied on their MFRs to the CS-16 AOC concerning the lunch-room incident. One night after my removal from the Academy, Cadet W passed my brother who was talking to me on his cellphone in the stairwell. As he walked past, Cadet W called Chaz a "piece of ****" and continued on to his room. Finally having had enough, Chaz immediately hung up the phone to pay Cadet W a visit. After he arrived at the enemy's lair, an hour-long argument ensued during which Cadet W shamelessly admitted to having lied in his MFR concerning the lunch-room incident. He not only admitted to lying but with a little grin on his face even went so far as to brag about the fact that he got away with it. He was obviously way out of line, and to this day it makes me wince when I contemplate the gravity of such moral depravity.

What I found most intriguing about the whole scenario was that Cadet W was the CS-16 honor officer. Here we had the squadron *honor officer* not only outright professing to be a liar but actually bragging about it! The *Cadet Honor Code Handbook* directive number 2.1.8.1 clearly states that it is the responsibility of the squadron honor officer to "Inform squadron AOC, MTL, and chain of command of all honor issues."[44]

However, as the honor officer himself was an admittedly brazen liar, it can only be assumed that he had been grossly neglectful of or abusing his honor responsibilities for quite some time. Regardless, it is the responsibility of every cadet, honor officer or not, to report alleged honor violations. One of Cadet W's buddies was present during the entire encounter. He was there when Cadet W bragged about how he and his cronies had gotten away with lying on their MFRs. Of course, the buddy chose not to report the flagrant honor-code violation. It would be reasonable to ask how the CS-16 AOC could threaten my brother with a Wing Honor Board for speaking the truth, whereas this Cadet W character could blatantly *admit to lying* and no one touched him, but that would be pointless, since the answer is obvious.

First and foremost, cadets simply do not turn in fellow cadets for honor-code violations unless they have a particular aversion for that cadet, or it is in their own best interest to do so, or both. Second, concerning issues that arise within the squadron, most AOCs across the Academy serve as mere lackeys for first- and second-class cadets, the legitimacy of the issue notwithstanding, so it would be astonishing to see an AOC take sides with a disliked freshman cadet over a first- or second-class cadet no matter what the issue.

Chaz's AOC wasn't concerned with the truth of the matter; he was just fulfilling his culturally imposed duty to support and defend the squadron's cadet leadership. It wasn't that Cadet W's loyal buddy didn't know he should inform the chain of command of any honor violations; he just didn't care. Here we were (my brother and I) the victims of incessant, unpunished harassment by Cadet W, yet as soon as I told him off because his AOC refused to do his job, I got slammed with the most

---

44 *United States Air Force Academy Cadet Honor Code Handbook* (USAFA, CO: United States Air Force Academy, 2003), Directive 2.1.8.1, August 2003, 17.

severe Form 10 possible. If I hadn't known what I did about the Academy at the time, I would have been shocked.

With this new Form 10 came 40 more demerits and confinements, which meant dozens more hours confined to my room. Although I had just completed 120 mind-numbing confinements and was certainly not looking forward to 40 more, I started working them off immediately. Not only did I start working them off right away; I even went about earning more than 120 *merits* by way of community service.

As a member of the USAFA Rodeo Club, I spent two Saturdays in a row helping out in the community. The first weekend I worked on base at the Boys' and Girls' Club carnival walking kids around on horses. The second weekend we traveled to the Pro Rodeo Hall of Fame complex in Colorado Springs in order to assist at the Special Rodeo. My job was to make sure the handicapped kids didn't fall off their horses or in any way hurt themselves while participating. It was a richly awarding experience. After the rodeo, one of the parents came to me with tears in her eyes and told me, "Thank you so much. That's one of the nicest things anyone's ever done for my daughter." Overwhelmed by something that I hadn't been exposed to in a long time—normal human compassion—I couldn't help getting teary-eyed.

The upperclassmen in charge of these two events wrote two separate positive Forms 10, each containing 60 merits for my service. I turned these two Forms 10 in at the same time as Cadet W's Form 10; mysteriously, only the negative Form 10 from Cadet W made it up the chain of command. Refusing to be cheated out of 120 merits, I had the same two upperclassmen write duplicate positive Forms 10 to be turned in for the second time. My element leader, responsible for their initial disappearance, claimed to have lost them while strangely having no trouble at all keeping track of the Cadet W Form 10, even though they were turned in at the exact same time. Considering his role in both the first and second SCRBs as well as the conflict-resolution meeting, I had a really hard time believing his story that "I don't know, I just lost them." Nonetheless, I turned them in again with his personal assurance that they would be processed as soon as possible. They were never processed. Not only were they never processed, later on most people (including my element leader) claimed to have never seen or heard of them, as if they were merely a figment of my imagination. It goes without saying that 120 merits was a rather large number, even *equivalent* to the number of *demerits* I had accumulated over the entire year. Their omission from my personnel file severely affected my standing at the Academy, and for that reason and that reason alone, I'm certain they were purposefully disposed of.

Although getting off probation was grueling, there was more to it than simply paying my debt to the Academy by working off tours and confinements. At that time I was on three different probations: academic, athletic and conduct-aptitude. All three of these, to varying degrees, were a product of my environment more than they were self-imposed. However, now that the Fourth Class System (and the extreme harassment associated with it) was a thing of the past for me, I could improve upon what had deteriorated into mere survival. I could get back into crisis-management mode and just maybe, with the right amount of effort and providence, turn the tide and provide for a brighter future.

Already more than halfway through the semester, I decided to focus on academics more than anything else. I went in for extra instruction almost daily until the end of the summer. A classmate of mine, who wrote a character letter on my behalf for my personnel file, described my effort in the scholastic realm best:

> Cadet Graney and I were in a summer math class together and from day one I could tell that Cadet Graney was a very diligent and hard worker. C3C Graney was not required to take that class, but he decided to take it in lieu of soaring or jump programs which he wanted to participate in a great deal. He knew his fall schedule would be tough, however, he wanted to put himself in the best situation he could to achieve academic success in the fall. This to me shows a lot of dedication because we as cadets already spend a tremendous amount of time on academics during the normal school year. Rarely would Cadet Graney miss going to extra instruction in the afternoon.

This was exactly the case, and because of this degree of effort I managed to bring my GPA up to a 2.12 by the end of the spring semester. This may not sound like much, but remember that the average GPA at the Academy at this time was a 2.3. I took the summer math class in order to position myself for greater academic success in the fall. I had to sacrifice participating in both the parachuting and gliding (flying gliders) courses in order to do so. Why would I choose to take a summer math class instead of parachuting from a plane for a large part of the summer?

Because I was determined to make things work at the Academy, and I knew that it was a necessary sacrifice to ensure myself a better future.

Another order of business was getting off athletic probation. I was not on athletic probation because of a lack of physical fitness on my part. I went on athletic probation just two months after competing on the intercollegiate Division I wrestling team. As I mentioned, I was put on athletic probation because the two times I was administered the PFT (physical fitness test) I was either stricken with illness or a disgruntled trauma victim. The first time I went on athletic probation, it was because I failed the running portion of the PFT by 0.5 seconds while suffering from exposure and flulike symptoms. This was very near that time that I was ordered to run around the terrazzo in a blizzard without proper cold-weather attire. I failed the running portion once again immediately following my Recognition victimization, a time during which my motivation had reached an all-time low—getting physically assaulted does that to a person. Nonetheless, never having had any problem with any other aspect of the PFT, I decided to focus on the run. In fact, I had continually scored higher on the PFT than most cadets *despite* a failing time on the run. Regardless, I established a running program which went into effect immediately. Weeks later, I was one of the first cadets across the finish line during the administration of the aerobic fitness test AFT (1.5-mile run), a sizable accomplishment considering the fact that there were more than 150 cadets running with me.

My greatest barrier to becoming a cadet in good standing was my conduct-aptitude probation. Although surmountable, it was going to take a considerable amount of stick-to-it-ive-ness to adhere to the probation guidelines. While on conduct-aptitude probation I lost all rank, position, and class privileges, so I had no phone, pager, civilian clothing, TV/VCR, or stereo. I had to enroll (once again) in behavioral-leadership counseling. I had to adhere to a whole host of rehabilitation guidelines, such as writing in a probation journal three times a week and monthly counseling with my element leader, flight and squadron commanders, and AOC, the catch to all this being that if I should fail to comply with any one of these regulations or guidelines, I would immediately fail the probation and be recommended for disenrollment. I jumped in headfirst. I wrote in my journal four to five times a week, abstained from the usual upperclassmen privileges, and met with counselors and my squadron chain of command. I volunteered in my new three- degree squadron and was accepted as the

B-2 element clerk responsible for taking accountability at every mandatory formation or meeting. I even completed my monthly counseling while being chased around in the woods during combat survival training (CST). I carried out everything that I had been ordered to do and more, and did it well.

Unfortunately, I did all this under the assumption that I had a legitimate chance to stay at the Academy. What I didn't know was that Major H had already clandestinely submitted paperwork to initiate the MRC process. So he knew all along, even all those times when he told me to just keep working, during our numerous probation counseling sessions, that he had already set in motion the process that would lead to my final dismissal and that I really didn't stand a chance of remaining a cadet at the USAFA.

My present feeling concerning this deceitful behavior on the part of Major H is genuine gratitude, believe it or not. I'm grateful that at a young age I was spitefully and repetitively stabbed in the back, as because of that experience I can now see danger coming from a much greater distance, giving me a better chance to prepare effective countermeasures.

My efforts were in vain, all the tours and confinements I worked off, the volunteer work, the conditioning, the studying, etc., all in vain. Soon after having watched the class of 2006 in-process, having been starved in the woods during CST, having my hat taken off my head, thrown on the ground, and kicked around by Cadet W's entourage during a midsummer altercation, and having triumphantly raised my GPA, MPA, and APA (Athletic Performance Average) to meet Academy standards, I received an e-mail saying I'd been slated for an MRC September 5, 2002. Ironically, it was on or around September 5 that I was scheduled to come off all three probations after almost six months of impeccable performance. I had done everything that could possibly have been asked of me and more, yet right when I started thinking more optimistically about my prospects at the Academy I received this "black spot" e-mail.

At the time of the e-mail, I was already well into my three-degree year, settled into a new squadron, rooming with my brother, and making things work. I was well liked by my new AOC Captain R, my classmates loved me, the four degrees (for whose training I was duly responsible) respected me, and I was only weeks away from becoming a cadet in good standing again. Right when I just about had everything back in order academically, athletically, and militarily, I was told that I would be going before a military review committee. This is why I made the analogy to Sisyphus earlier. I had struggled and strained to push the stone to the top of the hill, only to have some heartless degenerate kick it back down again. It was a huge blow, and it rattled me to the core.

Along with informing me of my imminent MRC, the e-mail also outlined the preparatory measures and provisions I needed to take care of prior to the review. First on the list was to meet with my new AOC, Captain R, in order to obtain a copy of my personnel file. Accordingly, I scheduled a meeting with him and in a matter of a day or two was sitting in his office. This wasn't the first time we had talked; he had conducted monthly probation counseling with me a few weeks earlier.

Our first encounter had been a little rocky because, without knowing anything about me, specifically the way I was treated as a freshman cadet, he initially chastised me for what he saw as an inappropriately negative attitude toward the Fourth Class System. After a heated, yet professional two- to three-hour discussion, he came to understand why I felt the way I did. I remember thinking at the time, *Finally* a man of integrity. Where has this guy been the last couple years? In fact, later on in a telephone conversation with my father, he specifically stated that after hearing about how I was treated as a freshman cadet in CS-17, there was no doubt in his mind why I might have developed a bad attitude toward the USAFA. He even went so far as to brag about my performance within the squadron, saying that it had been nothing short of impeccable, which he felt spoke highly of my character considering the kind of four-degree experience I had chalked up.

Furthermore, as if his understanding of my four-degree situation wasn't shocking enough (responsible leadership was a foreign concept for me at the time), before I left his office he recommended that I at least consider filing charges against my Recognition weekend assailant pursuant to my obligation as a professional military member to report criminal activity. As I listened to Captain R dispense advice, I was momentarily lost in contemplation of what life could have been like as a freshman cadet under the direction of this man as opposed to Major H. Apart from gratuitously contemplating what might have been, I couldn't help musing over the way my former AOC had handled the situation roughly five and a half months earlier.

It pains me to say that a decision to file such charges (an action first suggested by my father, then personally recommended by the Academy's very own inspector general's office, now reintroduced by my new AOC) had escaped me for so long. It wasn't a lack of courage that kept me from filing charges; it was the triumph of experience over expectation. I had no reason to believe that the security forces would do any better job of investigating the assault than had Major H and company months before. It was my unhealthy but well-founded skepticism that stalled the process so long. Nevertheless, I came out of that meeting with Captain R determined to fulfill my legal obligation and file charges against my assailant. In addition to the assault issue, I was tentatively scheduled for another meeting with the captain upon receipt of my personnel file from 34th Training Wing headquarters and ordered to seek legal counsel from the Academy IG concerning my upcoming military review committee.

I started by first ascertaining where exactly the 10th Security Forces were located, then thumbed a ride down there, having absolutely no idea what to expect. When I got there I entered an unobtrusive building marked "10th Security Forces" and found myself in an unwelcoming vestibule with no receptionist to be seen. After a moment of bewilderment, I walked up to an unattended bulletproof window and called out for assistance. A few minutes later an agitated young servicewoman came to the window and said, "What do you want?" I matched her tone. "To file a criminal report, if it's not too much of an inconvenience." After a brief stare-down, she left, then returned with form in hand. She flippantly told me to fill it out, sign it, and give it back to her. Although I wasn't 100 percent certain I was filling out the form correctly, I did the best I could and then submitted it without question in order to avoid any more friction between Ms. I-don't-like-to-do-my-job and me.

Then came the calm before the storm. After a few days of hearing nothing, I received an e-mail containing followup instructions. I set aside my surprise at the fact that they had actually contacted me and read the e-mail. I was instructed to return to 10th Security Forces HQ to complete an interview. Well, the interview turned out to be more like an interrogation, complete with hostile special investigators lurking in the darkness one moment and then hovering over my position the next, a single lamp barely illuminating the barren table at which I sat, provocative questioning and answering, and of course lots of ugly faces. It seemed that I was intentionally being made to feel as if underneath it all *I* was in fact the criminal, and that it was only a matter of time before I would reveal that I had killed Colonel Mustard in the library with the candlestick.

At any rate, these special investigators failed to find holes in my story, so I was promptly, albeit grudgingly, released from what felt like their custody.

The investigators took their sweet time coming to a verdict; so much so that they didn't come to a resolution until after my MRC had long since taken place. They questioned various witnesses who provided little to no redeeming information, mainly, I believe, because they were either basketball teammates of the accused, or suffering from stress-induced memory loss, or had been so institutionalized by the Academy that they argued in their affidavits that I had deserved to be physically assaulted because of my four-degree performance.

One of my classmates made this convenient statement: "My memory from this time frame is a little weak due to the enormous stress and pressure I was going through that came with Recognition."[45] I remember thinking when I read the police report months later that a memory failure of that kind should probably have medically disqualified my classmate from military service, as one day it could just possibly turn out to be slightly hazardous if not actually dangerous during high-stress military engagements in which he would most certainly participate.

Of course, I believe that there was no real memory loss; the only thing he forgot was his moral obligation to tell the truth, and in so doing he protected his teammate.

Another classmate and witness made this statement:

> That push was basically don't like Cadet Graney because he sometimes doesn't know his knowledge and doesn't pay attention on his uniform. Also, I think Cadet Graney doesn't (like) the fourth class roles as well.[46]

Along the same lines one more witness said this about the incident:

---

45 U.S. Air Force, Form 1168, Report of Investigation: SFAR Case Number: I2002090039, SFOI Case Number: 02-016, 25 OCT 2002.

Author's Note: Quote taken from an anonymous witness's affidavit, a personal statement written on an AF Form 1168.

46 Ibid.

> I felt that when I rejoined the group initially C3C Graney was not putting out all he could, therefore C3C Graney did deserve the extra attention he was getting, it also seemed like he may have had an attitude.[47]

Excellent logic, and well said at that. Therefore we can surmise, on the word of these cadets (now professional military officers), that it is morally permissible for our society to allow someone to be brutalized, as long as in the eyes of whoever is doing the brutalizing the victim deserves it. I disagree. Not only do I think my classmates were stunningly wrong in their official opinions, I also believe they have some serious issues to hash out if they are ever to function as responsible members of society.

Even as outrageous as these witness statements were, none was more dynamic than that of my assailant himself. The crux of his argument was that he was in effect *required* to attack me, that by virtue of his call of duty he *had* to do what he did, which happened like this, according to him:

> When Graney came to my station during Crossroads, I randomly picked him out and started to yell at him and tell him to get his chin in and what not. Throughout the [time] he ignored me and had an attitude on his face. So I did other things just to scare him like saying I took out 20 people before him and that his attitude will make him the 21st. It was all done just to scare with no intent to harm. So he came into my station and I had him and other 4 degrees doing pushups. I saw that he was not doing them right and I proceeded to yell at him some more but I got no response and nothing but attitude. Out of anger and frustration I head butted him and after I did I told him to get up. I then brung him over to talk to him and told him that if I showed him the disrespect he showed to me how would he react? He said he would do the same thing and he would be angry. So after he said that, I told him it's all a game, that I am playing a game, he is playing a game, soon it will be done and he can not worry. I gave him some motivational words and he left. I told a fellow cadet to watch out for this 4 degree because he has an attitude.[48]

---

47 Ibid.

48 Ibid.

This statement ranks high on the list of astonishingly stupid statements for two reasons. First of all, in an effort to justify his actions he, in effect, irreparably damaged his own reputation by pointing out that he had absolutely no self-control. He admitted that he could become physically violent at the drop of a hat merely due to the existence or presence of some sort of discomfiting entity (e.g., disagreement, dissatisfaction, frustration on some level—self-imposed or otherwise). He readily admitted that these ill feelings of his had the potential to produce an uncontrollable emotional response with destructive potential. The other reason was that he actually incriminated himself, the operative phrase being, "out of anger and frustration I head butted him."

Apart from directly incriminating himself in my assault and battery, there were other testaments to his guilt as well. Although there existed some disagreement between the three witnesses regarding the circumstances surrounding the incident, all except one (the one who claimed to have no memory of the incident) agreed on the fact that there was indeed physical contact between the assailant, Cadet J, and me. These same witnesses reported individually:

> … During this tirade, Cadet J's head struck Cadet Graney's … and being in Cadet Graney's face, he struck him.… To clarify the punch, it wasn't forceful like rearing back and stepping into a punch, but there was force behind it.… the punch was not like playing around.…

> … a moment later I saw that upperclassman pushed on Cadet Graney's chest, as a result, Cadet Graney leaned backward a little bit.…[49]

In addition to the assailant's own admission of guilt, corroborated by witness and complainant testimony (which is more than enough grounds for conviction in any court of law), there were two different cameras rolling during the assault. Mysteriously, security surveillance footage from the building where the incident occurred as well as a home video made by a CS-17 upperclassman documenting the whole Recognition affair (including the course at which I was assaulted) could not be found, nor could any of the dozens of copies of said video that had been widely distributed to my squadron's freshman class.

---

49 Ibid.

Even more mysterious than the elusive videos was the command decision to close the entire case in spite of a guilty verdict! Although investigators concluded that Cadet J was undoubtedly guilty of "head-butting victim during Recognition training in March 2002" (a violation of Article 128, Uniform Code of Military Justice)[50], someone up the chain of command (whose identity and motive have never been disclosed and remain unknown) decided to close the case. However discreet this unidentified individual, my painstaking analysis of the Academy leadership of the time, its structure and individual responsibilities, command climate, and the personnel who made up such an assemblage led me to believe that it could only have been one man, who carefully maintained a larger-than-life reputation, most assuredly as a result of years of meticulously cultivated interpersonal relationships and ambitious career jockeying—impressively low maintenance with suspiciously high impact, the former commandant of cadets, Academy graduate (Class of '78) General S. Taco Gilbert III.

Nonetheless, before General Gilbert even came into the picture, I was called before a military review committee. As previously stated, in preparation for such an occasion I was instructed by Captain R to seek legal counsel, an order that I promptly followed. Days later I found myself sitting in front of a lawyer whom I regard to this day as one of the most respectable individuals I ever encountered at the Academy, then Captain Mike Freimann. As we discussed my situation, the assault issue naturally came to the forefront of conversation. He genuinely commended me for deciding to report the assault but told me I shouldn't expect much to happen. He went on: "The reason I say that, Dave, is because things like that [physical assault] happen here all the time, and most of the time nothing is ever done about it." I wish I could say I was surprised by this statement.

I took a moment to stare out the window at the freshman cadets running around the terrazzo like madmen, yelling and being yelled at, and for a brief moment I was transfixed by the absurdity of the world in which I was living. When I came back to reality I changed the subject by asking about my upcoming MRC. That's when he told me that although I had been severely wronged by the Academy, if I valued my cadet career, the best course of action while in front of the committee would be

50 Ibid. (Taken from "Synopsis" Section 1-1).

to apologize and take responsibility for each and every Form 10 I had racked up as a freshman cadet, no matter how unjust that seemed to be. He told me that the board viewed any attempt at defending oneself as a lack of remorse, a lack of willingness to take responsibility for one's actions—therefore he said it would be best to just apologize.

Apart from flashing back to the conflict-resolution meeting months before, I remember thinking at the time, *How ironic, how pathetic.* Apologetic guilty cadets having a better chance at being retained than unapologetic innocent ones? Allow me to just say that being told while at the height of my frustration with the Academy's ineptitude that I must now plead for forgiveness, even though I was the injured party, to take responsibility for the injustice I had been served, to swallow my pride, and to ignore my sense of propriety in order to increase my chances of remaining a cadet, all that was almost more than I could take. In fact, it *was* more than I could take, though I wouldn't realize it until halfway through a MRC a few days later that lasted three and a half hours.

Without further ado, we painstakingly crafted a personal statement bent on the dissolution of whatever pride I had left, hashed out the MRC details, talked through some legal jargon, then called it a day. As I was standing up to leave, he stopped me in midsalutation to say, "You know, Dave, I've seen the system here ruin so many great guys who would have been good officers. Whatever happens at your MRC, don't let that slow you down. You're meant to do big things with your life."

I ignored the eeriness surrounding his encouraging words in order to appreciate the message and the messenger. I acknowledged the sound advice, then disappeared from his office.

My MRC was a rout even before it began. According to MRC guidelines, I was to have received my personnel file (officially known as a cadet personnel file or CPF] at least a few days in advance of the MRC, but by the time of my MRC I still had not seen it. Thus, if serious opposition had not been raised to postpone the initial MRC date, I wouldn't have had the chance to review my personnel file at all. Just as experienced drug traffickers, for purposes of self-preservation, change the location for a deal right at the last minute when doing business with an unreliable second party (in the movies at least), I believe Academy administrators sat on my personnel file in order to leave me unprepared going into my MRC. It seemed like just another scene in an ongoing play where once again I fell victim to the carefully orchestrated, Academy-leadership-sponsored Graney reprisal effort that had become so obnoxiously redundant.

Even after postponing my MRC by a few days I was still left with insufficient time to review my file. More unfortunate still, because I'd received my paperwork so late in the game, the three witnesses I asked to testify on my behalf hadn't had the chance to review my file at all. Therefore, these three witnesses came to the MRC having basically no idea what was contained within my personnel file. Although unaware of what felt to me like deliberate exclusion of *120 merits* from my personnel file and the extensive lies written about me therein, I did have a fairly good idea of what to expect from the MRC members. I expected to be hassled, badgered, insulted, degraded, and manipulated. My expectation turned out to be entirely accurate. In fact, I largely *underestimated* the degree and length to which I would be harassed.

Although it wasn't dark or stormy on the day of my MRC, it didn't really have to be; real-life horror stories take place no matter what the weather may be. As I walked across the terrazzo toward the 34th Training Wing headquarters, I let my mind wander. While crossing over the tour pad, I couldn't help letting out a frustrated laugh at the thought of the training-wing commander spying on my comrades and me through her office window as we marched tours months before. Though a momentary stress reliever, this muffled laughter quickly died out as my mind flashed back to my present situation. I knew very well that this would be one of the more antagonizing experiences of my life.

Ascending the stairs leading to the Training Wing floor, I felt that all too familiar preconflict adrenaline rush surging through me. My body was unconsciously going through the natural physiological alteration triggered by the mental recognition of an imminent threat or hostile environment. I didn't know it then, but I would need every ounce of mental and emotional energy I could muster to cope responsibly with the impending barrage.

Upon entering the foyer outside the 34 TRW/CC conference room where the confrontation was to take place, I was greeted by a pleasant young airman who directed me to a seat. I took a seat in the waiting area per instruction and found myself in the company of another beleaguered cadet. The fact that he was fidgeting with nervous anticipation, sporting the Academy service dress uniform, and rather frantically looking around the room like a frightened little schoolchild led me to believe that he had probably just come out of an MRC of his own.

No sooner had I reached this conclusion than I found myself engaged in random dialogue. This cadet wasted no time striking up conversation, asking me, "What are you in here for?" I stared blankly in his direction while I tried to figure out why I wanted to laugh. I realized that we were like two cellmates in prison meeting for the first time. In retrospect, we weren't much better off than criminals; both of us were considered guilty until proven repentant by our respective MRCs. At least those caught up in the American justice system are theoretically considered innocent until proven guilty.

This cadet told me he had been ordered before a MRC because he had purposefully blared his music at the highest possible volume from speakers strategically placed facing out from his dormitory windows during an Academy-wide vigil in honor of a recently deceased cadet. He had done it because he didn't like the guy. I was shocked. It's one thing to dislike somebody; it's another to desecrate the person's memorial service. I couldn't believe it. It was then that I realized there was probably more to Cadet W's comment to my brother, "Graney, if you died, I'd laugh at your funeral," than I had originally thought.

Before I could respond, my character witnesses started to arrive. My friend, religious leader, and mentor, Colonel P, was the first on the scene. He knew firsthand of the mistreatment I had endured throughout the year and had readily accepted the invitation to testify in my defense. We exchanged pleasantries, then sat down. Close behind him was my sophomore squadron cadet commander B, who had provided nothing short of exemplary leadership within the squadron; a cadet for whom I maintained a great deal of respect, as I believe he did for me. He, too, had accepted the call to testify on my behalf without reservation. Moments later my most loyal friend and ally (save my twin brother), Cadet X, entered the building, closely followed by the man I had come to view as my most vindictive and conniving enemy, Major H. Not far behind those two was Captain R, my sophomore squadron AOC and the antithesis of Major H.

Once all parties had assembled, the most awkward silence I've ever experienced settled over the waiting room; especially, it seemed, for Major H and me. One of the last things I had ever said to him had to do with his lack of character, and here we were to do it all over again. There was one break in the silence. All of a sudden the I-have-no-respect-for-the-dead cadet came out of the sentencing part of his MRC with a look on his face of "What just happened to me?" He turned toward me, looked me straight in the eye, and said, "Good luck, watch your backside." I didn't even respond. I just watched him walk away defeated, then exchanged a look of mutual disbelief with Cadet X.

Talking probation came to an end when my former and current, diametrically opposed AOCs were called into the conference room, signaling the start of the MRC. They were first to testify, and boy, did they testify. They emerged forty-five minutes later, both visibly fatigued. Major H shot this strange little smirk in my direction, then quickly scurried out of the building. Captain R, under no obligation to do so, accompanied me to a desk in the adjacent library. He sat and talked with me while each of my three witnesses took a turn testifying before the board. One by one they went in, testified, and left, each trying with encouraging words to disguise the "Thank God that's over, glad I'm not the one on trial" look in their eyes before leaving to go back to business as usual. Since there was so much anti–Cadet-Graney sentiment reverberating through the halls of the Air Force Academy at the time, simply being willing to testify on my behalf, let alone actually do so, was potentially damaging to a person's Academy reputation. My character witnesses, Captain R included, will never know how much I appreciated their willingness to place truth and justice on a higher pedestal than reputation and career advancement and come to my aid in my hour of need.

As the last of my three witnesses made his way toward the exit, it was clearly time for the main event. I steadied my breath, focused my intellectual energies, elevated my sense of awareness, and was walking through the door even before it was fully opened or my name had been called. I reported in and quickly took a seat at the end of a long conference table in a dimly lit room. Placed before me and every board member at that table were a copy of my CPF, my personal statement, and about eighteen character letters written on my behalf by friends and colleagues. This information was at their disposal and would be referenced ad nauseam by the end of our time together.

I was joined at the table by a whole crew of high-profile individuals; most notably the vice commandant of cadets, Colonel Eskridge (who would be leading the charade), Colonel Slavec, who had been a thorn in everyone's side ever since her arrival at the Academy, and representatives from the athletic and academic realms. If I hadn't already experienced two SCRBs, an ARC, and a soft-look MRC, I might have been intimidated; however, I was an old cat when it came to Academy disciplinary boards and their tactics, so I had no trouble performing under the heightened pressure of this hard-look MRC.

The vice commandant (whom I will refer to as the vice comm) was the first to speak. He melodramatically informed me that no portion of the MRC would be recorded. Then, after a short pause, he asked me, "Do you know why you're here?" as if to cut the crap and get right to the point. While I was giving him the most generic answer I could think of—that it was because of an accumulation of 126 demerits—he passionately interrupted me to ask the same exact question.

Before I was able to utter the first two or three words of the same answer to the same question, he cut me off: "No, you're here because everyone in your chain of command thinks you should be kicked out of the Academy. That's why you're here, Cadet Graney."

Not knowing how to respond, I simply muttered, "Okay, sir," to which he replied, "Okay? No, it's not okay, Graney! One hundred twenty-six demerits in less than six months is *not* okay!"

The MRC, barely a minute old, was already turning into a rout. I sat back in my chair, realizing that this was how it was going to be, and although in the back of my mind I was thinking about how much the vice comm could use a good jaw-check, I regrouped and refocused on the original game plan of acquiescence and apologies.

No sooner had I done so than commenced the second parley. Another brass sitting next to the vice comm started into me by asking questions regarding specific Forms 10 that I had received the preceding year. With the persistence of a dog chasing its tail and in what I felt was an unmistakably hateful tone of voice, he questioned me about every documented infraction contained in my CPF, hardly pausing even to hear my response. When they speak of badgering the witness in a court of law, it is this line of questioning that they are talking about. Figuratively speaking, I essentially spent the first hour or so subject to repetitive backhands to the face, slaps on the wrist, and bamboo strikes to the back of my legs.

Even so, I adhered to the original game plan. For the duration of this initial volley I patiently listened to this officer rant and rave, swallowed my pride, and apologized for as much as my self-respect would allow. However, as the onslaught reached its zenith (i.e., the point at which this officer emphatically asked multiple leading or rhetorical questions in a row without even the slightest hesitation between) I drifted away into something of a trauma-induced stupor.

While absent-minded, my thoughts ironically centered on some recent reading material: Plato's *Apology*. I had been sporadically reading from the book *Classics of Moral and Political Theory* for over a year by the time of my MRC, drawing wisdom from wise men's writings all along the way. I couldn't help thinking about the degree to which my own present situation resembled that of Socrates during his infamous trial thousands of years ago. Socrates and I had both been falsely accused by crooked members of disreputable institutions, he by the Athenian Government and I by the U.S. Air Force Academy. Whereas Socrates had been accused of being "a wise man, a student of all things in the sky and below the earth, who makes the worse argument the stronger" and "corrupting the young," I was accused of being that corrupted youth.[51]

Although there were many similarities with respect to the circumstances surrounding our two trials, there was one stark contrast, a blatant dissimilarity that I just could not ignore. Socrates made this statement at the outset of his trial:

> From me you will hear the whole truth, though not, by Zeus, gentlemen, expressed in embroidered and stylized phrases like theirs, but things spoken at random and expressed in the words that come to mind, for I put my trust in the justice of what I say, and let none of you expect anything else. It would not be fitting at my age, as it might be for a young man, to toy with words when I appear before you.[52]

Unlike Socrates, I had spent the entire first hour of my MRC toying with words, not telling the whole truth for fear of being kicked out of the Academy by injudicious MRC board members who would perceive any effort to defend myself as a lack of willingness to take responsibility for my actions. The more I thought about what I was doing, the more ashamed I felt for not having "put my trust in the justice" of what I said as Socrates so eloquently decreed. I realized that I had allowed myself to

---

51 Michael L. Morgan, *Classics of Moral and Political Theory*, 2nd ed. (Indianapolis, IN: Hackett Publishing Company, Inc., 1996), 6, 12.

52 Morgan, *Classics of Moral and Political Theory*, 6.

fear the injustice of several injudicious men and one equally injudicious woman over an even worse consequence; the condemnation by truth to fraudulence. I realized that it was no less wrong for me to *accept* responsibility for that for which I was not responsible than to not accept responsibility for that which I *was* responsible. I realized that either way it was simply unacceptable not to tell these board members the whole truth and nothing but the truth, regardless of their injudiciousness.

At any rate, irrespective of my hopes and dreams for the continuation of my Academy career, I came crashing out of my stupor bound and determined never to embarrass myself that way again. Although the feeling generated by apologizing for my own victimization was overwhelmingly agitating, it wasn't what brought down the apologetic façade; what did that was a newfound moral objection inspired by the writings of one of the greatest moralists and philosophers of all time.

I brought my eyes back into focus, returned my gaze to the brass addressing me, and cut him off to say, "Sir, if you really do want answers to your questions like you claim, you're going to have to show me some respect and allow me the opportunity to respond."

Before he could say a word, the vice comm broke in. "Well, I guess if you were in any way deserving of his respect—"

Switching the focus back to my original nemesis, I countered with, "Insult acknowledged, though you present an interesting notion, sir, to only do right by those whom you feel are deserving of your respect, unless of course I totally missed something."

His response came at once. "Yeah, Graney, you missed something all right, like the fact that when you're in the military you're supposed to follow orders."

I retorted, "Sir, I don't have a problem following orders. My Forms 10 are not the result of insubordination."

He broke in again. "Oh, is that right?"

I took back the floor. "Yeah, that's right, sir."

"Really, you think so?"

"No, sir, I know so."

After an exaggerated pause to allow for the exchange of hateful glances, the vice comm asked, "Well, then, what *is* your problem? You tell me, Graney, what's the *real* reason for your record number of demerits?"

I gathered my thoughts, then laid it down like a man possessed. Without reservation I explained the ulterior motives behind *every* Form

10 I had ever received. I told them about the 120 merits that had been purposefully withheld from my CPF. I spoke of confidential meetings turned public, fraternization, hazing, verbal abuse, manipulation, fraudulence, dereliction of duty, physical violence, and emotional instability; all the variables that factored into the equation. I made no excuses for anyone's behavior (including my own, for I was hardly the perfect cadet) and just said it how it was.

Without skipping a beat I transitioned from this "like it or not" dissertation concerning the illegitimacy of my Forms 10 to an impressive character defense, as I knew their only response would be to attack my credibility and question my integrity. Therefore, I maintained the initiative by addressing the issue before opportunity met desire. I started by telling them that I had never lied about anything *in my entire life*, including my tenure at the USAFA, that there was actually more reason to believe *my* side of the story than that of the vindictive, fraternizing, hazing, verbally abusive, manipulative, verifiably dishonest, professionally deviant, physically violent, and emotionally unstable upperclassmen from whom the negative documentation in my CPF originated.

My defense employed both altruistic persuasion and empirical evidence. With an air of attorneyship I presented my case in keeping with the deny-deny-counter-accuse-blame argument style. I appropriately denied allegation after allegation regarding my character, then methodically exposed both the inaccuracies behind the accusations and their disreputable sources, sparing none along the way.

My first target was the upperclassman who made sure to make his mark on my CPF more than once, saying things like, "Cadet Graney is the worst fourth-class cadet in the entire Cadet Wing." He also happened to be the cadet my roommate and I had discovered fraternizing with two of our female classmates. I explained to the board that while this cadet had *that* to say about me, another cadet (now an Army Ranger captain and two-time Iraq War veteran) had this to say about me: "If I were ever in battle, Cadet Graney is the individual I would want next to me."[53]

I quoted the cadet who I believe deceitfully withheld 120 merits from my CPF: "He (C4C Graney) has not demonstrated any leadership potential or capacity."[54] Although an opinion like any other, it was the

53 United States Air Force Academy Cadet Personnel File: David W. Graney.

54 Ibid.

opinion of someone I considered an underhanded cadet, and who could not have been more antithetical to the view of a demonstratively ingenuous cadet (now Air Force instructor pilot) who believed otherwise and expressed as much:

> David is a bright young man who understands things at a higher level. He is an outstanding person, and an individual for whom I have the highest respect. He has many qualities that will make him an *excellent leader and officer*. He has perhaps the best military bearing of anyone that I have ever met. [55]

My analysis continued relatively unabated until I had effectively brought into disrepute nearly every cadet responsible for the negative commentary found in my CPF, as well as providing rebuttal testimony concerning each and every character objection that had ever been raised about me. I pulled out all the stops and brought everything to the table. Mention was made of steroids, squadron leadership nearly drinking themselves to death, the shower course, the use of mind-altering medicinal concoctions, alcohol abuse, training infractions, sexual harassment, flight commanders who were responsible for my performance evaluations being kicked out of the Academy for honor-code violations, and of course physical assault.

The only man left unscathed preceding the finale to my verbal sonata was Major H, to whom I dedicated the closing movement. I knew quite well what the nature of his MRC testimony would be and that, despite what I viewed as his irresponsible leadership (even prejudicial to good order and discipline), he would likely be the prosecution's favorite witness. So I planned accordingly and saved my discussion of Major H for the end.

Stirring with energy, I introduced my former commanding officer into the picture and "threw it down," as they say, as never before. When the storm clouds parted I had figuratively, albeit categorically, nailed Major H to the wall. I believe I left no room for any *reasonable* doubt concerning the reality of what I viewed as his personal vendetta or his avid participation in what was turning out to be the effort toward my constructive removal from the Academy, the end product of well-coordi-

---

55 Ibid.

nated abuse and neglect spanning my entire freshman year. If I had been a character in a film at the time, moviegoers would have been proud of me, and there might even have been some sort of favorable outcome that might have left a better taste for dispassionate heroism in their mouths than the butter from their theatre popcorn. But Hollywood is to reality as oil is to water.

That being said, the reaction from the MRC board members was far from favorable. Their foregone conclusion, i.e., guilty verdict, easily *predating* the week of my MRC only gained that much more support, in that members of the board were not only disenchanted by my honest defense but *insulted* by it. Angered over having been forced to show even the slightest degree of respect, a fray the likes of which I had never seen before broke out immediately following the conclusion of my remarks.

They denied the reality of my assault, stating that my former commanding officer had claimed that it never happened. Apparently, contrary to what he claimed in conversations with both my father and me, Major H told the MRC that he *had* been present during the alleged assault, but that this supposed assault simply never happened! They told me I hadn't been treated *any differently* from any other four degree, and that instead of being mature and taking responsibility for my actions, I was essentially trying to blame my poor performance on everyone else, that I was trying to draw pity by creating an illusion of victimization to disguise my horribly deficient four-degree performance.

In the heat of the moment, one of the board members told me straight up (probably in much the same way she had spoken to underclassmen when *she herself was a cadet* at the Academy), "You don't belong here, Graney. Leave." When the fog lifted, I was instructed to exit left, the idea being to allow the committee time to deliberate and then determine my fate. There must not have been much deliberation, in that it seemed as though no sooner had I walked out of the hearing room than I was walking back in. These board members came to their decision faster than a Dick Wolf *Law and Order* jury coming back from a commercial break. I reported back into the room only to hear,

> Cadet Graney, it is the recommendation of this board that you be immediately dismissed from the Academy. Please excuse yourself. Meeting's over.

Rejecting the urge to karate-chop the smirk off the vice comm's face, I instead managed to salute him, turn around, and walk out; musing silently as I went. Such was the end of my MRC: an irresponsible foregone conclusion disguised as the reputable dispensation of justice.

I quickly exited the building then made my way out into the night. While crossing the relatively abandoned terrazzo I slipped into a deep trance that left me completely insensitive to my surroundings. In the midst of my distress I could not help thinking, *So this is how the story ends?* I felt like I had hit rock bottom. I was emotionally battered and broken, though despite my ailing heart, deep down inside I actually felt stronger in a way. I puzzled over this encouraging sentiment for quite some time until I finally realized I had known all along what I was feeling.

Isaac Newton taught the world that for every action, there is an equal and opposite reaction. I believe it is much the same with respect to human behavior and emotion. It is my opinion that for every action we take in our lives there is an equal and opposite psychological reaction or response, that there are inherent emotional consequences to every human behavior. That being said, the feeling I experienced walking away from my MRC was deep and abiding personal satisfaction, the natural result of proper conduct and honest living. Notwithstanding the firestorm from which I was still recovering, I felt relatively hale and hearty. Reminiscing about some of the things I had said at the MRC, I turned my thoughts once again toward Socrates, my affinity for the man becoming that much stronger as I repeated in my mind his last words in the Athenian courtroom. Socrates responded to his death sentence with these wise words:

> Perhaps you think that I was convicted for lack of such words as might have convinced you, if I thought I should say or do all I could to avoid my sentence. Far from it. I was convicted because I lacked not the words but boldness and shamelessness and the willingness to say to you what you would most gladly have heard from me, lamentations and tears and my saying and doing many things that I say are unworthy of me but that you are accustomed to hear from others. I did not think then that the danger I ran should make me do anything mean, nor do I now regret the nature of my defense. I would much rather die after this kind of defense than live after making the other kind.[56]

56 Morgan, *Classics of Moral and Political Theory*, 19.

"I would much rather die after this kind of defense than live after making the other kind." What an amazing display of moral courage and ethical rigidity. Although I'm not writing a treatise on ancient philosophers or their philosophies, it is my opinion that Socrates must have known that he had been convicted before ever stepping into the Athenian court of law. I believe if there were any uncertainty in Socrates' mind concerning his fate, it lay only with the type of punishment he would be dealt. Nonetheless, irrespective of any insightful premonition Socrates may have had, he admirably refused to deviate from the truth, regardless of the consequence. I had a similar mindset once I came to my senses during what amounted to my *own* trial. Afterward, I was much more content having jeopardized my Academy future by telling the MRC the truth than to have facilitated a better chance at retention by making a defense of the "other kind."

I made it back to my room on autopilot. My brother and roommate Chaz awaited my arrival. After a stiff gesture or two he was able to break the thinking spell that had come over me, and the debriefing began. We talked late into the night, the unsettling notion that my days were numbered looming over us all the while. Following a long pause in conversation we both fell asleep in a state of unrest, jaded beyond any previous benchmark of our Academy careers.

A few hours later I woke up to life after the fall, a time in which I experienced nearly the full range of human emotion. During this post-MRC era I felt everything from the blissful sensation of flying my own aircraft to the bitter frustration of having a research paper passionately thrown in my face by a belligerent history instructor. Violent disrespect, flagrant dishonesty, and sensational absurdity—all seasoned with a strange taste of comedy—would define my last days at the Academy.

I appealed the MRC decision, thus sending the case to the brigadier general commandant of cadets, the idea being that he, in all his wisdom, would thoroughly review the matter then make an objective, sovereign judgment. His executive responsibility was to either concur with the MRC decision, thereby sending the case to the superintendent (upon further appeal, of course), or to stop the bleeding and overturn the MRC decision, effectively retaining me at the Academy.

I requested a meeting with the commandant, only to be told by the person on the other end of the line, "The commandant doesn't meet with individual cadets." I asked again, albeit much more passionately, and to my surprise my request was granted. Shaking off the astonishment, I went to work preparing for our meeting. Over the next couple of weeks I formulated talking points, presented evidence to and obtained an officially signed document from the Academy inspector general's office stating that Major H had made a "purposefully inaccurate statement" (most people call it lying) on three separate occasions, then once again sought the advice of my legal counselor.

Going into the meeting with the commandant, my defense argument was rock solid. In addition to superior research and development, I had grown and matured under fire and forged my delivery and powers of persuasion in the foundry of hatred that had been my recent MRC. I went into the general's office on the day of our appointment ready for anything. Following a brief introduction, I spent approximately forty-five minutes straight explaining the debauchery that was my Fourth Class experience. It was a clearcut, to-the-point, no-nonsense analysis of my Academy career—engineered to sway even the most ardent adversary.

After I finished, he sat up in his chair and said, "Mr. Graney, you present a compelling argument. Tell me more about this assault." This was a good sign. Usually by the time I reached the conclusion of my remarks, someone wanted my head on a platter. Therefore, feeling as though I might actually be getting through to him, I described in great detail both the assault itself as well as the Air Force Academy's unseemly response.

Then came the kiss of death. The general leaned back in his chair, cocked his head to the side, and with a dash of Don Corleone he said,

> Cadet Graney, I believe you. This institution has not treated you fairly. However, I will of course have to hear the other side of the story; but let me promise you this. I will not make a decision on your case until the security forces investigation has been completed and I've had a chance to review the findings.

I was ecstatic. Hearing this gave me long-forsaken hope for my Academy career. I heard this and "sighed deeply in my spirit," as the Apostle Mark wrote. I would have sworn at the time that I had just gained an ally who was legitimately concerned with my welfare—and I would have been wrong! The *next day* this general's avowed consternation regarding my state of affairs proved to have been nothing short of full-blown lip service, sick entertainment for the panelists on my recent MRC if they could only have been there. The following day, General Gilbert delegated the appellate decision to his second in command and then left for two weeks on TDY (Temporary Duty Yonder).

His second in command just happened to be vice comm, the ranking officer on my MRC, the one who had made the decision I was now appealing. It was the essence of injudiciousness, analogous, for instance, to a superior court's relinquishing its appellate jurisdiction to an inferior court and instructing the court that issued the original decision to make the appellate decision as well, on behalf of the appellate court! The general's intention behind sponsoring such blatant injustice is a matter of speculation, though irrespective of his intentions, it could go without saying that I ended up on the losing end of that deal.

Gilbert's second in command simply concurred with his own decision (theoretically on behalf of the general), then sent the case to the Academy superintendent and Academy Board (now called Senior Executive Board), entrusting them as the final decision-making authority. Later the vice comm claimed he had excused himself from making the decision; however, as John Grady Cole in Cormac McCarthy's novel *All the Pretty Horses* would say, "There ain't but one truth. The truth is what happened, it ain't what come out of somebody's mouth." The truth is not what came out of vice comm's mouth; the truth is what really happened.[57]

I felt so betrayed. The man told me straight to my face exactly what he thought I wanted to hear, then effectively stabbed me in the back. Yet even with my Academy career once again hanging in the balance and feeling more and more desperate as the days passed with no word from the superintendent's office, I managed to keep up with my responsibilities—going to every class period and military formation, studying hard, and doing well academically and militarily. So much so, in fact, that my legal counselor, a public defender of sorts, felt inclined to write a letter to the superintendent on my behalf, stating:

> C3C Graney went five months while on probation without receiving a Form 10. He worked off 160 confinements while successfully improving his grades. He volunteers as an element clerk during which time he takes accountability at every mandatory formation and event. Finally,

57 Cormac McCarthy, *All the Pretty Horses*, Volume One of *The Border Trilogy* (New York: Alfred A. Knopf, Inc., 1992), 168.

> C3C Graney has helped out with numerous community service projects. This is a cadet who has the potential to be a great officer in the military.[58]

He also stated his feeling that if in the unfortunate event I were to be out-processed from the Academy, I deserved nothing worse than a "three" reenlistment/future commissionability rating. Future commissionability ratings range from one to five: one being reserved for excellent officer candidates (cadets) who, if they were to chose to return to military service, should be welcomed back with open arms; five being reserved for those officer candidates who should never be allowed back into the military under any circumstance, neither in the officer corps nor enlisted ranks. The MRC tacked on a "five" future commissionability rating to their recommendation for disenrollment, and the commandant (or actually his second in command) of course concurred. My legal counselor considered it a huge injustice to both expel me *and* give me a future commissionability rating that would prevent my ever serving in the military in any capacity. I think he believed he had been a real-time witness to a great injustice and therefore had to say something.

As I mentioned earlier, this time period was not all bad, just mostly bad. Guessing my days were limited at the Academy, and wanting to have some sort of memorable experience, an experience I would *actually want* to remember, I shifted some classes around to make room in my schedule for the Academy's glider program. Within a couple days of signing up I found myself down at the Academy airfield learning to fly and loving every minute of it. Twice a week I was at the airfield flying around in gliders, until the program was suddenly shut down.

The story I heard was that a cadet flying one of the Academy's stunt gliders had a wing fall off in midflight. While his aircraft was falling out of the sky, he had supposedly broken through the canopy, jumped out, and pulled his chute. Not too long after the incident, the lieutenant colonel who commanded the Academy's glider squadron was reassigned. Apparently the superintendent had lost confidence in his leadership, for he had to watch the entire fleet of Academy aircraft be taken out of service, grounded indefinitely due to safety concerns.

I guess sometimes it takes bad leadership to recognize bad leadership.

---

58 Captain Mike Freimann, letter to Lieutenant General John Dallager, 22 Oct. 2002.

My feeling at the time was simply, "Well, it was good while it lasted. At least *my* wing didn't fall off." They hadn't given our class parachutes.

That was a very stressful time for me. Sophomore coursework at the Academy is notorious for its difficulty, yet there I was studying hard, dealing with Academy administrators trying to kick me out, and I didn't even know if I was going to be around long enough to secure the academic credits for which I had been working so diligently. Add to that another random throw-down in a dormitory hallway because of a belligerent staff sergeant who understood that I was aware of his sexual exploits with one of the female cadets in his squadron. Add to that a history teacher who decided it was somehow necessary to break every rule of academic professionalism and attempt to publicly embarrass me by announcing to the entire class my below-average grade on a research paper, a paper I had written while trying to prepare myself for a meeting with the brigadier general commandant of cadets. Then, as if that weren't enough, the same teacher threw that paper in my face. Capping it all off was a completed security-forces investigation no one seemed to care about.

I felt as though my life was spiraling out of control; that I was inevitably going to lose that which I had worked so hard to obtain—the opportunity to graduate from the United States Air Force Academy, receive a commission, and go on to pursue a lifelong dream of flying military aircraft. I felt as though every second was precious, in that before too long I would have to say goodbye to both my brother and some of the best friends I had ever known, our relationships born of conflict and tried and tested in the worst of circumstances.

While one is a cadet at the Academy it's hard to imagine any other life. Life on the outside becomes something of an illusion. I think cadets almost forget what it was like to be a part of the normal world, and because of this, the idea of being thrown back out there always stirs a great deal of emotion. My last days at the Academy were spent in a state of uneasiness, with overwhelming apprehension, bitterness, and anger my constant companions.

Having gone two weeks without hearing anything from the superintendent's office, I sent a quick e-mail to the point of contact provided me requesting an update. This POC explained that we were all waiting for the Academy Board, which only met once a week, to convene, review my case, and then make that final decision I had been dreading for so long. Up to that point I had never heard of the Academy Board. Apparently (from what I was told by the POC) it was the Academy Board, not the superintendent, that made the final determination in cases involving upperclass cadets.

I battled through another week, supposedly waiting for the Academy Board to convene the week after, only to be notified by e-mail that the superintendent had sidestepped the board and made the decision himself. So, after I had waited three weeks for my appeal to go before the Academy Board, my case file ultimately never reached a conference table. The superintendent broke protocol, stole the Academy Board's thunder, and expelled me from the United States Air Force Academy.

Although shocking, there was nothing surprising about it. I would have had to be stupid in the extreme to have been surprised by either the general's assumption of power (completely uncalled for) or his ignorant decision to kick me out. The shock came with the understanding that everything I had gone through as a freshman cadet was now null and void, completely worthless in the truest sense of the word. I understood very well that other universities and future employers were not going to award me experiential credit or better pay for having been hazed for a year of my life at a service academy. The pain and frustration a person goes through as a freshman at the Academy means something only if that person stays and graduates from the Academy; otherwise it's just a story to tell to your civilian friends back home who can't help wondering what the hell happened to the guy they used to know.

Add to that the fact that finals were not even three weeks away, and because of my pending departure from the Academy I was going to lose more than twenty credit hours of college coursework for which I had expended considerable time and energy. With all hope dashed, I sank into a state of total despondency; a response in direct conflict with the belief of many of my accusers that I had never really wanted to be at the Academy at all.

This was the end game of my Academy experience. I think many people love to see a strong man stumble, and the amount of sadistic pleasure my expulsion must have brought to the hearts and minds of my enemies at the Academy was likely beyond measure; I believe I saw it in their eyes. Then again, dozens of friends and colleagues who felt quite differently came to pay their respects. They came to me, some a little emotional, to spend some quality time around a guy with whom they had undergone so much hardship. They wanted to see me one last time, and I them, before fading into memory. We all joked and broke out in the same stress-induced, therapeutic laughter that had eased our burden going all the way back to BCT I/II, sitting in our tents in Jack's Valley. In the end, though, the joviality dissipated, silence ensued, and the serious faces came out; we exchanged heartfelt pleasantries, and they left.

Out-processing from the Academy was a travesty. There was a laundry list of places around campus at which I had to either turn this in or sign that. One of these places was none other than the kingdom of chaos wherein stood the colossus of cloudy ideology—the Cadet Counseling Center. I returned to this old stomping ground in order to be psychologically evaluated. My standard out-processing evaluation turned out to be nothing more than another absurd, relatively one-sided conversation about the utility of the Academy training system drenched in condescension. The only difference was that by this time I couldn't have cared less if I tried, and I made that fact abundantly clear.

When asked, "How do you feel about being expelled from the Academy?" I merely quoted from the latest movie I had seen: "The Academy's more dead to me than my dead mother."

Wiping the amusement off his face, my questioner asked, "Well, do you have violent thoughts? You know, I mean like when you see people here that were mean to you, do you want to hurt them?"

Staring in amazement, I responded facetiously, "Well, to be honest with you, I have that feeling right now because of the way you're speaking to me. But no, I mean, apart from wanting to get up on the staff tower with a high-powered hunting rifle, no, I don't have any of those thoughts."

He immediately told me I'd better take the meeting seriously or else, and I cut in to say, "Or else what? You'll give me a Form 10? Or maybe you'll write something career-jeopardizing in my personnel file? News flash! We're past that stage. None of this matters any more. Write whatever it is you're going to write, and sign the paper so I can leave." Miraculously, he did just that.

Other aspects of out-processing weren't quite so obnoxious; some were even mildly humorous. On my last full day at the Academy, before boarding an airplane for home, I attended an AFA football game. I went not for General Deberry, but for the Gipper. I wanted to watch Notre Dame play football. Before every home football game AFA cadets are required to march onto the field as a show of support, an unavoidable mandatory formation if you're part of the Cadet Wing. Not being a part of the Cadet Wing any more, I said hello to all my friends in formation before the game, then proceeded toward the entrance to the stadium. One of the seniors in my squadron, fanatical about everything unimportant in life, chased me down and asked where I thought I was going. He obviously wanted me to be scared of his authority and jump back in line with the rest of the squadron, but because I was no longer a cadet I had nothing to fear and everything to gain, so I simply told him where I was going and where he could go.

He turned it into a huge standoff in front of the entire squadron, emphatically screaming at me to get in formation while I continued to refuse. I could have told him I was no longer a cadet, but that wouldn't have been as much fun, either for me or for my friends in the squadron whom this guy made a point of terrorizing along with me. The threats started to come: "Graney, get back in formation, or I'll have a Class D Form 10 nailed to your forehead before the game's even over. I might just kick your sorry *** along with it." I made fun of the movie *Top Gun* whenever the opportunity arouse, so I stepped into him and said, as much like Tom Cruise as I could possibly muster, "You know what? You're dangerous. Dangerous and foolish, and besides taking the shot when I am good and ready, I don't give a **** about you *or* your Forms 10!"

His demeanor became quite serious as he contemplated passing up watching Notre Dame play football and considering the severity of the multiple Forms 10 he was going to write alone in his bedroom, then he said, "Oh, is that right?"

Trying to contain my smile, I replied, "Yeah, that's right, tough guy. In fact, I want you to write me as many Forms 10 as you think your little pencil neck can handle, I want the book thrown at me. To tell you the truth, I'd eat Forms 10 for dinner right now if I had some, I want them that bad." I turned and winked at some friends while he started into me again, then left him there screaming and went to watch some football.

That night, having returned to the squadron, I was listening to my friend's postgame report (he's now a Texas high-school football coach) at the squadron CQ desk when along came a fellow three degree with a paper in hand. Without waiting for a break in conversation, he insisted that I sign the Form 10 and return it to the cadet with whom I had had the disagreement earlier that evening. I took the document and, without reading it, much less signing and returning it, I crumpled it and ate it. I chewed on it a couple times, then spit it out into the trash.

The messenger just about had a heart attack. In desperation he asked me, "What am I going to do now? What do I tell him?"

Looking him in the eye, I said, "Tell him I ate it." And that's exactly what he did. A few minutes later he returned with two pieces of paper in hand, both Forms 10: one to replace the original I had eaten and the other for having done so. Ignoring additional word-of-messenger threats to my nonexistent future at the Academy, I took both Forms 10, shredded them into little pieces, and then with festive jubilee threw them up in the air. I thanked him for providing the confetti for my going-away party, then told him to go away and not come back again.

He ran back to his boss who, on hearing the news, burst out of his room, ran over, and laid into me. After a few colorful sentences my friend informed him that I was no longer a cadet and that he might better spend his time harassing someone who might actually care. I wish I could have taken a picture of that cadet's face at the time. I would have kept the picture for use during life's saddest moments. The best part for me was watching him struggle to find another leg to stand on, for his entire game was built around threatening people with the power of the Form 10. Needless to say, it was entertaining to see him abruptly give up the fight and walk back to his room, evidently wildly frustrated and probably feeling more ignorant than he had in a long time.

My brother and I spent our last evening together strumming on the guitar and talking about life on the outside. The next morning I loaded my belongings into my sponsor family's car and drove to the Colorado Springs airport with my two brothers Chaz and Cadet X (the latter of course from another mother). I said goodbye to these guys, waved as they drove away, and turned my back on the only life I had known for the last year and a half. My time at the Academy had come to an end.

Few times in my life have I felt as alone and restless as I did sitting there in the Colorado Springs airport. Like Gary Allen, I watched airplanes take off and fly away as my entire Academy career spread across my mind. I thought of the old adage, "Fool me once, shame on you. Fool me twice, shame on me." I felt embarrassed to have allowed myself to think, while entirely cognizant of a wealth of evidence to the contrary, that my leadership at the Academy might have possessed the moral constitution to ultimately do the right thing.

Being out of aces, I had really had no options other than to merely hope for the best. Even so, I thought I should never have expected Major H to be able to appropriately handle an assault case. I should never have even remotely considered the unconscientious and wildly prejudiced twenty- and twenty-one-year-old cadets on the SCRB capable of coming to the right decision regarding my future at the Academy. I should never have presumed that Major H's next-door neighbor, BBQ buddy, and second group commander would be able or willing to see through the bull-**** that was my four-degree experience and not specifically engineer and mandate a probationary status fully equipped with a stipulation predisposed to usher in my demise.

I should never have expected fair treatment from MRC members, much less an honorable verdict. Nor should I have taken the commandant of cadets at his word when he told me that he would look into my case and not make a decision either way until the security-forces investigation was completed. And finally, I should never have counted on the three-star general and Academy superintendent to use those powers of discernment allegedly possessed by all such high-ranking military brass to stop the railroading job before it could carry me past the city limits. So many life lessons in so little time.

10

Vindication

"A man can be destroyed, but not defeated."
—Ernest Hemingway, *The Old Man and the Sea*[59]

It's amazing what people remember from their childhood. I read *The Old Man and the Sea* before entering the fifth grade, and although that was years ago, Hemingway's message weighs just as heavily on my mind today as ever. There are many ways of measuring defeat, though it would seem the only measure that counts is that utilized by the man himself—the measure of the man. Although a man may be destroyed in any number of ways, defeat is the product only of self-abandonment. Although the Academy had chewed me up and spat me out, I was nowhere near defeated. As far as I was concerned, it was merely a life lesson in rolling with the punches. I have never been the type to say uncle, surrender, and bow out. It's simply not in my disposition. I will fight the good fight and leave the rest in the hands of what powers may be. My post-Academy foray was no exception.

Almost as soon as I set foot on the plane that flew me back to Seattle, I was considering options and planning my next move. My parents and I had already been in communication with Senator Patty Murray's office; therefore, I thought, what better place to start? My parents had sent a letter to Senator Murray long before I was dismissed from the Academy. Their concerns at the time centered on the hazing to which both my brother and I had been subjected and the inaction of Air Force adminis-

59 Ernest Hemingway, *The Old Man and the Sea* (London: Granada, 1981), 89.

trators in dealing with criminal activity at the Academy—specifically my own criminal victimization. In their letter, they wrote,

> Because of the lack of interest and/or progress we perceive from the USAFA concerning this assault on our son, we would like to request the assistance of your office in investigating and adjudicating David's situation.[60]

My parents' perceptions were indeed correct, in that not only had the Air Force authorities failed to move on my case, they had already thrown it out! We wouldn't find out until months later that the Academy had never done *anything* about the assault. The matter was investigated, it was determined that my assailant had in fact intentionally head-butted and punched me, and then without further explanation the case was dismissed.

Not long after my return, I found myself seated before Senator Murray's military legislative assistant Muriel Gibson, who after hearing but a fraction of my experience at the Academy told me she felt wholly justified in having submitted a congressional inquiry on the matter to the DOD Inspector General's office months before. She had done so in response to my parents' Sept. 25, 2002, letter to her, which, in and of itself, was apparently enough to initiate a preliminary DOD IG whistleblower reprisal investigation.

We didn't stop there. E-mails were sent to U.S. Senator Allard's office in Colorado, and contact was established with various news media. In time I met with Ed Offley, a senior editor from *Defense Watch*, and spoke with a special-projects reporter from *The Denver Post*. Articles were later written and published concerning my experience at the Academy, and although we branched out to political leaders and the news media, we also continued to try to reason with the Academy administration. The problem, of course, was that Academy administrators were far from reasonable.

On November 3, 2002, my parents sent a letter to the superintendent of the Air Force Academy, then Lieutenant General John R. Dallager. It was both the culmination of a great deal of personal research on the part of my father and overwhelming frustration with delinquent Academy

60 William and Linda Graney, letter to Senator Patty Murray, Sept 25, 2002.

leadership as a result. The Academy bureaucracy was never very good to my dad (to put it nicely), often lying to him, insulting his intelligence, and even impeding his efforts to connect the dots surrounding my nightmarish AFA experience. This uncompromising belligerence on the part of Academy leadership contaminated almost every interaction my father ever had with the USAFA. However, two encounters specifically showcased the rigidity of the Academy administration's unprofessionalism better than the rest.

One of these encounters involved the Academy personnel responsible for processing Freedom of Information Act (FOIA) requests. In order to get a clearer picture of the official rationale behind my expulsion, my father insisted, by way of multiple FOIA requests, that any and all information and documentation having to do with the decision to remove me from the institution be released to him for review. Academy FOIA personnel did little more than lie to him, delay him, and insult him before finally processing the first request.

When a citizen of the United States of America files an FOIA request to a government agency, that agency is required by law to provide the information, assuming the information is releasable, i.e., nonsensitive or declassified, within twenty days of the date of request. Academy FOIA personnel initially told my father that they were under no obligation to provide the requested information, wanted to charge him thirty cents a page, and could not verifiably know when they would be able to get around to it. My father had to explain to them that they were indeed obligated by law, even the FOIA itself, to provide the requested information at no cost to him and within twenty days. Even so, none of the three FOIA requests my father submitted to the Academy was processed within the twenty-day deadline. As a matter of fact, the Academy took nearly *three months* to respond to one of those FOIA requests. When my father expressed his dissatisfaction with their careless disregard for their legal obligation to respond within the time period required by law, one of the Academy's FOIA workers became quite upset and sent an angry e-mail intended for her coworkers *to my dad* saying, "I mean seriously, who does this guy think he is?!"

The USAFA FOIA-request personnel weren't the only disturbance in the force. Near the beginning of my third-class year, my parents (who had, for some time, been respectfully prodding an inattentive and unresponsive Major H to fulfill his command responsibility and properly deal with the matter of Cadet J's assault and battery on me) decided to file a complaint with the AFA inspector general. It was this complaint that led to a personal recommendation from the AFA IG that I report the assault to the 10th Security Forces, a recommendation introduced by my father and reintroduced by Captain R, my CS-11 AOC. After hearing of this official complaint lodged with the AFA IG, my father received a phone call from a Major J, who introduced himself as the deputy to the commandant of cadets, General Gilbert. Major J went on to tell my father, a thirteen-year Army combat engineering officer (of which Major J was aware), that the questions and concerns he presented to the AFA IG could have been better handled if my father had only understood and followed the chain of command. He followed up by criticizing my dad for not having first contacted my freshman squadron AOC, Major H.

Not only did this Major J have an unclear picture of the situation, he also had, in my opinion, missed out on a great deal of intellectual development somewhere down the line. For an officer to think it necessary to explain the chain of command to a man with thirteen years' military service is bone stupid, and no less insulting. Furthermore, as a civilian, my father was not required to adhere to the Air Force Academy chain of command. Civilians have the right to complain to or about whomever they please, *including the man who outranks the entire military establishment*—the commander-in-chief, the president of the United States.

After having this reality explained to him by my father, Major J became agitated and did what many people do when proven wrong: he pointed fingers. He pointed his finger, figuratively, at my and my brother's behavior, saying, "Mr. Graney, do you know about all the bad things your sons have done?" My dad responded confidently, "How about you elaborate." Major J went on to say that according to the records, Charlie (my brother) had failed to take his coat off quickly enough when he was instructed to do so in Mitchell Hall, on the day he was pushed and shoved around by three freshman squadron upperclassmen. He then accused *me* of assault, in that I had knocked a cadet on his back during Recognition training, when, as instructed, I hit the hand-held football body bag the cadet was holding. Then came one of the most ironically preposterous statements I've ever heard: "The Air Force Academy just can't tolerate this type of behavior, Mr. Graney, because people can get hurt."

I think this man had a loose wingnut somewhere upstairs. "Charlie didn't take his coat off fast enough." Was he serious? Had he really said that? Had he actually told my father that my brother's alleged tardiness in taking his jacket off was one of those "bad things" my brother and I had done at the Academy? Was he truly accusing me of assault? Was he, in reality, saying that my hitting the football body bag like the six-year veteran football player I was constituted one of the "bad things" I had done? Yes. That's what he was saying, and my father couldn't help cringing. It was myriad frustrating interactions like this that led my father to submit the formal complaint to General Dallager.

The November 3 letter addressed approximately twenty-two issues of abuse, crime, and dereliction of duty at the USAFA (basically all the same issues discussed in this work). The letter was compelling enough, because of the truth behind the allegations, to spur what then Lt General Dallager called a "fact-finding inquiry" into the matter, to be carried out by the AFA inspector general's office. A few months later, we received the results of the inquiry attached to a letter from Dallager dated March 3, 2003. In the letter, Dallager explained that thirteen of the twenty-two allegations had been either "substantiated" or "partially substantiated," and that command action had been taken to correct the problems. Although "command action" sounds convincing, Academy leadership did nothing more to correct the issues my parents presented in their letter of November 3, 2002, than they did to remedy the correlative sexual assault problem, which by this time had been festering at the Academy for over a decade.

USAFA Sexual Assault 1993-2003

[Sexual assault] is a problem at the USAFA which threatens the foundations of the institution. Female cadets may be at high risk for physical or sexual abuse because of the institutional culture at USAFA which has not addressed the existence or severity of the problem. Cadets who have been sexually or physically assaulted are at high risk for further damage because of this culture as well as the lack of coherent institutional measures to address the problem...."[61] (Extract from a four-page point paper submitted by a USAF investigator to the USAFA by then AF Chief of Staff Gen. Ronald R. Fogleman, spring of 1996)

61 Department of Defense, Inspector General, "Evaluation of Sexual Assault, Reprisal, and Related Leadership Challenges at the United States Air Force Academy, Report No. IP02004C003" (Arlington, VA: Inspector General, Department of Defense, 2004), 95.

Women were first admitted to the Academy in 1976, and ever since then sexual harassment has been an accepted reality at the institution. Year after year, Government Accountability Office (GAO) reports have shown that the vast majority of female cadets are sexually harassed on a continual basis while at the Academy. From 1993 to 2002 there was an average of 14 alleged sexual assaults a year; worse yet, according to a DOD IG May 2003 survey of Academy cadets, 80.8% of females who said they had been victims of sexual assault at the Academy did not report the incident.[62] Like a runaway train, sexual assault at the Academy was out of control and bound for disaster.

Apart from the emotional and physical wreckage this relatively unabated sexual harassment and assault caused along the way, the disaster for the Academy came on January 2, 2003, when an e-mail under the pseudonym Renee Trindle was sent to various high-profile recipients including former Secretary of the Air Force Dr. James G. Roche, former Chief of Staff of the Air Force Gen. John P. Jumper, Senators Wayne Allard and Ben Nighthorse Campbell, other U.S. Congressmen, and media representatives. The e-mail asserted that there was a significant sexual assault problem at the USAFA and that it had been largely ignored by the Academy's leadership.[63]

Although surprising to some, many of the individuals listed above had been very much aware of the problem for months, if not years, by that time. Senator Allard had heard accounts of physical assault from me and my family along with reports of sexual assault from numerous female cadets as well—and though the circumstances surrounding our individual victimizations bore only slight resemblance to each other, the common thread tying all our experiences together was the dereliction of duty on the part of Academy leadership that allowed these things to happen. Fur-

---

62 Panel to Review Sexual Misconduct Allegations at the U.S. Air Force Academy (The Fowler Panel), "Report of The Panel to Review Sexual Misconduct Allegations at the U.S. Air Force Academy" (Arlington, VA: Panel to Review Sexual Misconduct Allegations, September 2003), 1. http://www/defenselink.mil/news/Sep2003/d20030922usafareport.pdf

Author's Note: References a May 2003 survey of Academy cadets brought to the Fowler Panel's attention by the Department of Defense Inspector General.

63 U.S. Air Force Inspector General, "Summary Report Concerning the Handling of Sexual Assault Cases at the United States Air Force Academy" (Washington, DC: Air Force Inspector General, Sept 14, 2004), 1.

thermore, at least one of the congressmen on the list *actually participated in drafting the e-mail*—and it would be remiss of me not to mention that neither Secretary Roche nor General Jumper was unfamiliar with sexual assault problems at the Academy.

Shortly after the Renee Trindle e-mail went out, these senior Air Force leaders took action, though not, I would say, because of a supreme adherence to the call of duty. These leaders took action because the national media, having also received the Trindle e-mail, was already reporting across the country that numerous female cadets had been sexually assaulted while attending the USAFA, that Air Force management generally covered up the crimes and did not punish the offenders, and that female cadets were frequently punished for reporting sexual assaults.[64] Female cadets told their stories to Barbara Walters on *20/20*, the *Oprah Winfrey Show*, and CNN, effectively leaving Air Force leaders with no choice but to act, with their national reputation on the line.

Secretary Roche wasted no time directing the general counsel of the Air Force to establish a high-level working group whose mission it would be to review sexual misconduct allegations at the Academy, more specifically, cadet complaints concerning the Academy's program of deterrence and response to sexual assault. The working group, led by Mary L. Walker, spared nothing (except for their professional credibility) in investigating the matter. It was bewildering for me, as well as a great many others, to read that the working group found "no systemic acceptance of sexual assault at the Academy, institutional avoidance of responsibility, or systemic maltreatment of cadets who report assault" after roughly 170 pages of their own material that would indicate otherwise.[65] Ultimately, Mary Walker was accused of "shielding" top Air Force brass from public criticism by intentionally "avoiding any reference to the responsibility of Air Force Headquarters for the failure of leadership which occurred at

---

64 Department of Defense Inspector General, "Evaluation of Sexual Assault, Reprisal, and Related Leadership Challenges at the United States Air Force Academy, Report No. IP02004C003," i.

65 *Working Group Report*, "Report of the Working Group Concerning the Deterrence of and Response to Incidents of Sexual Assault at the U.S. Air Force Academy" (Washington, DC: Headquarters, Department of the Air Force, 2003), 165.

the Academy" by members of a followup independent review panel (the Fowler Panel).[66]

Suspicious of the Air Force's ability to properly investigate itself, Congress passed H.R. 1559 (signed into law by the President of the United States on April 16, 2003), establishing a panel to review sexual misconduct allegations at the USAFA.[67] Not long after, former Congresswoman Tillie Fowler was chosen by the secretary of defense to lead a seven-member panel of private citizens specializing in the proper treatment of sexual-assault victims and/or handling of sexual-assault cases, whose cumulative list of credentials stretched out the door. This panel worked through the summer of 2003 meeting and discussing the issues with current and former Academy leaders and cadets, senators, congressmen, and sexual-assault experts. The panel held multiple public hearings at the City Hall in Colorado Springs, Colorado, reviewed thousands of documents, and met in closed session with DOD/AF inspectors general and their deputies. And although provided with less time and information than the working group, they were somehow able to develop an accurate synopsis with straightforward conclusions regarding sexual assault at the Academy. The panel found "a chasm in leadership during the most critical time in the Academy's history—a chasm which extended far beyond its campus in Colorado Springs ... [a chasm] that helped create an environment in which sexual assault became a part of life at the Academy."[68]

How is it that two high-level investigative panels, assigned to analyze *the same issue* and dealing with the same people and the same information, could produce such diametrically opposed conclusions? The answer is simply the difference between objectivity and subjectivity. It's really not all that hard to figure out which of the two is the biased review when you read them, especially when you come across comments dripping with excessive flattery such as this:

---

66 Fowler Panel, "Report of The Panel to Review Sexual Misconduct Allegations at the U.S. Air Force Academy" (Arlington, VA: Fowler Panel, September 2003), 4.

67 Ibid., 9.

68 Ibid., 1.

> In closing, I would like to communicate to you on behalf of the Working Group that it has been an honor to serve you and the Department of the Air Force in conducting this important review.[69]

The same obsequious mentality that caused Mary Walker to write such an ingratiating memo to the Secretary of the Air Force is what caused the working group to fail to hold Academy administrators accountable for their failures of leadership in its June 17, 2003, report. It's this same culture of unaccountability within the Air Force at large that compelled Secretary of Defense Robert Gates to effectively terminate former Chief of Staff Gen. T. Michael Moseley and Secretary of the Air Force Michael W. Wynne in early June, 2008, in response to the Air Force's gross mishandling of nuclear weapons. In 2006 the Air Force mislabeled nuclear warhead fuses, which led to the accidental shipping of classified components to Taiwan. Then in late August 2007 the Air Force accidentally transferred six nuclear-tipped cruise missiles from Minot Air Force Base, N.D., to Barksdale Air Force Base, LA. Nobody even discovered the mistake until thirty hours later! That kind of unaccountability is pathetic, and everyone knows it.

Regardless of what anyone may say, sexual assault *was* a problem at the Academy. Though one may truthfully say sexual assault is a problem at many universities across the country, there's no doubt Academy leadership fueled the fire by failing to appropriately respond to sexual assaults at the institution. Failure to establish or maintain effective policies, programs, and practices to deter and respond to incidents of sexual assault constitutes a sexual-assault problem in and of itself, and the Academy definitely lived up to that level of incompetence.

It was a defining moment in the early 1990s that really paved the way for the next decade of sexual-assault problems at the Academy. Near the beginning of 1993, former Superintendent Lt. Gen. Bradley C. Hosmer changed sexual-assault policies and procedure at the USAFA in order to (with any luck) ensure greater victim confidentiality and support. Although well intentioned, Gen. Hosmer set the Academy sexual-assault program on a course for disaster. Hosmer's unauthorized deviation from the standard UCMJ definition for sexual assault, military reporting pro-

69 *Working Group Report*, "Memorandum for the Secretary and the Chief of Staff of the Air Force from the General Counsel of the Air Force," June 17, 2003.

cess, and criminal response measures utilized by the rest of the *entire operational Air Force* set in motion a cascade of miscommunication, misunderstanding, and noncooperation between the members of Academy leadership responsible for handling sex crimes.

Although confusion drove the bus for the next ten years, signs warning of considerable sexual deviancy among cadets and an inadequate USAFA sexual-assault response program were evident everywhere. Even predating the unauthorized administrative overhaul of the sexual-assault program in 1993, a November 1992 GAO report indicated major sexual-harassment problems at the USAFA. In the report, the GAO commended the military and naval academies for "their efforts to clarify the objectives of their Fourth Class Systems to eliminate remaining elements that serve no demonstrated developmental purpose" and recommended the Air Force Academy do the same, the reasoning being that by decreasing the amount of hazing-like treatment wrought by the Fourth Class System, the Academy would also see a decrease in sexual assault just as West Point and Annapolis had.[70] The Department of Defense rejected the GAO's recommendation, saying there was no need for such action. They were obviously wrong, and their decision would come back to haunt them.

Left unabated, the problem festered. Two years later the GAO blew the whistle once again. In its January 1994 report, the GAO indicated that women were subject to harassment at all the service academies at a level that "portended a serious threat to the mission of the academies to educate and train future military officers."[71] Once again, the AFA did nothing, at least, nothing helpful.

In that same year, female cadets with no confidence in the Academy's formal reporting system formed an unofficial and secret support group for victims of sexual assault. That red flag—the superintendent not

---

70 GAO Report, "DoD Service Academies: More Changes Needed to Eliminate Hazing," 5.

71 Fowler Panel, "Report of The Panel to Review Sexual Misconduct Allegations at the U.S. Air Force Academy," 15.

Author's note: The Fowler Panel report references the GAO Report, "DoD Service Academies: More Actions Needed to Eliminate Sexual Harassment" (Washington, DC: U.S. Gov't Accountability Office, Jan 1994)

only knew of the group's existence but had actually *attended* one of their meetings—was followed by yet another disturbing GAO report in 1995.

By this point the GAO was sounding the alarm like a broken record. Careful to maintain their tradition of irresponsibility and culture of unaccountability, Academy administrators listened to the GAO's advice about as much as people, by and large, listen to broken records. The 1995 GAO report was a followup report to its 1994 investigation of sexual harassment at the academies and concluded that not only had there been no improvement at the Air Force Academy, but the problem had grown *significantly worse.*[72]

Apart from GAO reports, ominous social-climate surveys, and repetitive objections from the Air Force Office of Special Investigations (AFOSI) concerning its exclusion from the sexual-assault reporting process, the following warning signs were exceptionally blatant. In 1998, a year after codifying the sexual-assault program first introduced in 1993, the chief of sexual-assault services at the Academy provided a briefing entitled "We Have A Problem" to all of the Academy bigwigs (superintendent, commandant, vice commandant, training group commander, and athletic director) in which it was reported that 24% of female cadets claimed to having been sexually assaulted since their arrival at the Academy.[73] After such a briefing these leaders would have had to claim insanity to explain how they could have thought the Academy's new program was successfully addressing sexual assault at the USAFA, but still they did nothing.

The Fowler Panel, in its September 2003 report, said:

> On June 3, 1996, General Anderson, General Roadman and Colonel Hall [AF Surgeon General, Deputy Surgeon General, and psychiatric consultant to the Surgeon General carrying out the review of AFA sexual assault at the time—respectively] met with then–Chief of Staff of the Air Force General Ronald R. Fogleman. At the meeting, Colonel Hall briefed General Fogleman regarding sexual assaults at the Academy, and asserted that "the problem of sexual assault and victimization continues at the Academy in large measure due to a cultural or institu-

72 Fowler Panel, "Report of The Panel to Review Sexual Misconduct Allegations at the U.S. Air Force Academy," 16

73 Ibid., 24.

> tional value system. This climate promotes silence, discourages victims from obtaining help, and increases the victim's fear of reprisal." Colonel Hall also stated that the Academy lacked a coordinated policy linking the various support agencies into a safety net for the traumatized victim, and expressed concern about the policy that allowed victims of assault to determine if they would identify the perpetrator or press charges.
>
> On June 4, 1996, General Anderson followed up on the meeting of the previous day and sent a note to General Fogleman reiterating his concerns. In the note, General Anderson stated that "there are CRIMES here—FELONIES.... this patient [the Academy] needs major surgery, not just a band aid."[74]

Could it get any clearer than that? Seriously, could there really have been any room for doubt in the minds of Academy leaders that sexual assault was a major problem at the institution, that their rogue sexual-assault scheme might just possibly have been a failed program? Especially after such a statement as, "there are CRIMES here—FELONIES...this patient needs major surgery, not just a band aid." If that weren't enough, around the same time the chief of the Administrative Law Branch, General Law Division, Air Force Judge Advocate General's Office, sent a prophetic memo to the chief of the Military Justice Division that would have impressed even the French apothecary Nostradamus. In the memo, Colonel Sanborn, referring to the AFA's peculiar sexual-assault program, stated that the "Air Force would take a drubbing from parents, Congress, the press, you name it, if we pursue this particular policy."[75]

Sadly, an entire decade of AFA leaders failed to heed ample warning signs. Academy leadership failed to developed a comprehensive approach to solving the problem of sexual assault, which led to not only what Colonel Sanborn described as "a drubbing" from parents, congress, and the press in 2003, but the deterrence of sexual-assault reporting, hindrance of the investigative process, and, most unfortunately, the commissioning of any number of sexual assailants into the United States Air Force.

---

74 Ibid., 20-21.

75 Colonel Jarisse J. Sanborn, USAF, Chief, Administrative Law Branch, Memorandum to Chief of the Military Justice Division (JASM), General Law Division (AF/JA), April 22, 1996.

What was so wrong with the Academy's sexual-assault program? The AFOSI said it best: the Academy sexual-assault program was "unbalanced, reinforced a 'system within a system,' jeopardized the safety of other cadets and the ability to bring the offender to justice, and could result in the commissioning of an unsuitable officer."[76]

Between 1993 and the 2000 two policies in particular plagued the Academy sexual-assault program: amnesty and victim confidentiality. Amnesty was a discretionary policy, intended to encourage cadets to report sexual assaults. The policy provided that cadets would "generally not be disciplined for self–identified violations of cadet instructions that may have occurred in connection with an assault."[77] The idea was that by assuaging the fear of punishment for lesser indiscretions linked to an alleged sex crime, the victim would be more willing to report the sexual assault itself. The second policy, victim confidentiality, was intended to afford victims of sexual assault greater privacy, safety, and mental and emotional wellbeing by allowing cadets to report sex crimes only if they wanted to. It also provided that when cadets reported a crime, they were only required to divulge information they felt comfortable sharing, even to the exclusion of their own names and that of the assailants, if they so desired.

These two unsanctioned programs, unwisely instituted by Air Force Academy leadership, were a total bust. For a number of reasons, these programs missed the target entirely and had an effect opposite to the one desired. When the USAFA superintendent implemented his new sexual-assault program in 1993, incorporating amnesty and victim confidentiality, he failed to inform all of his senior staff, the commandant included, that he had done so. He also intentionally excluded the Cadet Counseling Center from the program, leaving USAFA counselors wholly unaware that an amnesty program even existed. Not only that, but apparently the program depended on Academy nurses to spread the word, and from there via word of mouth among cadets.[78] Furthermore, some years later, when the successive superintendent formalized the program, that

76 Fowler Panel, "Report of The Panel to Review Sexual Misconduct Allegations at the U.S. Air Force Academy," 18.

77 Ibid., 88. (See also: USAFA Instruction 51-201, paragraph 2.8.3)

78 DoD IG, "Evaluation of Sexual Assault, Reprisal, and Related Leadership Challenges at the United States Air Force Academy, Report No. IP02004C003," 27.

superintendent failed to issue any guidance for requesting or approving amnesty, resulting in years of inconsistent command decisions and subsequent mistrust of the Academy's sexual-assault program in the Cadet Wing. It was this state of affairs that led the DOD IG to conclude in its report of December 3, 2004, "the program was not well understood by cadets or by USAFA officials, and the application of program requirements was inconsistent."[79] The DOD IG wasn't the first to say it. The June 2003 Working Group Report concluded that the Academy's amnesty program "was not well understood by cadets or leadership, and uncertainty as to its efficacy reduced any effect it may have had in encouraging reporting."[80]

The policy of victim confidentiality fared no better. With a flavor of criticism, the working group, Fowler Panel, and inspectors general (both Air Force & DOD) all expressed serious concern regarding the Academy's confidential reporting process. On the subject of "limited confidentiality" the Working Group stated,

> This practice precluded command and investigative organizations from having access to some information that may have resulted in the timely investigation and prosecution of assailants. Further, it suggested to cadets that command could not be trusted to respond appropriately, a concept antithetical to military principles and the training of future military leaders.[81]

The Fowler Panel reiterated the working group's concerns, stating that the Academy's confidentiality initiative:

> ... had the potential of preventing command and law enforcement authorities from learning of serious criminal conduct. It also could interfere with the collection of evidence required for the success of any future prosecution. This problem occurred at the Academy and was exacerbated over time, as it appears that those individuals responsible for receiving confidential victim reports may not have fully satisfied their responsibility to encourage victims to formally report assaults.

79 Ibid., 27.

80 *Working Group Report*, "Report of the Working Group Concerning the Deterrence of and Response to Incidents of Sexual Assault at the U.S. Air Force Academy," 166.

81 Ibid., 165.

> Instead, some counselors may actually have *discouraged* victims from reporting.[82]

The DOD IG, referencing the unfortunately long period of time (four months on average) between the date of an alleged sexual assault and the reporting of it to AFOSI, stated,

> The delays were inherent in the confidential sexual assault reporting program that USAFA implemented unofficially in 1993, and formalized in 1997.[83]

The Academy's amnesty and confidentiality initiatives were disastrous, ill-starred programs from the get-go. However, these two failed programs were not the only factors working against the Academy.

The Academy not only espoused a unique sexual-assault reporting process, it even maintained its *own definition* of sexual assault inconsistent with the law and statutory Air Force policy. The unique definition of sexual assault was codified along with the unique sexual-assault reporting process in 1997 and, according to the Working Group Report, was responsible for years of "inaccurate perceptions, expectations, and even inaccurate reports of assault" among cadets.[84]

Furthermore, the Sexual Assault Services Committee (SASC), the focal point for oversight of the sexual-assault processes at the Academy, had since its inception in 1995 progressively deteriorated. On the eve of the 2003 sexual-assault media frenzy, the SASC was meeting on a biannual basis as opposed to the quarterly timeline of former years, and when it did meet, apparently failed to keep official records. The commandant at the time, Brig. General Gilbert, didn't even know he was the committee chair in charge of the committee, and the SASC had allegedly ceased reporting its business to senior Air Force Academy leadership. The SASC

---

82 Fowler Panel, "Report of The Panel to Review Sexual Misconduct Allegations at the U.S. Air Force Academy," 76.

83 DoD IG, "Evaluation of Sexual Assault, Reprisal, and Related Leadership Challenges at the United States Air Force Academy, Report No. IP02004C003," ii.

84 *Working Group Report*, "Report of the Working Group Concerning the Deterrence of and Response to Incidents of Sexual Assault at the U.S. Air Force Academy," 22.

had lost the initiative in the fight against sexual assault at the Academy, and its members had apparently resigned themselves to that.

Arguably the most significant counterproductive element within the program was the deliberate exclusion of the AFOSI from the sexual-assault reporting process. For more than a decade, 1993–2003, Air Force Academy leaders sustained this sexual-assault response program even though it undeniably impeded AFOSI detachment 808 from doing its job. The AFOSI has always been charged with "initiating and conducting independent investigations of serious crimes, including investigations of alleged sexual assault."[85] Albeit, when the USAFA installed its unique reporting process in 1993, Academy administrators effectively drew the AFOSI out of the picture.

A huge part of the problem was a program entitled "Cadets Advocating Sexual Integrity and Education" or CASIE, the chosen medium for both sexual assault reporting and education at the Academy around the start of the 21st century. The CASIE program was instituted with the sexual-assault victim in mind, its principal intention being to increase sexual-assault reporting at the Academy in connection with the institution's amnesty and confidentiality initiatives. The program afforded cadets an avenue through which to report their victimization confidentially, without having to press charges or divulge any details of the assault; including their own names and those of their assailants. Finally having been filled in regarding amnesty and victim confidentiality at the Academy, the Cadet Counseling Center (CCC, the entity responsible for the CASIE program) was then required to inform the commandant of any reported sexual assault, no matter how vague the details. At that point, USAFA senior leadership, in consultation with legal advisors from both the 10th Air Base Legal Office and Academy Legal Office, would generally do nothing for want of actionable information. Cases were referred from the CCC or 34th Training Wing to AFOSI only with the permission of the aggrieved cadet. Therefore, until that exceptionally rare go-ahead was given, USAFA leadership (in harmony with the beast *they created*, i.e., the irregular sexual-assault procedures they illegitimately instituted) was not allowed to take action. However, if the go-ahead was given, then the case would be handed over to AFOSI, investigated, and sent back to legal per-

85 Ibid., 113. (See AF Instruction 71-101V1, paragraph 1.1)

sonnel. From there it was up to Academy administrators to pursue either administrative punishment or prosecute under UCMJ.

Cadets across the Academy were taught that they should report sexual assaults through the twenty-four-hour CASIE hotline and that the CASIE program personnel could best provide for their physical and psychological needs in the traumatic wake of a sexual assault. Although this sounds rather copacetic on the surface, the history of the matter suggests otherwise. In retrospect we see that something was very wrong with this whole arrangement.

First of all, Air Force Regulation (AFR) 124-4 concerning "initiating AFOSI Investigations and Safeguarding, Handling, and Releasing Information from AFOSI Investigative Reports" dated November 29, 1989 (predating the Academy's unauthorized deviation from standard sexual-assault reporting procedures), *required*, not recommended, that USAFA commanders "… refer matters and offenses that fall within AFOSI investigative responsibility …"[86] This instruction resurfaced a few years later, in paragraph 8.5.1 of Air Force Policy Directive 71-1, "special investigations, criminal investigations and counterintelligence," September 7, 1993, which reiterates every Air Force commander's obligation to "… Refer to AFOSI all criminal matters and offenses for which AFOSI is responsible."[87]

Just like the rest of the Air Force, USAFA commanders were required *by law* (regardless of the victimized cadet's wishes or unauthorized AFA sexual-assault policies to the contrary) to inform AFOSI of any and all sexual assaults they knew of, the purpose being to afford AFOSI the opportunity to carry out proper and timely investigations that would provide sufficient evidence to identify and punish sexual criminals under UCMJ. It was not AFA leaders' prerogative to establish alternate avenues through which to report sexual assaults, regardless of the rationale. For all legal intents and purposes, the CASIE program's very existence contravened U.S. statutory and Air Force policy requirements, in that its *main charter* was to exclude AFOSI from the reporting process, thereby preventing the OSI from learning of sexual assaults at the Academy.

Contrary to some lines of reasoning, this most recent claim is far

86 DoD IG, "Evaluation of Sexual Assault, Reprisal, and Related Leadership Challenges at the United States Air Force Academy, Report No. IP02004C003," 16.

87 Ibid., 56.

from speculative, in that, for one, an Academy administrator admitted as much. During an interview with DOD IG investigators, this individual confessed to having deliberately instituted a program that purposefully excluded AFOSI from the sexual-assault reporting process, saying,

> … we couldn't tell the OSI not to investigate, and that's why we needed a system where they didn't find out. …[88]

Not only was it illegal to intentionally exclude the investigative body primarily responsible for investigating serious criminal activity and providing victims with the emotional and physical support services needed, it was also very ineffective. By excluding AFOSI from the reporting process, Academy administrators engendered an environment in which sexual criminals had little to fear. The Air Force Academy's unauthorized policy of allowing cadets to report crimes of a sexual nature confidentially and incompletely, to an entity other than their chain of command or AFOSI, contributed to years of categorical administrative failure to appropriately respond to sexual assault. Shoddy investigations, improper administrative and prosecutorial decisions or nondecisions, and ever-increasing sexual misconduct followed.

Finally, who were the men behind the masks? The truth of the matter is that no part of this administrative failure could have been possible without the contributions of an incredibly inept officer corps (collectively speaking) who made it happen day in and day out. Some may still question how exactly these leaders neglected their command responsibility. The answer comes from the Department of Defense Inspector General:

> The USAFA process for sexual assault reporting abrogated command responsibility for decisions, and shifted the responsibility to the youthful cadet victims already traumatized by the events and possibly lacking the objectivity to make valid decisions. The process contravened DoD and Air Force Policy. The senior Air Force officers who created, contributed to, or abided the new program generally ignored persistent senior staff and AFOSI warnings against the policy. Most importantly, they also generally ignored the need for a management system or process to measure program effectiveness and provide oversight. As a re-

88 Ibid., ii.

sult, they did not comply with Title 10 section 8583, "Requirement of exemplary conduct," which requires all commanding officers and others in authority in the Air Force –

(1) To show in themselves a good example of virtue, honor, patriotism, and subordination;

(2) To be vigilant in inspecting the conduct of all persons who are placed under their command;

(3) To guard against and suppress all dissolute and immoral practices, and to correct, according to the laws and regulations of the Air Force, all persons who are guilty of them; and

(4) To take all necessary and proper measures under the laws, regulations, and customs of the Air Force, to promote and safeguard the morale, the physical well-being, and the general welfare of the officers and enlisted persons under their command or charge.[89]

Against that stated official Air Force performance standard, the Academy leaders of the decade 1993–2003 did not measure up. Although failure of this magnitude ordinarily involves multiple guilty or responsible parties, a few in this particular situation deserve special attention.

In addition to former AFA brass responsible for the Academy's deviation from standard Air Force policy and procedure regarding sexual assault, the 2000–03 era USAFA administrators' leadership performance unquestionably warrants its own crack of the paddle. It was the same kind of underwhelming lack of concern General Dallager showed for my parents' twenty-two specific complaints dated November 3, 2002, that largely accounted for mission failure (regarding sexual assault) in the years 2000–2003. Senior Academy leadership from 2000 to 2003 failed to oversee a proper, legally sound, and effective sexual-assault program, not just because of the flawed system they inherited, but on account of their own incompetence, careless disregard, and general disinterest concerning criminal activity at the Academy. This indictment may seem far-reaching, but as *Reading Rainbow*'s LeVar Burton would say, you don't have to take my word for it. The 2003 Fowler Panel reported:

During his appearance before the Panel, Secretary Roche acknowledged the possible unfairness of holding recent leaders accountable for an in-

89 Ibid., 42.

> stitutional climate that evolved over time. Although the immediate past leaders of the Academy cannot be blamed for the situation they found when they arrived at the Academy, they should be accountable for any failures of leadership that occurred on their watch. Clearly, the leaders who arrived at the Academy had lengthy service in the operational Air Force and should have been vigilant in evaluating the Academy's non-standard sexual assault reporting procedures. The fact that the Academy's program departed from the procedures used in the regular Air Force should have heightened the Academy leadership's awareness of the potential for unintended consequences.[90]

While serving as an Army combat engineering officer, my father held various command and staff positions. At the start of his company command, a colleague warned my father: "Good luck with that! Those guys [the men soon to be under his command] are notorious for drug and alcohol abuse." Moments after the change of command ceremony concluded, my father ordered a drug search. Military policemen immediately brought out the drug-sniffing dogs and methodically searched the premises. The search pulled in a handful of soldiers, all possessing illegal narcotics, to be punished by way of nonjudicial UCMJ Article 15. The outfit had no more drug problems for the remainder of my father's two-year tenure. The moral of the story? Blaming your own leadership failures on those who came before you is antithetical to good military order and discipline, not to mention pathetic, in my opinion. Simply passing the buck does not relieve a person of command responsibility; it just makes him or her look like a gutless wimp.

The Fowler Panel went on:

> General Dallager and General Gilbert failed to exercise the judgment, awareness and resourcefulness necessary to realize that there was a sexual misconduct and social climate problem in their command that directly impacted the welfare and safety of their cadets. The Panel is unimpressed with assertions made by some that General Dallager and General Gilbert should not be held accountable for an institutional culture they inherited. The responsibilities of command required that

---

90 Fowler Panel, "Report of The Panel to Review Sexual Misconduct Allegations at the U.S. Air Force Academy," 38.

> Academy leaders take the necessary steps to understand the scope and dimensions of the issue and be suitably informed to take appropriate actions.[91]

I would take it one step further and say that, by and large, it really wasn't an issue of awareness or the lack thereof. There really is no question that these two generals were aware of the Academy's problems of sexual misconduct and social climate. According to their own belated admissions, they *knew* the program had the potential for jeopardizing the welfare and safety of their cadets. Knowledge of the decadent social atmosphere at the Academy and corresponding volume of sexual assaults was not the issue—it was their inaction in the face of such knowledge; it was their commonly accepted belief that there were no "true rapes" (as Colonel Slavec put it) taking place at the Academy; it was their perception that false accusations of sexual assault were a significant problem at the Academy (despite DOD IG assertions to the contrary).

No, the issue was not the culture they had inherited but what they did with that inheritance. These leaders allowed a bad situation to get worse; they allowed their preoccupation with reputation and career advancement to impede their judgment. I believe these leaders chose to allow their trepidation over the way that high-profile legal action might affect their politicized careers to deter them from effectively dealing with sexual assault at the Academy. Furthermore, although AFA administrators would never have admitted as much outside of their own close circles, it was their general opinion that most female cadets who reported sexual assaults were in some sort of disciplinary trouble themselves, or, according to one Academy official, couldn't make it in a man's world, so they cried "Rape" to avoid the long arm of the 34th TRW adjudicatory system, thereby essentially "making up for their own deficiencies" by rather arbitrarily casting blame elsewhere, e.g., alleging sexual assault.[92]

This scene from the past turns even uglier considering, as the Working Group Report stated,

---

91 Ibid., 38.

92 *Working Group Report*, "Report of the Working Group Concerning the Deterrence of and Response to Incidents of Sexual Assault at the U.S. Air Force Academy," 117.

> Whether either or both legal offices [were] involved [in sexual assault cases] depended mainly upon personnel within the training group recognizing that the more serious forms of discipline may [have been] appropriate. The recognition may [have been] affected by differing views among leadership about the appropriate use of cadet discipline for actions that could also [have been] considered crimes. (Over time, cadet discipline has been used for a variety of actions, which, if proven, could qualify as UCMJ violations.)[93]

A perfect example of this would be my assailant, Cadet J. Even after reading a sworn affidavit from Cadet J himself saying, "out of anger and frustration I head-butted him" (clearly a physical assault punishable under UCMJ), General Dallager, in all his wisdom, decided to merely issue a Form 10, and that was only after significant prodding on the part of my family to do something about the assault. On average, female cadet sex-crime victims fared no better in their pursuit of justice.

The 2000–2003 Academy administration's failure to establish or maintain effective policies aimed at deterring and responding to incidents of sexual assault was in fact systemic acceptance of sexual assault and maltreatment of cadets who reported assault. Their collective declaration that they were unaware of the extent of the sexual-assault problem at the Academy was unmistakable evidence of institutional avoidance of responsibility. My experience and the experiences of many of my contemporaries has led me to believe that the 2000–2003 USAFA leadership just didn't concern themselves much with criminal activity in general, sexual assault being no exception.

Nevertheless, there I was in exile, a former AFA cadet looking from the outside in. I had petitioned the Academy. I had contacted multiple United States senators. At the insistence of a fair-minded military legislative assistant in Senator Patty Murray's Seattle District office, a preliminary whistleblower reprisal investigation had been initiated by the DOD IG in Washington, DC. I had told my story to the media. I had done everything that both my parents and I felt appropriate. The time had come to do what I had never envisioned myself doing: choose an alternate career path.

So I did what any lonely desperado not quite ready to accept his fate

---

93 Ibid., 125.

would have done; I went to Alaska. Not only did I go to Alaska, but I went to the far reaches of civilization even by Alaskan standards. I found myself working eighteen-hour days (124-hour work weeks) in the fish and crab industry in Dutch Harbor on Unalaska Island. It was cold, dark, wet, windy, and exactly what I needed. I channeled my frustration with my Academy experience through every swing of the hammer to a crab cage, every heavy box of frozen fish I tossed around, or the hundreds of thousands of crabs I killed with my bare hands. It was exhausting work, perfectly mind-numbing physical labor, and painfully therapeutic.

As I worked away the anger month after month surrounded by the Bering Sea, the Academy saw a number of developments. Unbeknownst to me, my protestations and those of dozens of victimized female cadets had started something of a reformation at the Academy, aided of course by a great deal of media attention, concerned citizens, and action-oriented U.S. senators and congressmen. It was against the backdrop of Iliuliuk Bay that I read news of the Trindle e-mail. It was Rudi Bakhtiar from the CNN newsroom who first informed me, through a rather dysfunctional television tube, of a sexual-assault scandal at the Air Force Academy, as it had come to be known. At the same time I learned of the space shuttle *Columbia*'s disastrous fate over the Lone Star state, I learned of the establishment of Mary Walker's working group.

Around the time that I inquisitively stepped on an industrial scale (usually reserved for unprocessed seafood) and realized I had gained thirty pounds of muscle throwing boxes around all day and night, I learned of a March 6, 2003, Senate Armed Services Committee hearing regarding sexual assault at the Academy. Not long after, I was sitting by myself on a pew in Dutch Harbor's historic Russian Orthodox Church reading my mail when I first found out, by way of news from home, that Senator Allard felt the sexual-assault scandal at the Academy was *worse* than the 1991 Navy Tailhook scandal. Just moments after watching a coworker break his back against the railing of a surging crab boat, I listened to my dad tell me about how the Air Force was considering high-level personnel changes at the Academy. He informed me that on or about March 24, 2003, Senators Wayne Allard (R-CO) and John Warner (R-VA), in an official statement, recommended the replacement of almost the entire senior staff at the AFA. It was their belief (Senators Allard, Warner, and John McCain as well) that current Academy brass had failed miserably to take effective action regarding allegations of sexual assault and rape at the

AFA. Listening to hours of evasive testimony from senior AFA leaders in committee had apparently left these senators exceedingly disappointed.

Soon after, I found out that only a couple of days after these recommendations Secretary of the Air Force Dr. James G. Roche and Air Force Chief of Staff General John Jumper announced the dismissals of Air Force Academy Superintendent General John R. Dallager, his second-in-command Brig. General S. Taco Gilbert III, Vice Commandant Colonel Robert D. Eskridge, and Commander of the 34th Training Wing Colonel Laurie S. Slavec, as part of what they were calling "Agenda for Change." These four individuals were dismissed for what congressional leadership viewed as a systematic coverup of sexual assault, intimidation, and punishment of victims at the hands of AFA leadership; specifically General Gilbert, whom Senator Allard described as the "common thread" tieing dozens of reports of mishandled sexual assault cases together.[94]

Months later the Fowler Panel put it this way, speaking first of General Dallager, then Gilbert, and finally Colonel Slavec:

> The Panel concurs with the decision of the Secretary of the Air Force to retire *General Dallager* in a lower grade. General Dallager failed to exercise the degree of leadership expected of commanders. He did not recognize indicators of problems, nor did he aggressively pursue solutions to those problems. Having been at the helm of the Academy for several years prior to the recent allegations, General Dallager is the Academy leader bearing ultimate responsibility for the failure to adequately respond to sexual assault issues.
>
> *General Gilbert* failed to fully ensure the safety and security of the cadets under his command. Like General Dallager, General Gilbert failed in his leadership responsibilities by not seeking to acquire information on sexual misconduct issues and by failing to take responsibility for finding solutions. As the commander responsible for the safety of the Cadet Wing, it is not enough for General Gilbert to say that others were in charge of the Academy's sexual assault response program. General Gilbert had the responsibility to be informed about sexual assault and gender climate issues at the Academy, and he did not take the steps required to become fully informed. His inaction in this regard

94 Cathy Booth Thomas, *The Air Force Academy's Rape Scandal*, *TIME*, Mar. 06, 2003. http://www.time.com/time/magazine/article/0,9171,1004371-3,00.html

jeopardized the safety and security of the cadets under his command with respect to sexual misconduct issues.

The Academy's instruction mandates that the Cadet Counseling Center inform the commandant of a reported sexual assault immediately "… because the commandant is the commander responsible for both cadet victims and cadet perpetrators. This general officer must ensure the safety of each cadet and the good order and discipline of the entire Cadet Wing." That same instruction put General Gilbert in charge of the Academy's Sexual Assault Services Committee, but apparently General Gilbert failed to learn about this key responsibility. The Panel understands the practice at the Academy before General Gilbert's assumption of command gave responsibility for the SASC to the vice commandant. Nevertheless, as the senior commander, General Gilbert was obligated to take charge of sexual misconduct issues. General Gilbert failed to execute his responsibilities and directly contributed to mission failure.

Colonel Slavec was overly aggressive in discharging her command responsibilities and alienated AOCs, MTLs and cadets. Although Colonel Slavec sought to enforce disciplinary standards, she contributed to the breakdown of good order and discipline within her command by taking such aggressive actions that her subordinates viewed her as unfair and overly harsh. Specifically, she created an environment where the perception of fear, punishment and reprisal among the staff and cadets became an accepted reality. Colonel Slavec's leadership style and treatment of some victims of sexual assault had a negative impact on the willingness of cadets to report incidents of sexual assault.

Additionally, while Colonel Slavec was in the first line of responsibility for enforcing disciplinary standards, she was unaware of the definition of sexual assault, held her own definition of a "true rape" as requiring some level of violence, and seemed to hold the attitude that cadets claimed sexual assault only to receive amnesty. As the member of the leadership team closest to the Cadet Wing, Colonel Slavec was in a key position to become aware of the problem of sexual assaults. Instead, her inflexible and insensitive attitudes and actions exacerbated problems in the Cadet Wing. Colonel Slavec failed to establish a safe and secure military training environment and failed to execute her command responsibilities in a fair and impartial manner. Through her ineffective leadership, Colonel Slavec directly contributed to mission failure.

The "Agenda for Change" was not simply a knee-jerk reaction to intense congressional pressure for an Academy shakeup. It was also a response to Mary Walker's two-month preliminary Working Group Report. Its stated objective was to:

> ... bolster those processes and systems that guide honorable conduct ... ensure cadets understand and exercise the spirit of these values in the context of their future in the Air Force ... [to administer] discipline with measured judgment and in accordance with core values.[95]

The intent was that in so doing they might succeed in curtailing the rampant sexual deviancy and other unbecoming behavioral patterns that had for so long defined Air Force Academy culture.

The "Agenda for Change" made its debut simultaneously with my early retirement from the fishing industry. As I boarded the plane that would take me home, Secretary Roche hashed out the details of his virgin initiative before the Senate Committee on Armed Forces on March 31, 2003. On April 1, 2003, Secretary Roche repeated his plan, this time in the Rayburn Congressional Building in front of the House Armed Services Committee. The plan called for a number of rather drastic changes that didn't sit well with the image-conscious, tradition-based Association of Graduates, an old guard led by individuals who had gone to the Academy "back when it was hard." Many were the same guys who called themselves "The Last Class with Balls," as any number of them were among the last male-only graduating class at the Academy. However, despite their sometimes vehement objection to progress, the "Agenda for Change" went forward, thanks in large part to the structured leadership of General Gilbert's replacement, then Brigadier General Johnny A. Weida. General Weida quickly became the face of change at the Academy as he energetically went about his grand task of implementing said AF Headquarters–mandated provisions. Until the confirmation and arrival of then Major General John R. Rosa, Jr., in July 2003, General Weida wore two hats, that of commandant of cadets and that of acting superintendent. Along with his fellow administrators, newly appointed Vice Commandant of Cadets Colonel Debra Gray, and 34th Training

95 *Working Group Report*, "Report of the Working Group Concerning the Deterrence of and Response to Incidents of Sexual Assault at the U.S. Air Force Academy," 117.

Wing Commander Colonel Clada A. Monteith, General Weida seemed to have genuinely attempted to get the Academy back on track.

Change had come to the Academy whether anyone liked it or not. Administrative roles were defined and duties reassigned as part of "Agenda for Change" policy directives and initiatives. An Academy Response Team (ART) was established comprising medical, legal, counseling, and command elements to better deal with sexual assault. Academy counselors now had to be licensed mental-health practitioners and could no longer hide sexual assault from 34th Training Wing command. Cadets were now required to report sexual assault to their chain of command, which was now more educated and better trained. USAFA leadership was to actually prosecute likely criminals under UCMJ. AOCs were given UCMJ command-level authority and responsibility commensurate with their rank. Under guidance from the general counsel of the Air Force, definitions of sexual assault consistent with standard Air Force–wide definitions were applied to the Academy. AFOSI was now allowed to do its job and take the reins during criminal investigations. Basic Training was changed to emphasize fair treatment and mutual respect among cadets. The Fourth Class System was changed slightly, restricting third-class cadets (college sophomores) from interacting with freshman cadets. The rules of engagement were changed concerning on-the-spot corrections, theoretically to make it a more demonstrative activity vs. a punitive engagement. Recognition weekend and tours were temporarily suspended. Academy billeting was rearranged (rooms occupied by female cadets were all clustered in the same vicinity, near the women's bathrooms). Furthermore, no cadet was allowed to enter the room of a cadet of the opposite sex without knocking and then waiting for the door to be opened by the cadet occupying the room, and once invited inside, the door had to remain wide open.

Twenty-four-hour security patrols were instituted in the cadet dormitories, and alcohol infractions began ending cadet careers with much greater frequency. In order to encourage the reporting of sexual assault, amnesty from Academy discipline arising in connection with the alleged offense was extended to all cadets involved, with the crucial exceptions of the alleged assailant, any cadet involved in covering up the incident, any cadet involved in hindering the reporting or investigation of the incident, and the senior ranking cadet in attendance. Those found guilty of falsely accusing someone of sexual assault were now to be prosecuted to the full extent of the law. Rape kits were to be made available at the Cadet Clinic and Academy Hospital. A cadet-on-cadet mentoring program was introduced to facilitate greater respectability throughout the Cadet Wing. The "Bring Me Men" sign on the wall above the ramp leading to the cadet area was removed to make the Academy appear more female-friendly, and an assessment of Academy processes to deter, stop, or deal with sexual assault was to be conducted every three years by Air Force Headquarters.[96]

In addition to actionable policy changes, the "Agenda for Change" outlined goals for culture and climate change at the Academy as a whole. It was Air Force Headquarters' desire to see the Academy "operationalized" for the reason that many key congressional leaders expressly believed the Academy needed to start resembling the operational Air Force rather than a parochial college fraternity. Accordingly, Air Force leaders developed the Officer Development System (ODS); a new training guidance engineered to bring the AFA in line with standard operational military policy and procedure.

The changes were reflected in USAFA Cadet Wing Instruction and prominently published in the Cadet Wing Manual. Cadet life at the Academy would never be the same again. Athletes were technically required to participate in military training. The beat-downs of yesteryear were a thing of the past. In order to engender greater professionalism, military order, and discipline within the ranks, cadets were to interact respectfully. Compliance with training rules of engagement was no longer a suggestion but supposedly a required component of every training objective. In theory, the ODS, as part of the greater "Agenda for Change" was to revolutionize the Academy experience; and to some degree it did.

One thing's for sure, though—as integral as these improvements were to the Academy program, the "Agenda for Change" didn't do much to change my situation. Although even amidst all this administrative upheaval the lines of communication had managed to stay open between the parties involved in my case. After receiving Dallager's letter of March 3, 2003, my dad, frustrated with what he perceived to be another unsatisfactory AFA response, reiterated his concerns not only to Dallager but to the President of the United States as well. With the audacity of a Martin Luther, my father made clear to both offices that the Academy

96 Secretary of the Air Force Directive, *The Air Force Academy: Agenda for Change* (Washington, DC: Headquarters, Department of the Air Force, 2003)

had unequivocally done me wrong and caused irrevocable damage that warranted some sort of corrective action. Unsurprisingly, we never heard back from the White House. Undoubtedly, that letter never made it past the pay-grade of the volunteer intern in the correspondence office of the EOP. However, we did hear back from Dallager just prior to his forced retirement.

In his letter of April 21, 2003, General Dallager responded to my father's followup questions as best he could (covering for such vast institutional delinquency couldn't have been easy), then made this somewhat encouraging statement:

> As of April 11, 2003 the DOD is still conducting its investigation. My inspector General office has completed its inquiry and has attempted to answer all questions and follow-up questions in as detailed a manner as we can provide. The new 34 TRW vice commander, who chairs the MRC boards, is currently evaluating David's MRC package and process to determine if a new MRC is warranted. I am awaiting that decision as I consider my options as disenrollment authority.[97]

As soon as I finished reading the letter thoughts raced across my mind. Another Military Review Committee? Why? What would be the point? Where would that take place, at the Academy? Was I to actually believe that there was a chance of being readmitted to the Academy? At this stage in the game, would I really even *want* to go back to the Academy? Either way, not too long after this letter from General Dallager I received a followup letter from General Johnny Weida, then acting USAFA superintendent, stipulating my options concerning a second MRC. The letter provided a date and time for this second MRC and instructed me to inform the Academy if I wished to proceed.

In the past, when faced with such an issue, I would have at least run it by my Washington State liaison officer, with whom my family had maintained healthy contact throughout my short Air Force career; however, utterly disgusted with Academy delinquency, this career Air Force officer had relinquished his post in protest. Therefore, I merely conferred with friends and family and ultimately decided to go through with it, although I was only willing to conduct the MRC via teleconference, for the reason

---

97 Lieutenant General John R. Dallager, letter to Graneys, 21 April 2003.

that I had no desire whatsoever to waste my own money (money hacked out of the Alaskan wilderness) traveling to the Academy chasing a prayer of vindication.

Over the next few weeks we (Academy support personnel and I) hashed out the details of this second MRC and ultimately settled upon a mutually agreeable date, time, and location (means of communication). The parties involved had been notified and the scene set. The only thing left to do was to settle upon and implement a few preparatory measures. Without undue delay, I wrote a personal statement, prepared important documents for presentation, composed a list of actionable demands and requests I considered necessary for justice to be served, and formulated responses to questions I knew would be asked by MRC members. In my personal statement I highlighted every point and detail concerning my unfortunate Academy experience, drawing heavily, appropriately enough, from previous MRC arguments. I took these preparations very seriously. Only with exceedingly great care and diligence did I orchestrate my case against the Academy, a case that probably could have held up even in a court of law.

This second MRC took place via teleconference from the Army Corps of Engineers' Seattle District office building in the early summer of 2003. I knew very well going into it that the MRC would not be a pleasant experience. I also understood that it would probably not yield many positive results. However, these were the cards I had been dealt, and I had no choice but to try my hand despite the odds against me. Once inside the building and past security, I inspected the battlefield—a room containing nothing other than a table, a chair, the video teleconference module, and a pull-down projection screen. On the other end of the line, as displayed on the screen in front of me, was what I recognized as an empty conference room in the 34th Training Wing tower of the Air Force Academy in Colorado Springs, Colorado. It was a familiar scene. Just seeing the Academy again brought back a swarm of ugly, repressed memories that, until this point, I had relegated to the back of my mind. In an instant, my exasperation with the AFA resurfaced and got my juices flowing. It was a familiar feeling.

Having arrived quite early, I spent some time going over talking points, gathering my thoughts, and emotionally preparing myself for the ensuing conflict. Soon thereafter my concentration was broken by movement on the screen in front of me. The MRC members were beginning to file into the room. One by one they made their way to their seats and settled in for the show. Unaware that I could see and hear them at this point, some made comments that otherwise they wouldn't have done, revelatory comments exposing their disbelief in the necessity of a second MRC for a guy like me. Disrespectful and offensive statements commanded the moment until it dawned on one of them that I might actually be able to hear them. This individual muttered something under his breath, after which all eyes were on me. Paying little heed to the adverse reaction they would most certainly have as a result of such an embarrassment, I immediately hung them out to dry. I said something to the effect of, "Great. Well, now that I know what I'm dealing with, how about we get on with it." Like children too emotionally volatile to acknowledge their own guilt, one of them attempted to regain the initiative, saying something like, "Cadet Graney, do you know why you're—"

I cut him off. "Sir, I'd really appreciate it if you would address me by the appropriate title; *Mr.* Graney. I'm no longer Cadet Graney, as you took that title from me."

With the man stunned and confused as to how to respond, the new vice comm spoke. "Mr. Graney, you make some serious allegations here in your personal statement. Do you have anything to back them up?"

Earlier I had sent three documents to the Academy for these board members' review, and with this comment it was obvious that they had not even glanced at two of them. As frustrating as this realization was for me at the time, I managed to lock it up and respond. "Ma'am, it appears you haven't read the entirety of the materials I submitted. I know this, because if you had you wouldn't have asked me that question. I'm not going to lie. This is very disappointing."

Before she could respond, another member of the board spitefully interjected. "Cadet Graney—excuse me, Mr. Graney, you were just asked a question by a colonel in the Air Force. You might want to think about answering the question."

Experienced as I was in regard to USAFA MRC scare tactics, I explained to this individual the futility in ordering me around as a civilian. I also informed the board that it was my understanding that the reason behind submitting documentation for review was for such documentation to actually be reviewed. I then said that as long as the three documents I had provided them remained unread, I would be unwilling to proceed further.

Although noticeably perturbed, these board members swallowed their pride and spent the next twenty to thirty minutes reading my unapologetic ten-page personal statement, a memorandum for record from the USAFA Inspector General evidencing the lying ways of my freshman squadron AOC Major H, and the police report in which my assailant, Cadet J, admitted to having head-butted me out of "anger and frustration." When it appeared that these documents had been thoroughly reviewed, I opened the floor up for discussion. Back and forth we went for nearly two hours and, trust me, at no point was there ever a shortage of insults, snide remarks, or colorful body language. These MRC members tried every stunt and pulled every trick in the book in what seemed to me an effort to discredit a man who, by this point, could not have been more impervious to such sophomoric examination.

Despite their best efforts to the contrary, with the assistance of truth, justice, and prior experience, I incontrovertibly seized the moment by meticulously doing and saying everything that needed to be said and done. All things considered, it was a huge moral victory for the good guys, and the peace of mind it engendered was intoxicating. My experience has been that there's just something strangely enchanting about hopeless moral determination, and this was no exception.

As the MRC drew to a close, I was asked what I felt would be appropriate reparation for the damages I had sustained. I could hardly believe my ears. I remember thinking at the time, Did the vice comm really just ask me that? Is this some sort of sick joke? Irrespective of my well-warranted suspicion, I answered the question. I asked to be reinstated to the Academy, or at least provided the opportunity to go back to the Academy should I wish to do so. I asked for a corrected personnel file illustrative of the gross mistreatment and abuse I had been subjected to as a freshman cadet. And I asked for my future commissionability rating to be changed to reflect my true officer potential.

The MRC members exchanged mystified glances across the table, then at the sound of the vice comm's voice abruptly turned and listened. The vice comm broke the awkward silence with, "Well, Mr. Graney, these aren't same-day-type decisions, of course. Let's go ahead and wrap this meeting up. You'll hear from us soon enough."

Following her lead, I thanked the committee members for their time, encouraged them to do the right thing, then promptly dismissed myself. Turning off the teleconference module brought a huge sigh of relief. This second MRC had proven to be as intellectually challenging as the first MRC had been emotional. I had "left it all on the field," as they say in football vernacular, and could now only wait to see if the score would reflect my performance. Although experience told me not to hope for much, expectation wanted more.

I spent the next couple of weeks both considering the would-be results of my MRC and preparing to move to Buenos Aires, Argentina. Just before shipping out to South America for the next fifteen months I received word from the Academy that my future commissionability rating had been changed from a "5" to a "3" and that my DD214 form had been modified to reflect as much. They would not be readmitting me to the Academy, and my personnel file would remain the same. It was the final letdown.

This marked the end of my struggle with the United States Air Force Academy. Although I still awaited word concerning my DOD reprisal investigation, instinctively I knew it would also amount to nothing. The DOD investigator, Marge Trevino, had already hung up on my dad on the phone and insulted my intelligence in an earlier conversation. This was clearly a woman who not only lacked professionalism (her boss ultimately sent us a written apology for her subordinate's incompetence) but also gave the impression that she simply didn't like doing her job. It seemed as though everything was an inconvenience for this woman, and for all these reasons I felt rather confident that it was just a matter of time before I would hear from the DOD that, as in O.J. Simpson's murder trial, there just wasn't enough evidence to cast that guilty verdict. On that note, I went to Argentina.

I was less than two months into my foreign residency when I heard, of course, that the DOD had found the evidence against the Academy insufficient to warrant further investigation. This news fell upon deaf ears, as the Academy was more or less dead to me by that point. I was a world away, entirely immersed in another culture, speaking a different language. I simply didn't care, although I must say I did find it amusing to read a quotation (sent to me by my mother) from a newly assigned general-grade officer to the Academy. This was it: "The only time you should yell at someone in the Air Force is if someone's just thrown a grenade in your foxhole." I remember thinking, *Well, isn't that about right?* Unbelievable. I couldn't help snickering at the absurdity of it all. Here I had spent my entire AFA career being chastised for upholding the belief that incessant yelling at subordinates was nothing more than abusive, counterproductive, and contrary to good military order and discipline—and now here comes this new guy espousing the same ideology that had been at least partially responsible for my expulsion from the Academy not even a year before. Interesting twist of fate, I'd say.

> The circumstances of men's lives do much to determine their philosophy, but, conversely, their philosophy does much to determine their circumstances.[98]

As I've said before, my philosophy going into the Academy was the product of familial, religious, and community environs that championed the just life. This philosophy was completely at odds with that of the 2001–2003 era's AFA culture, an ideological friction which, of course, determined my unfavorable circumstances within the 34th Training Wing. I say life is a funny thing, in that, had I entered the Academy even a year later with the same exact mindset, there most likely would have been far less conflict of opinion. Change at the AFA came a little too late for me. Nevertheless, that was the lot I had been cast and, as we all know, there's never much use in complaining.

After a great deal of community service, establishing a deeply personal rapport with Los Porteños (the people of Buenos Aires), and lots of soccer, it was time to come home. I said goodbye to some of the best people I've ever known, then flew nonstop from Buenos Aires to Dallas, TX. As soon as I arrived on American soil I got down and kissed the earth beneath me. Although I loved Argentina, it was great to be home. I remember a Southern debutante type who witnessed the scene asking me, "Wow, happy to be here? Where you coming from, stranger?" With a smile on my face I said, "It doesn't matter, all that matters is that I'm home!"

The choice was mine at this point whether to go back to school or make some money somehow, somewhere. I looked into an offshore oil rig in Prudhoe Bay on the north shore of Alaska. I was tentatively hired as a deckhand on an Alaskan fishing boat leaving out of Fisherman's Terminal in Seattle. I submitted applications to lumberyards, warehouses, and just

---

98 Bertrand Russell, *A History of Modern Philosophy* (New York: Simon & Schuster, 1945), xiv.

about every other blue-collar employment within the job market. Ultimately I went with none of them, did a complete 180, and went back to school. By this point it had been three years since I was last in college, and I felt it was past time to go back. My average AFA GPA did me no favors among college and university admissions staff who had no understanding of the difficulty of the AFA curriculum. Consequently, I ended up going to a little-known college in Orem, UT, where I hoped to gain a spot on the wrestling squad and maybe even an athletic scholarship.

This transition, my return to academia, marked the beginning of a daunting uphill climb back to professional respectability. Despite the circumstances surrounding my expulsion from the Academy, the fact that I had been involuntarily dismissed from that institution severely stunted my professional development for a time. Many employers thought twice about hiring a guy like me, and most didn't think to hire me at all—even for supplemental income–type jobs.

Finally, I found a job as a lift operator and snowboard instructor at Park City and worked like a madman. I studied my college course material at every opportunity. Even within my frozen-over mountain-top hut I could be found studying, because I was bound and determined to succeed on some level.

In due course I completed my Psychology 101 class with well over a hundred percent in the class, leading my instructor to request me to be his paid teaching assistant for the following semester. I accepted the offer, quit work at The Canyons, and executed my TA responsibilities as best I could. I prepared study guides, lectured in class, graded papers, submitted test questions, led numerous study sessions, and calculated final grades. The instructor was impressed with my effort and voluntarily wrote me a letter of recommendation reflecting as much. I used that letter of recommendation to apply for an internship in U.S. Senator Bennett's office in Washington, DC, *three times.*On denying me for the third time because of the black spot that they considered my Academy experience to be, they laughed and sent me away without even an interview.

I went straight from there to Senator Hatch's Provo office, uninvited and unscheduled, and found myself speaking with a staff member there who, it just so happened, had heard of me through a mutual professional acquaintance. We talked for almost two hours. I left Senator Hatch's office that day under consideration for an internship in the Washington, DC, office for the fall of 2005.

I wouldn't know the result of my rather informal application until I had spent the next three to four months working on a cattle/horse/buffalo ranch in Cimarron, New Mexico. I spent the duration of this career interruption doing everything from branding, shoeing, and vaccinating, to bull-riding at the county rodeo, tracking lost horses on distant ridgelines, and dating the town sweetheart. I was thrown off more horses than I can remember, had my finger partially ripped off, had a horseshoe nail go through my hand, was kicked through a fence by a horse, and almost got struck by lightning while riding through a thunderstorm.

Unfortunately, this country song I was living came to an end when a hot-blooded, emotionally disturbed coworker attacked me for simply asking him to get off his rear end and help me out. This kid was sitting on a fencepost heckling me as I struggled to load a 300-lb horse carcass onto the bed of the work truck by myself. Because of this altercation I was asked to leave the ranch, while the coworker was left with a broken nose, loose teeth, and a different mindset concerning who to pick fights with.

Auspiciously, two weeks later I found myself on an airplane from Seattle, WA, to Ronald Reagan International Airport to begin work in Senator Orrin Hatch's office. It was just the break I needed. Work at the U.S. Senate released me from the professionally stifling steel trap that had been my unfortunate AFA experience. Working as an intern for media, environment, health policy, and casework matters there led to work at Cable News Network (CNN). My performance as the Pentagon Unit intern in the newsroom and on the set of Wolf Blitzer's *Situation Room* led to another internship in the U.S. House of Representatives. After graduating from Utah Valley University months later, I took a job working to develop the Standard Operating Procedures (SOPs) & Organization Manual for U.S. Coast Guard Sector Corpus Christi. The winds of fate then took me to Arizona to clerk at a law firm, then San Diego to work on a state assembly campaign, and eventually the U.S. Department of Commerce.

I applied to return to the Academy twice during this three-year professional and educational roller coaster, though to no avail, even with a congressional nomination secured both times. Why was I unable to gain readmittance to the Academy? Because the unfortunately sustainable institutional culture of unaccountability, cronyism, and lack of professionalism the Academy is known for remains relatively intact. Recent polls have shown that around 20 percent of the Academy's male population still think women don't belong there. Sexual harassment is still prevalent. Hazing continues. The Fourth Class System (though now called the Four Class System) still exists. Freshman cadets still get the runaround, running the strips, chewing only seven times before swallowing, at attention all the time, knowledge bowls, training sessions, etc. The honor system is still broken and the conduct adjudicatory system ineffective, and both are susceptible to abuse in the same ways as always. Although the practice was temporarily suspended, cadets still march tours and go through a modified version of Recognition. Upperclassmen still issue demerits at random and harass each other incessantly. Though vastly improved in many areas, I believe the Academy continues to be the professionally depraved, morally polluted institution it has been for years, as evidenced by its drug and alcohol problems, sexual harassment and assault, cheating scandals, and religious shenanigans that are still making headlines.

Some may say, "Why fret about this? That's just the way the system operates. That's just the way the military is. Does the situation at the Academy really warrant attention? Is it truly as bad as you make it seem? What's the point in fighting this battle? Do you really expect to change anything? Nothing's going to change, nobody cares. Get over it."

The point in fighting is that injustice anywhere is a threat to justice everywhere, as Martin Luther King, Jr., so eloquently taught. Additionally, the way in which we train our future military officers directly affects our collective wellbeing as a nation. If someone cares about this country, logic requires that she or he should also be concerned with the state of affairs at our service academies. This is the reality of the situation.

This book was not written as an attempt to garner sympathy. It was not written to bash the military or even the Air Force Academy itself. I did not tell my side of the story hoping to somehow clear my name in the book of life, because I consider society's stamp of approval largely overrated. In light of the inequities of this life, I hope for justice in the next. I wrote this book to deliver a message. It is a means to an end, that end being to stimulate thought on an individual basis and provoke action that might ultimately engender revolutionary change at our nation's service academies. For all the reasons mentioned in this work, I believe the Air Force Academy is operating under a false pretense. Even considering the changes of 2003–04, I believe the AFA is failing to produce socially and professionally adept military officers. I believe social and professional ineptitude on such a grand scale does not just warrant attention but, to the concerned citizen, serves as a call to action. I believe as responsible, patriotic Americans we need to take it upon ourselves to address problems within our society, not just because it's the right thing to do but because the stakes are high and the consequences great. At some point, one way or another, societal problems (such as wayward military installations) affect everyone's way of life. We owe it to ourselves and future generations to salvage failed institutions such as the Air Force Academy. Our very future depends upon it.

The German philosopher Arthur Schopenhauer once said,

> All truth passes through three stages. First, it is ridiculed. Second, it is violently opposed. Third, it is accepted as being self-evident.

While serving as a cadet at the Air Force Academy I was ridiculed incessantly for the truths I espoused, and undoubtedly, the message contained herein will face violent opposition. However, given some time, I believe the truths of which I speak will be accepted as self-evident.

I hope the reader of this work comes away with a heightened sense of awareness. I hope the reader agrees with me that there is indeed right and wrong in the world, that there is such a thing as moral obligation. I hope the reader stands convinced that there are more important things in life than mere political, professional, and social survival, and that one's foremost allegiance should always be to truth and justice. I hope the reader agrees with me that there is a time for action and a season for change. I believe the season for change at our service academies is now. *Positive change is always in season.*

Documentation

1. John Diedrich, "Some Air Force Cadets Using More than Gliders to Get High," *The Gazette*, (Colorado Springs, CO) November 19, 2003. Find Articles.com. 08 April 2009. http://findarticles.com/p/articles/mi_qn4191/is_20031119/ai_n10027593/
2. Graham Allison, *Essence of Decision*, (Upper Saddle River, NJ: Addison-Wesley Educational Publishers Inc., 1999), 4.
3. *Working Group Report*, "Report of the Working Group Concerning the Deterrence of and Response to Incidents of Sexual Assault at the U.S. Air Force Academy," (Washington, DC: Headquarters, Department of the Air Force, 2003), 92.

   Author's Note: The *Working Group Report* integrated, by reference, privileged materials, including the statement of then-Major General Steven R. Lorenz, Exhibit 52, at 47-48.

   See Also: Defense Technical Information Center, Fort Belvoir, VA. http://oai.dtic.mil/oai?very+getRecord&metadataPrefix+html&identifier+ADA488305
4. S. L. A. Marshall, *The Armed Forces Officer*, (Washington, DC: U.S. Government Printing Office, 1975), 68.
5. Marlene Steinberg, MD, *The Stranger in the Mirror: Dissociation—The Hidden Epidemic*, (New York: HarperCollins Publishers Inc., 2000), 15.
6. Donald Rumsfeld, Pentagon Briefing, March 23, 2006, Author's notes.

See also: Ruttenberg, Jim, "In Farewell, Rumsfeld Warns Weakness Is 'Provocative'," nytimes.com, December 15, 2006. http://www.nytimes.com/2006/12/16/washington/16prexy.html

7. Marshall, *The Armed Forces Officer*, 192.
8. *Working Group Report*, "Report of the Working Group Concerning the Deterrence of and Response to Incidents of Sexual Assault at the U.S. Air Force Academy," (Washington, DC: Headquarters, Department of the Air Force, 2003), 26-30.
9. Marshall, *The Armed Forces Officer*, 41.
10. Government Accountability Office Report, "DoD Service Academies: More Changes Needed to Eliminate Hazing," GAO/NSIAD-93-36 (Washington, DC: U. S. Government Accountability Office, November 1992), 11.

    See also, referenced in GAO Report: S.E. Ambrose, *Duty, Honor, Country: A History of West Point* (Baltimore, MD: The Johns Hopkins Press, 1966).

    P. Benjamin, *The United States Naval Academy* (New York: G.P. Putnam, 1900).

Captain W.D. Puleston, *Annapolis: Gangway to the Quarterdeck* (New York: D. Appleton-Century Co., 1942).

11. United States Air Force Academy Cadet Handbook, *Contrails* (USAFA, CO: United States Air Force Academy, 2001-2002), 16.
12. GAO Report, "DoD Service Academies: More Changes Needed to Eliminate Hazing," 76.
13. Edward Smith, Susan Nolen-Hoeksma, and Barbara Fredrickson, *Atkinson & Hilgard's Introduction to Psychology,* 14th ed. (Florence, KY: Thomson Learning, Inc., 2003), 461-463.
14. Ibid., 461, 462-463.
15. Ibid., 461-462, 627.
16. GAO Report, "DoD Service Academies: More Changes Needed to Eliminate Hazing," 66.
17. Ibid., 55.
18. United States Air Force Academy Cadet Handbook, *Contrails*, 17.
19. Ibid., 63. (Quote taken from his graduation address to the West Point class of 1879.)
20. GAO Report, "DoD Service Academies: More Changes Needed to Eliminate Hazing," 60.
21. Ibid., 74-75.
22. Marshall, *The Armed Forces Officer*, 160.
23. Government Accountability Office Report, "DoD Service Academies: Comparison of Honor and Conduct Adjudicatory Processes," GAO/NSIAD-93-36 (Washington, DC: U.S. Government Accountability Office, November, 1992), 11.
24. Ibid., 33.
25. Ibid., 27.
26. Jaime Holguin, "Expelled Cadet Awaits Pentagon Ruling,"*CBSNews.com*, Sept. 25, 2002. http;//www.cbsnews.com/stories/2002/09/25/eveningnews/main523248.shtml
27. Meg Kissinger, "From Outcast to Officer, Fight with Academy Ends in Exoneration," *The Milwaukee Online Journal,* Aug 1, 2004. http://www.jsonline.com/news/wauk/aug04/247965.asp
28. Bruce Murphy, "Air Force Overrules Cadet's Suspension," *The Milwaukee Journal Sentinel*, Dec 23, 2003.
29. Government Accountability Office Report, DoD Service Academies "Status Report on Reviews of Student Treatment,"T-NSIAD-92-41 (Washington, DC: U.S. Government Accountability Office, 2 June 1992), 9-10.
30. *Manual for Courts-Martial United States*, (Washington, DC: Department of Defense, 2005), Section IV Rule 401, pages 111-119.
31. GAO Report, "DoD Service Academies: Comparison of Honor and Conduct Adjudicatory Processes," 38-42.
32. Ibid., 38. (1989 study done for Assistant Superintendent of the U.S. Coast Guard Academy.)
33. Marshall, *The Armed Forces Officer*, 44.
34. Steinberg, *The Stranger in the Mirror: Dissociation—The Hidden Epidemic,* 1.
35. Leon Festinger, *A Theory of Cognitive Dissonance* (Evanston, IL: Row, Peterson, 1957), 3.
36. Ibid., 16.

37. Cadet Captain Vaughn Brazil, *Recognition 2002: Concept of Operations* (USAFA, CO: United States Air Force Academy, 10 March 2002), 9.
    Author's Note: This document was for "Internal Use Only" but a copy of the directive *may* be obtained from the USAFA; however, the requestor must submit a Freedom of Information Act Request (FOIA).
38. James S. Olsen and Randy Roberts, *My Lai: A Brief History with Documents* (New York: St. Martin's Press, 1998), 22-23.
39. United States Air Force Academy Cadet Handbook, *Contrails*, 185.
40. C/Capt Vaughn Brazil, *Recognition 2002: Concept of Operations*, 28.
41. Ehud Barak, *The Middle East: Today and Tomorrow*. (World Leaders Forum, Obert C. and Grace A. Tanner Humanities Center, Kingsbury Hall, University of Utah, Feburary 14, 2007), citation is from Author's notes.
42. John R. Dallager (then Lieutenant General), letter to the Graneys, 21 April 2003.
43. Marshall, *The Armed Forces Officer*, 151, 176.
44. United States Air Force Academy Cadet Honor Code Handbook, (USAFA, CO: United States Air Force Academy, 2003), Directive 2.1.8.1, August 2003, 17.
45. U.S. Air Force, Form 1168, Report of Investigation: SFAR Case Number: I2002090039, SFOI Case Number: 02-016, 25 OCT 2002.
    Author's Note: Quote taken from an anonymous witness's personal statement/affidavit written on an AF Form 1168.
46. Ibid.
47. Ibid.
48. Ibid.
49. Ibid.
50. Ibid. (Taken from "Synopsis" Section 1-1).
51. Michael L. Morgan, *Classics of Moral and Political Theory*, 2nd ed. (Indianapolis, IN: Hackett Publishing Company, Inc., 1996), 6, 12.
52. Morgan, *Classics of Moral and Political Theory*, 6.
53. United States Air Force Academy Cadet Personnel File: David W. Graney.
54. Ibid.
55. Ibid.
56. Morgan, *Classics of Moral and Political Theory*, 19.
57. Cormac McCarthy, *All the Pretty Horses,* Volume One of *The Border Trilogy* (New York: Alfred A. Knopf, Inc., 1992), 168.
58. Captain Mike Freimann, letter to Lieutenant General John Dallager, 22 Oct. 2002.
59. Ernest Hemingway, *The Old Man and the Sea* (London: Granada, 1981), 89.
60. William and Linda Graney, letter to Senator Patty Murray, Sept 25, 2002.
61. Department of Defense, Inspector General, "Evaluation of Sexual Assault, Reprisal, and Related Leadership Challenges at the United States Air Force Academy, Report No. IP02004C003," (Arlington, VA: Inspector General, Department of Defense, 2004), 95.
62. Panel to Review Sexual Misconduct Allegations at the U.S. Air Force Academy (The Fowler Panel), "Report of The Panel to Review Sexual Misconduct Allegations at the U.S. Air Force Academy," (Arlington, VA: Panel to Review Sexual Misconduct Allegations, September 2003), 1. http://www/defenselink.mil/news/Sep2003/d20030922usafareport.pdf
    Author's Note: References a May 2003 survey of Academy cadets brought to the Fowler Panel's attention by the Department of Defense Inspector General.

63. U.S. Air Force Inspector General, "Summary Report Concerning the Handling of Sexual Assault Cases at the United States Air Force Academy," (Washington, DC: Air Force Inspector General, Sept 14, 2004), 1.
64. Department of Defense Inspector General, "Evaluation of Sexual Assault, Reprisal, and Related Leadership Challenges at the United States Air Force Academy, Report No. IP02004C003," i.
65. *Working Group Report*, "Report of the Working Group Concerning the Deterrence of and Response to Incidents of Sexual Assault at the U.S. Air Force Academy," (Washington, DC: Headquarters, Department of the Air Force, 2003), 165.
66. Fowler Panel, "Report of The Panel to Review Sexual Misconduct Allegations at the U.S. Air Force Academy," (Arlington, VA: Fowler Panel, September 2003), 4.
67. Ibid., 9.
68. Ibid., 1.
69. *Working Group Report*, "Memorandum for the Secretary and the Chief of Staff of the Air Force from the General Counsel of the Air Force," June 17, 2003.
70. GAO Report, "DoD Service Academies: More Changes Needed to Eliminate Hazing," 5.
71. Fowler Panel, "Report of The Panel to Review Sexual Misconduct Allegations at the U.S. Air Force Academy," 15.

    Author's Note: The Fowler Panel report references the GAO Report, "DoD Service Academies: More Actions Needed to Eliminate Sexual Harassment" (Washington, DC: U.S. Gov't Accountability Office, Jan 1994)
72. Fowler Panel, "Report of The Panel to Review Sexual Misconduct Allegations at the U.S. Air Force Academy," 16.
73. Ibid., 24.
74. Ibid., 20-21.
75. Colonel Jarisse J. Sanborn, USAF, Chief, Administrative Law Branch, Memorandum to Chief of the Military Justice Division (JASM), General Law Division (AF/JA), April 22, 1996.
76. Fowler Panel, "Report of The Panel to Review Sexual Misconduct Allegations at the U.S. Air Force Academy," 18.
77. Ibid., 88. (See also: USAFA Instruction 51-201, paragraph 2.8.3).
78. DoD IG, "Evaluation of Sexual Assault, Reprisal, and Related Leadership Challenges at the United States Air Force Academy, Report No. IP02004C003," 27.
79. Ibid., 27.
80. *Working Group Report*, "Report of the Working Group Concerning the Deterrence of and Response to Incidents of Sexual Assault at the U.S. Air Force Academy," 166.
81. Ibid., 165.
82. Fowler Panel, "Report of The Panel to Review Sexual Misconduct Allegations at the U.S. Air Force Academy," 76.
83. DoD IG, "Evaluation of Sexual Assault, Reprisal, and Related Leadership Challenges at the United States Air Force Academy, Report No. IP02004C003," ii.
84. *Working Group Report*, "Report of the Working Group Concerning the Deterrence of and Response to Incidents of Sexual Assault at the U.S. Air Force Academy," 22.

85. Ibid., 113. (See AF Instruction 71-101V1, paragraph 1.1)
86. DoD IG, "Evaluation of Sexual Assault, Reprisal, and Related Leadership Challenges at the United States Air Force Academy, Report No. IP02004C003," 16.
87. Ibid., 56.
88. Ibid., ii.
89. Ibid., 42.
90. Fowler Panel, "Report of The Panel to Review Sexual Misconduct Allegations at the U.S. Air Force Academy," 38.
91. Ibid., 38.
92. *Working Group Report*, "Report of the Working Group Concerning the Deterrence of and Response to Incidents of Sexual Assault at the U.S. Air Force Academy," 117.
93. Ibid., 125.
94. Cathy Booth Thomas, *The Air Force Academy's Rape Scandal, Time Magazine,* Mar. 06, 2003. http://www.time.com/time/magazine/article/0,9171,1004371-3,00.html
95. *Working Group Report*, "Report of the Working Group Concerning the Deterrence of and Response to Incidents of Sexual Assault at the U.S. Air Force Academy," 117.
96. Secretary of the Air Force Directive, *The Air Force Academy: Agenda for Change* (Washington, DC: Headquarters, Department of the Air Force, 2003)
97. Lieutenant General John R. Dallager, letter to Graneys, 21 April 2003.
98. Bertrand Russell, *A History of Modern Philosophy* (New York: Simon & Schuster, 1945), xiv.

CPSIA information can be obtained
at www.ICGtesting.com
Printed in the USA
BVHW070403011219
565262BV00003B/327/P

9 781604 943955